The March Of Faith The Story Of Religion In America Since 1865

Winfred Ernest Garrison

The

MARCH OF FAITH

The

MARCH OF FAITH

*The Story of
Religion in America
Since 1865*

by

Winfred Ernest Garrison

HARPER & BROTHERS PUBLISHERS

NEW YORK *and* LONDON — MCMXXXIII

Contents

Acknowledgments

Grateful acknowledgment is made to the following publishers for their courtesy in granting permission for the use of quotations from books of which they have the copyright:

From *The Beginnings of Critical Realism in America*, by Vernon L. Parrington, copyright, 1930, by Harcourt, Brace and Company, Inc.

Harper & Brothers, *Will America Become Catholic?* by John F. Moore.

Houghton Mifflin Company, *The Marital Spirit*, by Walter Millis.

John Murphy Company, *A Retrospect of Fifty Years*, by Cardinal Gibbons.

Little, Brown & Company, *The Adams Family*, by James Truslow Adams.

The Macmillan Company, *The Rise of American Civilization*, by Charles A. and Mary R. Beard, and *History of the Councils of Baltimore*, by Peter Guilday.

Willett, Clark & Company, *Catholicism and the American Mind*, by W. E. Garrison.

Introduction

Religion is not merely one thing among many things, or one interest among many interests—business, politics, science, art, education, literature, and the like. It is a way of harmonizing all these in the pursuit of the highest ends. And then it is also a way, or perhaps many ways, of conceiving of those highest ends, and a set of institutions especially devoted to realizing them.

So, in a history of religion for a particular period and place there must be not only something about the churches and about what people do and say in the churches, but also something about business and politics, science and art and the rest—and these last not merely as forming the social and cultural background against which the picture of religion is to be drawn, but as a part of the very substance of the history of religion.

But there are practical limits to the inclusiveness of any study in the history of religion, however comprehensive it may be in theory. In actual practice the story of religion must omit or touch lightly much which under this large definition might logically be included in it and must devote itself chiefly to the consideration of these four kinds of material: first, the growth and changes of the institutions of religion, that is to say the churches; second, the development of ideas about religion, that is to say theology, using the term in its most general sense; third, the effect of religious institutions and ideas upon behavior; and fourth, some consideration of social, political, economic, and cultural conditions as these have affected, or have been affected by, or have been expressions of, those factors which are "religious" in the more specific sense.

As I prepare to write this book with the materials in hand collected through some years of research and organized under such headings as have seemed suitable, I am aware that the organization of the data is almost certain to seem loose and sometimes almost random to persons with orderly and systematic minds. But that is the way life is. To conceive of history as a "stream" which one may follow downward and see all the scenery in one continuous trip—only in this case one would like to think of it as a stream that flows upward—is to over-simplify the facts. If it is a stream at all, it is a stream with many interlacing currents and many engaging tributaries and much hinterland on both banks which invites exploration, and profitable traveling always involves some zigzagging and backtracking.

The period since 1865 has been chosen as a field for this study because in many respects both the churches and the nation as a whole took a fresh start after the Civil War. In how many ways this was true will be evident as we proceed. It may be sufficient here, as confirmation of the impression that a new era began with 1865, to note that since that date the following things have occurred: almost all of the settlement of the country and the planting of the churches west of the Mississippi River; by far the greater part of that urbanization which has transformed America from a country overwhelmingly rural to one on the point of becoming predominantly urban; the rise of those conditions which quickened the social conscience of the churches; the vast increase in the numbers and prestige of the Roman Catholic Church; the entire impact of modern science and biblical criticism upon religious thought and the rise, for better or worse, of the new theology; a new attitude toward denominational divisions, interdenominational relations, and the unity of the church; the rise of the religious education movement; a new sensitiveness of the church to its international responsibilities, not only as a propagandist of Christian institutions, but as a promoter of good will; a deeper concern with moral, social, and economic problems, which has brought to an acute point a new aspect of the old question as to the proper relation between church and state.

And besides, the period since 1865 forms just about the normal lifetime of one person. Men who were very young then are very old now. Those of middle age have heard from their older contemporaries much that they have not themselves seen. So that for those who are neither very young nor very old, these years may be considered as our fathers' times and ours.

The

MARCH OF FAITH

Chapter I

JULY 1, 1865, A CROSS SECTION OF THE COUNTRY

Since every beginning, even at so crucial a date, must be arbitrary and abrupt, let us make a cross-section of the United States in the middle of 1865 and see what kind of country this was and what was going on at the opening of our epoch. So far as possible, let us note what was happening in the first week of July, 1865.

July 1 was Saturday and the moon was in its first quarter. An intense heat wave from the prairie states to the Atlantic seaboard had been followed by heavy downpours of rain, after which it may be presumed that the sweltering country had peace for a season.

Peace had also but recently returned to the war-vexed nation. In fact, the Civil War was not yet officially ended, though the fighting was over and President Johnson's general amnesty proclamation had been issued on May 29. Just a week before that, Jefferson Davis had been captured and confined in Fortress Monroe, and just a month later the trial of four conspirators for complicity in the assassination of President Lincoln ended in their conviction. They were executed on July 7. General Lee had gone to a country house in Cumberland County, Va., to spend the summer months (*Chicago Times*, July 1, 1865).

President Johnson, his administration now ten weeks old, was still high in favor with the friends of the Union. He was being as heavily beset by pardon-seekers as Lincoln had been by office-seekers. For this reason or some other, he was unwell for a few days before and after July 1, and the door of his private office was temporarily closed to visitors.

The heart of the country was still bleeding for the death of Lincoln, but along with grief there had come, as soon as the numbness of surprise had passed, the rising of a great tide of bitterness and resentment. Many good people of the North, ordinarily sane and judicious, could not but believe that the assassination was the result of a conspiracy in which practically the whole South was implicated. This combination of grief and grievance was to furnish strong popular support to the harsh policy of reconstruction devised by politicians for ends of their own. Charles Sumner was still a mighty man in the Senate; Benjamin Wade and John Sherman were there also; but it was on the whole a Senate of mediocrities.

The soldiers were returning from the front by thousands, and the good people of the cities assumed the responsibility of making some sort of provision for their immediate needs. "Our veterans are arriving by hundreds every day. The city is filled with blue uniforms and the citizens seem never weary of giving them welcome. The 'religion of bread and butter' is being devoutly attended to in these days; indeed, the quantity of the meals provided daily at the Soldiers' Rest is something astonishing" (*Chicago Times*, July 1, 1865).

The return of the soldiers was not altogether an uplifting influence. The women camp-followers who had been practicing their old profession in the rear of the army in the field followed it also on its return to the cities. Bishop Simpson was doubtless dealing in rhetoric rather than in exact statistics when he said, in a speech at Cooper Union in 1866, that there were more prostitutes in New York than members of the Methodist Church. But the superintendent of police thought it worth while to reply that, at the time of the last official count, in January, 1864, there were only 599 houses of prostitution and 72 concert-halls of equivalent character. This, however, was before the army of women who had followed the army in the field had been demobilized and returned to the cities.

The hope which idealists had cherished of a revived spirituality and a finer humanity after the nation had passed through the crucible of war was, as usual, doomed to disappointment. Rebecca Harding Davis, describing conditions as an eye-witness, wrote: "When Johnny comes marching home he is a very demoralized member of society and hard to deal with. You cannot take a man away from his work in life and set him to march and fight for five years without turning his ideas and himself topsy-turvy. The older men fall back into the grooves more readily than the lads who have been fighting." And nearly all who had been fighting were lads. Something like half of the soldiers in the Northern army were under eighteen years of age.

The Fourth of July, 1865, was a great day. President Johnson had been expected to deliver an address at Gettysburg, but his illness prevented and he sent a letter instead. The celebration in Boston was on an extensive scale and was graced by the presence of Admiral Farragut. In Washington the day was officially given over to the Negroes. New York's festivities involved the society of the Cincinnati, the veterans of 1812, and Tammany Hall, which was already functioning profitably, for itself, under the leadership of Boss Tweed. The wounded soldiers were to be brought from Central Park Hospital to view the parade, "Rev. Dr. Adams" was to be the orator of the day, and "Old Trinity chimes will ring out a beautiful selection ending with Yankee Doodle" (*New York Herald,* July 3, 1865). New York was not yet too big or too sophisticated to have a community celebration and a Fourth of July oration by a popular preacher. P. T. Barnum delivered the Fourth of July address at Bridgeport, Connecticut. That tinseled prophet was not without honor in his own home town. In all the principal cities of the North the day was observed as a time of special rejoicing for the deliverance of the nation from the danger of division and the beginning of a new era in the national life. There had not been such a Fourth since the semi-centennial.

Wherever the soldiers were still in the field the celebration took on a special character and, at least in some cases, was marked by an effort to restore the spirit of good will between the two armies. If I may draw from my own family records, my father, then a cavalry major in the Union army, was appointed by the general in command of the division encamped at Camden, Arkansas, and receiving the surrender of the Confederate troops, to deliver the Fourth of July address to a vast audience of both Union and Confederate soldiers. The youthful major, who was expecting to enter college as a freshman that fall, gave unofficial assurance that, the war being now over, enmity would cease with hostility, and that the North, having fought to prove secession impossible, would treat the men of the South as fellow citizens in a common country. If they only had!

The college commencements and commemorations of the year, whether before or after the Fourth, were marked by the same sense of the eventfulness of the moment. Lowell delivered his "Commemoration Ode" at Harvard, and William Lloyd Garrison was made an honorary member of Phi Beta Kappa. Phillips Brooks, then twenty-nine years old and rector of the Church of the Holy Trinity in Philadelphia, leaped into fame by his prayer at the same Harvard Commemoration at which Lowell presented his "Ode." President Johnson received an honorary degree from Columbia.

In 1865, Henry Ward Beecher was nearing the middle point in his forty-year pastorate of Plymouth Church, Brooklyn. He was then easily the most conspicuous figure in the American ministry, and his prestige had been greatly enhanced by his service as unofficial ambassador to England to win sympathy for the Union cause. He had been graduated from Lane Theological Seminary, Cincinnati, of which his father, Lyman Beecher, was then president, and after Presbyterian pastorates at Lawrenceville, Indiana, and Indianapolis, had been called to Brooklyn in 1847, where he almost immediately became a commanding figure. His prominence in the national scene is indicated by the fact that he was the orator of the day at the great celebration on April 14, 1865, when the flag was raised again over Fort Sumter on the fourth anniversary of the firing upon it. It was on the evening of that day (Good Friday, as it happened) that Lincoln was shot. A few days before this Fourth of July, 1865—on June 24, to be exact—the *Brooklyn Eagle* reported a speech by Mr. Beecher in Boston arguing for Negro suffrage and ridiculing the idea of making ability to read and write a qualification for the franchise.

Lyman Abbott, who was to become Beecher's colleague and then his successor in editing the *Christian Union* (which later became *The Outlook*) as well as his successor at Plymouth Church, was a young man just closing his pastorate at Terre Haute, Indiana.

John H. Vincent, later a Methodist bishop and the founder of Chautauqua, was minister of a church at Thirteenth and Wabash Avenues, Chicago. General Grant, passing through Chicago on his had refused to make him captain of the company which he had raised in 1861, picked up Vincent on the way and took him along to make the speech. Somebody had to make it, for Grant couldn't, and it was fitting enough that Vincent should, for as an inconspicuous young Methodist minister in Galena four years before he had delivered the oration which had sent to the front the Galena company, with Grant in the ranks.

Mrs. Eddy, then Mrs. Patterson, spent the year 1865 in Lynn. She had been treated by Dr. Quimby off and on for the past three years, had lectured a few times on his system of healing, had experimented with spiritualism, getting messages from her brother, and had recently gone to Lynn to rejoin her dentist husband. Dr. Quimby died in January, 1866, and it was later in that year that she "discovered Christian Science."

The New England Olympians of letters were still living. James Russell Lowell, at forty-six, was joint editor of *The North American Review*, and his *Biglow Papers* were appearing from time to time in *The Atlantic Monthly*. Oliver Wendell Holmes, at fifty-six, was professor of anatomy and physiology in Harvard Medical School. His *Humorous Poems* were published in this year. Whittier, the most intensely religious of the group, at fifty-eight had ceased to take an active part in public affairs, but much of his reputation was based on his patriotic and anti-slavery verse. In this year he published *National Lyrics* and the next year *Snowbound*. Emerson, no less religious but less Christian, sixty-two and full of honors, had already written everything of importance that he was ever to write and his years of lecturing were long past, but it was not until the following year that he achieved an honorary degree from Harvard. His lectures and essays had opened a new dimension to the spiritual consciousness of America, had prepared the way both for some philosophic thinking more exact and less rhetorical than his own and for all the cults of courage and affirmation that were to come after, and had fastened upon millions the habit of being thrilled and uplifted by noble words that they could not understand.

Walt Whitman, a splendid pagan of Quaker origin, had served during the last two years of the war as an army nurse. The immediate literary fruit of this experience was *Drum Taps*, published in 1865, now incorporated in *Leaves of Grass*. He described it as "a little book containing life's darkness and blood-dripping wounds and psalms of the dead." But there were other and more alarming qualities in his verse which led to his dismissal from a small post in the Interior Department. The Treasury Department, however, less squeamish, gave him a clerkship which he held for the next eight years.

Longfellow, the Zeus of the Olympian fellowship around Boston and the exact antithesis of Whitman in everything but hair and beard, was fifty-eight. He had resigned his professorship at Harvard eleven years before and was living in Cambridge, radiating sweetness and light, and working on his translation of Dante which was to appear two years later. We even know exactly how far he had got with that task, for on June 16, 1865, declining an invitation to the White Mountains, he wrote to James T. Fields: "The Dantesque notes move along so slowly that I cannot bear to put any impediment in their way. We have just reached the twentieth canto and fourteen more remain." (It must have been the "Inferno," for that is the only one of the three parts that has thirty-four cantos.)

Commodore Vanderbilt, seventy years old, had acquired a fortune of ten million dollars in the steamboat business before he began to transfer his attention and his capital to railroads shortly before the outbreak of the war. He already had the New York and Harlem Railroad and the Hudson River Railroad, but he did not obtain control of the New York Central until 1867.

Peter Cartwright, who had run for Congress against Lincoln, was now eighty years old but still a vigorous presiding elder in Illinois, a backwoods circuit rider, evangelist, debater, and Campbellite-killer. He had preached fourteen thousand sermons up to ten years before and then lost count. In his later years he had added to his other activities that of a lecturer on a country-wide scale. He was guest of honor at a dinner given by James Harper, of Harper & Brothers, Publishers, in New York in 1862 and had walked out on it, with frank and caustic words, when one of the guests criticized Lincoln. In January, 1865, he held a huge meeting in Keokuk, Iowa, raised the debt on a church, and made enough money by one lecture to buy a lot for a parsonage. That summer, about July, he was in St. Louis where a testimonial purse and a laudatory poem were presented to him.

He had become a figure of international renown as the embodiment of religion on the frontier, and even the European intelligentsia had been made acquainted with him through two articles, not by him but about him, in the *Revue des Deux Mondes.*

Alexander Campbell, seventy-seven years old and within a year of his death, had outlived his mental powers and was telling visitors at Bethany about his trip to Jerusalem, which he never took, but the membership of the religious movement which he had started had grown to a quarter of a million.

Another preacher, a glance at whose career helps one to realize what was going on in the American church and especially the transition from frontier conditions to world-wide interests, was William Taylor. A Tennessee backwoods Methodist preacher sent to California in 1849, he had remarkable success as a street preacher in San Francisco for several years. Returning to the East, he evangelized in the eastern states and Canada, supporting himself by the sale of his books. Then he went to England and to Australia and to South Africa, evangelizing all the way. Just where he was in 1865 would be hard to tell. Perhaps in the West Indies, where he stopped for a few months on his way via Europe and Australia to India, where he arrived in 1870. After fourteen years there and in South America, where he did mission work independent of any board, he attended the general conference as a lay delegate and was elected Bishop for South Africa where he served for a dozen more years. What a man! Let us say that he was in the West Indies in July, 1865, though he may have been on any continent in either hemisphere.

Anthony Comstock, having returned to New Canaan, Connecticut, after two years in the army, had gone to New Haven where he was clerking in a grocery store and looking longingly toward the great city. He had not yet captured his first lewd book or made his first raid on an indecent show, but he was soon to begin.

Henry C. Potter, afterward Bishop of New York, was thirty years old and rector of St. John's at Troy. His uncle, Horatio Potter, then Bishop of New York, was having his famous controversy with Doctor Tyng.

Neither cultural nor economic development had been at a standstill during the Civil War. The old University of Chicago, then spoken of as a young institution, had "added $175,000 to its material resources in the past two years," including astronomic equipment which even the eastern press considered noteworthy (*Independent*, March 2, 1865). Edward Everett Hale announced in a letter from Indianapolis that arrangements had been made for the reconstruction of Antioch College (*Boston Transcript*, July 1, 1865). A Gothic stone church, seating over a thousand, was built in Chicago for $50,000.

The Congregational National Council had had a meeting in Boston during the last week in June at which it had voted to raise $750,000 for the evangelization of the West and South; and at a session held at Plymouth in connection with a pilgrimage to the shrine of the Pilgrims, the famous Burial Hill Declaration was adopted. The council "today defeated a resolution in favor of prohibitory legislation against rum selling on the sensible ground as stated by Rev. Dr. Bacon that the cause of temperance had been wrecked on the rock of the Maine law" (*Boston Transcript*, June 26, 1865). This Rev. Dr. Bacon was Leonard Bacon, who was minister of the First Church of New Haven for more than forty years, one of the editors of the *Independent* and as vigorous an opponent of Neal Dow's ideas of prohibition as he was of William Lloyd Garrison's ideas of abolition.

Nevertheless, temperance found many advocates in the church, and pledge-signing was a prominent feature of the campaign against alcohol. The women also were beginning to take a part in the temperance movement. Their organization still lay ahead and the power of that organization was but faintly foreshadowed in the feminine appeals for sobriety, generally either whimsical or hysterical, at this period. "Young ladies should never consent to lock arms with a walking jughandle," declared a spinsterish temperance lecturer who had never locked arms with anybody, "or throw their arms around the neck and put their lips to the filthy mouth of a living brandy bottle" (*Brooklyn Eagle*, June 26, 1865). Medical as well as moral cures for inebriety were being offered. An advertisement asserts that "4,000 drunkards have been cured within the last three years by the use of the radical cure for drunkenness prepared by Dr. Beers."

The last stage of the slavery controversy and the war itself had wiped out the Know-Nothing party and, for the time, put an end to the effort to stampede the country into political measures against

Roman Catholicism. Suspicion of Catholicism still continued, however, and just now it was finding expression in some of the activities of the Christian Union Association, which, although it existed to find a basis of union among the churches and not to combat Roman Catholicism, according to the statement of its secretary, nevertheless gave occasion for the feeling that the latter was its real purpose. But it also promoted exchanges of pulpits among ministers of different denominations. Since some Episcopalians had joined the association and their fraternizing called forth the protest of their bishops, the immediate result was to produce more trouble in the Episcopal church than union among the others. It was this matter of pulpit exchange that occasioned the dispute between Bishop Horatio Potter and Doctor Tyng.

The system of renting pews, which was still maintained by most of the older churches, came into conflict with the newer democratic tendencies, and the problem of satisfying strangers who wanted seats at church without offending irascible pew-holders was causing enough trouble to provoke journalistic comment. A conservative suggestion from an editor who was radical on nearly everything else was that the pew-holders' reservations should be good only until the services began or else that strangers should be allowed to sit in the gallery (*Independent*, Oct. 19, 1865).

A slight, but still very slight, tendency was observable toward more liturgical worship in the non-liturgical churches. When a selection of psalms for responsive reading was produced it was remarked that "whether or not the Methodists are prepared to adopt even so simple a liturgy remains to be seen."

Orthodoxy was still strongly enough entrenched in the churches to take vigorous action against those who departed even slightly from its canons. A Congregational council in Maine refused to install a minister in Portland because he thought that "the punishment of the wicked *may* not be eternal, but end in annihilation, and that the heathen and others not having had the privilege on earth *may* in another world have the offer of salvation." He held these lax opinions in abeyance and did not preach them and he was sure that those who died impenitent were hopelessly and permanently damned, but the council thought his doctrine was dangerous even as a private opinion.

Universalism, in however mild and modified a form, had been one of the most pestilent heresies from the standpoint of the older puritanism. Now that humanitarian ideas were on the increase, it seemed particularly hazardous to permit any loose views as to the promptness and finality of judgment.

In the matter of morals and manners, also, the more conservative felt that there was ground for alarm. Not that too much weight should be given to the laments of a single critic, but the following words at least indicate how one correspondent felt about it: "The state of religion in our church is very low. The deaths and dismissions were last year greater than all the receptions. The young people fall off to the Episcopal, the Methodist and the Baptists. In the Episcopal church they find pomp and ceremony, while they are permitted full indulgence in all fashionable worldly amusements. In the Methodist church, the more active and enterprising find more of life and freedom and, seemingly, more of religious devotion. In the Baptist church, with immersion and close communion, they find a stricter order and a greater separation, with more that is distinctive. Not a great many therefore are left for our church. As the aged must die and the young do not join, the consequence is that the church must grow more and more feeble and, unless a change takes place, the church must become extinct" (*Independent*, January 19, 1865).

Religious journalism was represented by 407 periodicals, according to the enumeration in 1870. The number was probably in the neighborhood of three hundred in 1865. In both the number of periodicals and in circulation, the religious press had shown more increase during the twenty years preceding than had the secular press. The religious papers were, in fact, just coming into their golden age so far as circulation and influence were concerned. Almost all of them were, of course, denominational. The most conspicuous exception was the *Independent*, edited by Theodore Tilton, who had succeeded Beecher in the editorial chair in 1863. It was still nominally a regular Congregational paper but covered a wide variety of interests and two or three years later definitely cast off its denominational allegiance. In 1865, besides publishing regularly Beecher's sermons, which were for the most part expository, devotional, and strongly religious, never pulpit lectures, it was printing articles and editorials on a wide range of

social and cultural topics. But Tilton's reputation for brilliant journalistic writing has been undeservedly obscured by his later follies and
misfortunes.

Advertisements throw a bright light on contemporary customs and
conditions: "Situation wanted by a respectable boy fifteen years of age
as barkeeper" (*New York Herald*, July 3, 1865). "Strayed—a dark red
cow from Quincy Street" (*Chicago Times*, July 1, 1895). Tonsorial
fashions are reflected in the advertisement of a tonic which will grow
"whiskers and mustache in four weeks—a full set" (*Chicago Times*,
July 1, 1865). The *Brooklyn Eagle* advertises a business college as "the
only place in the city where ladies have the rare opportunity of taking
the same courses as men."

But the day of the ladies was coming. "Vassar Female College" was
preparing to open in September, 1865, with Dr. John H. Raymond as
president, but "the departments of physical training, anatomy and
physiology will be placed in the hands of lady professors." Advocates
of equal suffrage for women were few, but Lucy Stone and Susan B.
Anthony were in the field. In arguing for suffrage for Negroes,
Horace Greeley also approved suffrage for women whenever they
wanted it; and the *Independent* not only declared in favor of equal
suffrage but ventured the apparently absurd prediction that it would
come within the lifetime of men then living, as it did. The churches,
however, never got excited about suffrage for women as a moral issue
and the interest in it which they developed a little later was chiefly
due to the belief that it would aid the temperance cause.

In 1865, the United States was a country composed of thirty-six
states. Accurate census statistics for that year are not available, but in
1860 the population was thirty-one million. New York was a city of
813,000 people; Boston had only 177,000; St. Louis and Cincinnati
were practically tied at about 160,000, and Chicago had amazed the
country by growing from approximately nothing to 109,000 in the last
thirty years. It continued to awaken the amazement, if not the admiration, of the world by an almost three-fold increase during the decade
of the 'sixties. Minneapolis was a town of 2,500 and Kansas City was
negligible. The Homestead Act of 1862 had stimulated the westward
movement and with the close of the war a general real-estate boom
was in progress. The papers, even the religious papers, contained con-

stant references to the surprising acreage of western lands that were being taken up.

One may get something of the feeling of the exuberant spirit and rapid change of this period by noting the conditions in a few western states. Minnesota was still so primitive that it had experienced an Indian uprising in 1862 in which eight hundred whites were killed. At the close of the war Scandinavians began to pour into the state in great numbers and to settle the land in its central and western parts. This fact and the rapid building of railroads started Minneapolis on its way to becoming a great milling center.

Colorado still had less than forty thousand inhabitants, most of whom had come in the rush following the discoveries of gold near Boulder and Idaho Springs in 1859. Denver was a mining town and wars were still being waged with the Cheyenne and Arapahoe Indians. But the University of Colorado had already been incorporated by the territorial government and the ambitious settlers had made an unsuccessful attempt to form a state government in 1864.

Texas had about 700,000 people scattered over its vast area and the increase during this decade was not rapid. Its leading industry, cattle raising, did not make for great increase in population, there were no gold discoveries, and agricultural development came later. The last battle of the Civil War was fought at Palmito on the Rio Grande on May 13, 1865, a month after Appomattox.

California was a curious compound of the almost baronial life of the great wheat and barley ranches and the hectic excitement of its mining camps. Los Angeles was still a drowsy village untouched by the newer influences, while San Francisco was a brawling and tumultuous city of more than 100,000 people. In the 'sixties the original gold excitement had been reinforced by the Bonanza silver strike, and California probably had more money in proportion to what it had to do with it than any other American community ever had before or since. The Central Pacific was being built eastward from San Francisco and the state was enjoying the lively hope that it would soon be connected with the East by rails.

The whole country was, in fact, greatly excited about new methods of rapid transportation and communication. Cyrus Field was still laying trans-Atlantic cables, in the hope of getting one strong enough to stand the strain. His first one had broken while being laid in 1858; his second broke on August 2, 1865; the third held, and the first news flashed over it was the peace at the end of the Austro-Prussian War in July, 1866. Before the Atlantic cable was completed, plans were afoot for a cable to China by way of the Hawaiian Islands, and a telegraph line was being built toward Bering Strait with a view to uniting Europe to America via Asia. The Suez Canal was opened on August 15, 1865, but to small boats only.

The increased speed of travel had already begun to take its toll in accidents and there were critics who complained that the new trains and steamers were not much less deadly than war. "The returning soldiers are being daily slaughtered by steamboat disasters and railroad accidents while on their way to their homes. Twelve hundred homeward bound soldiers were dispatched by the sinking of one steamer on the Mississippi; by way of exchange, a couple of hundred Confederate soldiers have been drowned. If railroads cannot slaughter as many at one time they make up by the frequency of their accidents" (*Brooklyn Eagle*, July 24, 1865). Railroad management was, however, more interested in the opening of new territory and in the consolidation of short lines into systems than in the prevention of accidents. In July, 1865, the consolidation of four roads produced the Toledo, Wabash and Western, which was the only road between Lake Erie and the Mississippi under single management and with a uniform gauge.

The civic pride of the municipalities which were expanding at such startling rate only occasionally permitted the recognition of those hard facts which bulk so large in the comments of visitors from afar. In a burst of frankness, the *Chicago Tribune* declared: "The municipal affairs of Chicago are all at loose ends and nobody knows what is the matter. But everybody understands that we have the foulest streets and dirtiest river and most inefficient police and most nauseous water, the most fogyish board of public works and board of health in the world" (July 4, 1865). And instead of the beautiful and cleanly Washington that we know there was a city of which it was said: "The sanitary condition is so bad that the mayor and other city officials called on the Secretary of War today and asked that the bone-boiling establishments and deceased horses be removed from within the city limits" (*Chicago Times*, July 1, 1865). Allowing for a certain amount of rhetorical exaggeration, it must be believed than sanitary conditions in general were rather bad when it could be said that "the air of the whole country is poisoned by the effluvia of rotten garbage and the decaying carcasses of the war" (*Chicago Times*, July 3, 1865).

That was not the worst that the war had left. It had left the South impoverished and embittered; the North triumphant, enriched, and arrogant; the churches divided; religion confused by its identification in the South with a lost cause, in the North with a ruthless political policy under the sacred name of patriotism. But there was the West! The watchword of the hour was Westward Ho! But before we can follow Greeley's advice—"Go west, young man, and grow up with the country"—or trace the trails of those who did follow it, we must pause to consider the part that religion played in relation to the policies of reconstruction.

Chapter II

THE DAYS OF RECONSTRUCTION

The condition and the activities of the churches after the Civil War were determined partly by the state of the country and partly by the attitudes which the churches had taken on the great divisive issues before and during the war. Religion reflected both the mood of recovery, expansion, and optimism which dominated the North, and the desperate and heroic determination to go on living in spite of disaster which characterized the South; both the surge of prosperity and the pinch of poverty. What was equally significant, the echoes of war antagonisms reverberated through the churches, as they did through politics, long after the sounds of actual conflict were stilled.

The slavery question had divided the Methodist, Baptist and Presbyterian churches into separate organizations as it divided the country into two warring sections. The country was reunited by force, but no appeal to arms could nullify the secession of the southern churches or the sectionalism of the northern ones. Even God could not immediately join together what man had put asunder.

Slavery was the first great issue in social morality which the churches had taken with complete seriousness. To be sure, the church had always had its code of individual morality. It had always raised its voice against murder, theft, lying, and adultery. But no one came to the defense of these sins, though many practiced them. In slavery the church confronted an issue that had two sides. As it faced this issue, it rediscovered the fact that religion was concerned with other things than the salvation of individuals. It had once known this, but Jonathan Edwards and the Great Awakening had concentrated attention upon saving individuals from hell. After a brief but energetic participa-

tion in public affairs in the years just before the Revolution, when the
New England puritan clergy preached independence, the churches
had returned—in the great western revival and the evangelistic efforts
which followed it, and in the struggle for the maintenance of Calvinistic orthodoxy—to a view of religion as detached from the society
within which it existed. Horace Bushnell had pointed out the relation
of Christianity to its social setting. He made it clear that not only the
family but also the community and the nation furnished environment
by which the character of souls was determined, and were therefore
within the scope of the church's legitimate interest. But it was in the
slavery issue that the churches generally rediscovered the community
as a fact of vital religious significance.

When the war came, almost all the churches threw themselves into
the struggle with complete abandon and loyalty on one side or the
other, and conviction about the wickedness or righteousness of slavery
immediately passed over into patriotic devotion to the political and
military organizations which were arrayed for and against it. The
southern churches were already convinced that slavery was an institution ordained by God. Partly to defend it and partly to sustain what
their section of the country deemed a just political cause, they were for
the Confederacy—not, as they came to think, because their personal or
sectional interests were involved, but because it was the will of God.
The northern churches, opposing slavery as sinful and secession as
treasonable, similarly interpreted their support of the union as obedience to a divine command. The Protestant Episcopal and Catholic
churches had refrained from passing judgment on slavery. In the
Episcopal and Old School Presbyterian assemblies some voices were
raised even against passing resolutions of loyalty when the crisis came.
The Episcopalians divided calmly only after the ordinance of secession
was passed and as calmly reunited when the war was over. The
Methodists and Baptists had divided hotly on the slavery question
fifteen years earlier and the Presbyterians divided on the war.

There was apparently no thought on either side about the ethics
of war. Only the Quakers and a few minor sects which were generally deemed curious and fanatical saw any impropriety in settling

gentle lady who wrote the Battle Hymn of the Republic, felt no incongruity between the concepts of battle and hymn, and all the Christians of the North thrilled with holy enthusiasm at the picture of God "trampling out the vintage where the grapes of wrath are stored." Christ was made to do duty as the great exemplar of warfare in a righteous cause, if not as a recruiting officer for this particular struggle: "As he died to make men holy let us die to make men free." That he had not died in an effort to kill his enemies did not appear to spoil the analogy. The gentle poet and physician, Oliver Wendell Holmes, wrote:

> O Lord of Hosts, Almighty King,
> Behold the sacrifice we bring.
> To every arm Thy strength impart,
> Thy spirit shed through every heart.
> Thine are the scepter and the sword;
> Stretch forth Thy mighty hand, *etc.*

On the other side a southern writer with equal confidence and equal piety affirmed:

> In the name of God we'll meet you,
> With the sword of God we'll greet you,
> By the grace of God we'll beat you.

Horace Bushnell, so far in advance of his contemporaries in regard to conversion and Christian nurture that he was deemed half a heretic, was as orthodox as the best on this point: "Peace will do for angels, but war is God's ordinance for sinners."

The *Independent*, which had waved the flag with the utmost vigor throughout the war, carried at its editorial masthead early in 1865, when the contest was virtually decided, these words: "Our view of peace. We agree with Patrick Henry: 'Men may cry peace, peace, but there is no peace.' Now on to Richmond." And when Richmond fell, a dithyrambic double-leaded editorial, which even now can scarcely be read without the imagined accompaniments of drums and trombones, shouted: "The city of Richmond . . . Babylon the Great, Mother of Harlots and Abominations of the earth . . . Rejoice over her, thou Heaven, and ye holy apostles and prophets; for God hath avenged you on her" (*Independent*, April 6, 1865). But in another column on the same page, Beecher wrote of his proposed visit with officers of the government to Fort Sumter to raise the flag: "If any man goes supposing that he accompanies me on an errand of triumph and exultation over a fallen foe, he does not know the first letter of my feelings." The actual spirit of the North lay somewhere between the kindly attitude of Beecher and the apocalyptic ravings of Tilton. But the reconstruction program which the northern churches generally supported had more in common with the latter.

Already a movement was on foot to enact a "Christian" amendment to the United States Constitution acknowledging the sovereign power of God, the place of Christ as ruler of nations and "his revealed will as the supreme authority." Originated by the United Presbyterians, this had been approved by the Old School Presbyterian general assembly and by the Methodist Episcopal general conference. A critic objected that the proposed amendment "looks like an attempt to blend the constitution, the declaration of independence and the catechism into one." But even such a blending would scarcely have gone farther than the attitudes which the churches actually took with regard to the war. It was on these allied issues of slavery and secession that the churches first began to exercise an influence in politics.

If the participation of the churches in the events of the day divided some of them and embittered the internal relations of others, it undoubtedly increased their prestige among those who were outside of all of them and who valued religion for what it could do in advancing causes in which they were interested. Not only at home but also abroad the spokesmen for religion became advocates of the Union cause. Henry Ward Beecher in England and Archbishop Hughes in France had served as unofficial ambassadors to create favorable sentiment.

President Johnson came into office with the admiration and support of most of those who were to become his bitterest enemies. Their support was based upon the expectation that he could pursue a rigorous policy toward the South. "We thank God that the new president who has ennobled himself in a single week into the complete confidence of the people stands already illustriously pledged to deal an unrelenting punishment to crimes against the Republic," said the editor of the *Independent* (April 27, 1865), and he called for a "vow before heaven to fulfill a three-fold duty: first, to slavery, annihilation; second, to rebellion, unconditional surrender; third, to treason, the extreme penalty of the law." These are the requirements of "the ethics of the New Testament."

The questions upon which the churches contributed their share in the molding of public opinion and in the ultimate determination of policies were these: first, slavery; then, the granting of suffrage to the newly enfranchised Negroes; after that, the restoration of political rights to the southern whites, the general conditions of Reconstruction and the punishment of those who had lately been in arms against the Federal government; and finally, the impeachment of the President when he favored milder policies than those which were approved by either the politicians or the churches in the North. And along with these political questions—all interpreted of course as high moral issues upon which the most solemn sanctions of religion were invoked— was the question of the evangelization of the South, from which it was deemed that true religion had departed when the southern churches became apostate by the defense of slavery.

The slavery question itself was, of course, already virtually settled, though it was not without vigorous opposition from northern congress- men and by barely the required two-thirds vote (119 to 56) in the House of Representatives, that the thirteenth amendment was sub- mitted in January, 1865. But aside from some opposition to the amendment on grounds of political expediency or of constitutional law, what the war had done to popular sentiment in the North was to transform it from a somewhat vague and largely prudential dis- approval of slavery into an absolute denunciation of it. The North in general had been chiefly concerned to check the further extension of slavery and to prevent the slave-owning states from securing a predominance of power in Congress. Opinion in some of the churches had gone beyond this and declared slavery essentially sinful. But to the mind of the majority, slavery was simply an obnoxious institution which supported a society having economic interests and cultural patterns other than those of the North which therefore ought to be held in check. Abolitionists before the war were considered fanatics even in the North. The war made the whole North abolitionist. A note of absolutism had entered the North's denunciation of slavery which had not been there before. The result was the Thirteenth Amendment.

The granting of suffrage to the Negroes was a different thing from granting them liberty, but because it had come to be taken for granted that they would of course get their liberty, the great "moral issue" now came to be the suffrage question. On broad humanitarian grounds it seemed plausible that in a country dedicated to the proposition that all men are created equal no race should be disfranchised. Besides, the Negroes had helped to win the war and deserved something for that besides a bare grant of the freedom which they ought to have had all along. And especially there was the feeling that without the right to vote the Negroes of the South would be unable to maintain their other rights. The whole economy of the southern states had been constructed with a view to the interests of the slave-owning whites. Now it must be reconstructed so as to guard the interests of the freedmen. But was it safe to entrust that task to the southern whites alone? It is easy to see how the moral urgency of emancipation came to be translated into moral urgency for Negro suffrage. Politicians with little or no concern for either morals or religion might have their own reasons for desiring to put the control of the southern states into the hands of grateful blacks rather than resentful whites, and they might utilize the moral and religious appeal, as they did, to throw the cloak of sanctity about their most nefarious policies. But it must be recognized that on the whole the sentiment of the religious people of the North in favor of granting suffrage to the Negroes and limiting for a time the political rights of those who had so recently fought to divide the union and perpetuate slavery was sincere and high-minded. There seemed no other way to guarantee to the Negroes that their newly acquired freedom would be anything more than an empty word.

It was not wholly illogical, nor is it an evidence of insincerity, that the North was more enthusiastic about Negro suffrage in the South than in the North. As a matter of fact, few of the northern states had permitted Negroes to vote before the war and not all of them were convinced that such a rule should be made nation-wide and constitutionally binding after the war. There were many who, waving aside doctrinaire considerations of the theoretical equality of all men, saw that the Negroes were not qualified to exercise the rights of citizenship and did not want to grant them such rights in their own states but felt that it was the least of two evils to grant them in the southern states.

In the North the personal and economic rights of Negroes would be protected anyway; in the South they would not be unless the Negroes had votes. Such was one argument.

Closely connected with the granting of suffrage to the Negroes was the question of restoring political rights to the whites who had lately been in arms against the union, of restoring representative government in the southern states, and of punishing or pardoning those who had been the leaders in secession. Upon all of these points the policy of President Johnson began almost immediately to diverge from that favored by the leaders of his party. The complexities and bitternesses of the struggle between the President and the radicals need not here be detailed. The significant thing for our purposes is that the northern churches were almost solidly on the side of the radicals. Republican preachers made their pulpits platforms for the advocacy of Negro suffrage and a stern policy toward the erstwhile "rebels." Religious journals held up to scorn "the unwashed democracy who hate godliness and cleanliness with equal cordiality (and) properly regard the Republican party as led by the piety and worth of this nation, by the people who detest grogshops and Sabbath breaking and gambling saloons and dance halls" (*Christian Examiner,* November, 1866). Beecher favored Negro suffrage but, in advance of his constituency in this as in so many other things, argued for a generous attitude toward the South and split on this point with the *Independent* which had for years been his organ. When Beecher came out for Johnson, the paper solemnly chided him for "putting a great reputation to the ignoble use of debasing his country," and in an adjoining column castigated the President with scorching and stingingly clever rhetoric. In the same issue John G. Whittier expressed his admiration of the southern loyalists and his wish to see the southern states back in the union "in the speediest manner consistent with the safety of the union; in other words, whenever the rights of all their inhabitants are secured and the monstrous inequality of representation growing out of slavery has been so adjusted that a rebel in South Carolina shall not have double the political power of a loyal man in one of the New England states." This had special reference to the Fourteenth Amendment which was then pending (*Independent,* September 6 and 13, 1866). Beecher's brother, Rev. Edward Beecher, felt impelled to write him an open letter declaring that readmission of the southern states to the union without the disfranchisement of the rebels and the grant of Negro suffrage would tend "to enslave the freed-men and plunge us into another civil war. . . . What good reason have we to trust in the generosity and magnanimity of slavery-begotten aristocracies?" But Beecher undoubtedly voiced the Christian sentiment of the North when he said that the granting of full suffrage rights to the Negroes was the great moral duty of the hour and that it was absurd to consider literacy an essential qualification to the exercise of that right.

In only six northern and western states did the Negroes have the vote before the war. In 1865, while the Thirteenth Amendment was pending, Connecticut, Minnesota and Wisconsin defeated proposals for Negro suffrage in state elections. The Fourteenth Amendment, introduced in 1866 and adopted in 1868, reduced the congressional representation of states which did not give the ballot to the Negro. This went over easily in the North because it meant little to states that had few Negroes and, pending legislation on the suffrage question, diminished the political power of those which had many. The Fifteenth Amendment, giving the franchise to Negroes, was adopted in 1870, partly as a result of idealistic and humanitarian sentiments, but much more as a means of keeping the South under the control of the Republican party. This political motive was also capable of lofty interpretation, for it was possible to say that only so were the rights of Negroes and southern loyalists safe. But both of these motives together were not able to hold New York in line, for that state, after voting favorably, withdrew its ratification and Georgia added its at the last moment to make the necessary quota.

Rev. Mr. Newman, opening a session of the southern loyalists' convention, prayed God to "deliver us from the rule of bad men, especially from him who through Satanic agency has been raised to authority over us"—meaning Johnson (*New York Herald*, September 6, 1866). Parson Brownlow, ordained Methodist minister and Governor of Tennessee, said: "The Devil is in the people of the South and in the man at the White House in particular. If we are to have another war, I want a finger in that pie. I want your army to come in three divisions, the first to kill, the second to burn, and the third to survey the land into small parcels and give it to those who are loyal in the North" (*New York Herald*, September 11, 1866).

Southern missionaries of northern churches wrote back for publication horrendous accounts of the animosity of the South toward the freed Negroes. Parson Brownlow, visiting the North, said: "I find here at the North you do not need and many of you do not want Negro suffrage. We are not so. We want the loyal Negroes to help us vote down the disloyal traitors and white people" (*New York Herald*, September 12, 1866). Brownlow's quarterly had denounced Lincoln in 1864 for his pocket veto of the Davis bill proposing a radical substitute for Lincoln's program of reconstruction proclaimed December 8, 1863. Brownlow, minister as he was, went even farther than most in his unscrupulous methods of securing the adoption of the radical reconstruction program. In his first message as Governor of Tennessee early in 1865, he had opposed suffrage for the Negroes and had suggested colonizing them somewhere outside of the United States, but before the Fourteenth Amendment was submitted he outradicaled the radicals. Alarmed by the poor showing of his party in the congressional election of August, 1865, he forced the passage of an act disfranchising all whites who could not take oath that they "rejoiced at the defeat of the Confederacy." This was followed by a resolution, also pushed by Brownlow, that Jefferson Davis, General Lee and other Confederate leaders "had justly forfeited their lives and ought to suffer the extreme penalty of the law and be held infamous forever." Three days after receiving the Fourteenth Amendment from Washington he issued a call for a special session of the Legislature to act on it. When the Legislature was slow in assembling—called on June 19, it was to meet July 4—he asked Federal military aid to compel the attendance of members. Washington refused to sanction this, but Brownlow had two members of the lower house seized on writs of habeas corpus (which were declared illegal as soon as they got to a judge) and carried into the House. Even then there was no quorum but he insisted on the passage of the act anyway.

The northern New School Presbyterian general assembly in May, 1865, without discussion or dissent, passed resolutions declaring the rebellion "a crime against the state and a sin against God," and demanding that "it should be punished by the judicial power of the nation in the infliction of penalty upon its guilty authors." The support given to the southern cause by southern ministers is "one of the most astonishing moral perversions to be found in the history of this sinful world. . . . In the event that any of these ministers should apply for admission into the presbyteries, the assembly advises the presbyteries not to admit them or in any way to recognize them as ministers of Christ until they have given satisfactory evidence that they have sincerely repented of their sin."

The Old School Presbyterian general assembly had kept the southern presbyteries on its roll in the hope of restored fellowship, but the *North Carolina Presbyterian* repudiated the idea of return and said that being "subjugated to the civil power" of the North is not so bad as it would be "ever to strike hands with them again in common ecclesiastical association."

Except in the minds of the most rabid, the character of General Lee commanded respect and there was no great desire on the part of the church people generally for criminal action against the military leaders of the South. The case of Jefferson Davis, however, was different. Upon him was focused as much of the resentment and hatred of the victors as could be concentrated upon any one man. While the church assemblies for the most part were not disposed to foul their records by the explicit mention of his name, it was he who was chiefly in mind when they passed resolutions sternly demanding the punishment of traitors, and the only question for most Christian patriots was whether he ought to be shot or hanged. Immediately after his capture, the *Independent*, voicing a sentiment which was common among the church people of the North, said: "The great criminal is in our hands. Guilty of treason, guilty of perjury, guilty of barbarity, guilty of murder—such is the indictment against Jeff Davis. What shall be the punishment? . . . On whatever charge he may be tried, let his trial be dignified, passionless and impartial, and after the sentence let the death penalty be solemnly executed."

Admiration for Lee, coupled with a genuinely benevolent desire to advance education in the ruined South, led many northerners to lend their sympathy and financial aid to Washington College, of which Lee became president, at Lexington, Va. But powerful voices were also raised against this weak indulgence in sentiment. William Lloyd

Garrison, writing in 1868, said: "The South is shattered, disorganized, bankrupt, helpless; still animated by a demoniacal spirit toward all that pertains to free institutions and the general popular enlightenment, still disloyal in spirit and conduct; still wishing to rule in Hell rather than serve in Heaven. Cursed by her old slave system beyond all that imagination can depict or language express, she is both morally and intellectually incapable of self-recovery and needs help in every way and of every kind." But, he adds, neither countenance nor cash should be given by northerners to Lee's college until and unless Lee and the state of Virginia show themselves utterly repentant—which he thinks highly improbable.

The attempt to impeach President Johnson was merely one aspect of the effort of radical Republicans to put into effect a rigorous policy toward the beaten South. The attacks upon his character, as "drunkard, rebel and repudiator," were merely incidental to the main campaign. The legend of Johnson's intoxication at the time of his inauguration and of his habitual drunkenness was doubtless conceived in the minds of those who had personal and political motives for blackening his character as a means of putting him out of the way. It was widely believed and played a part, though a subordinate part, in alienating from him the sympathy of the church people. Beecher believed the rumor and helped to give it currency, but he never took the pains to contradict it even when it was found to be false, though he was more nearly in harmony with Johnson's reconstruction program than any other conspicuous churchman. The alienation of the religious mind rested upon more serious grounds. It was because the whole secession enterprise with its championship of slavery had come to be interpreted as apostasy from God and an insult to Christ that no quarter could be given to the culprits, no confidence could be placed in the apostates, and no support could be given to one who was disposed to show consideration for them.

Within six months after his inauguration the suspicions of the radicals began to be aroused and the religious press began to echo the uneasiness of the radical Republican secular press at the President's failure to initiate strong measures. He had been expected to "punish treason." Instead of that there came reports of from 100 to 500 pardons a day. Still inflamed by the assassination of Lincoln, the loyal mind could not be satisfied with the execution of the four conspirators found guilty of that crime, but must have vengeance for the greater crime of which that crime was a mere incident.

But, though a mere incident, it was one which raised devotion to the twin causes of Federal unity and Negro enfranchisement to a higher moral level, furnished ground for considering the enemies of these causes as the enemies of God and all righteousness, and threw a halo of sanctity about every measure that could be proposed for the humiliation and punishment of the South. Old atrocity stories were revived and given full credence. "The massacre at Ft. Pillow, the slow torture to death of our captured soldiers and the attempt to lay New York in ashes" were made the subject of renewed bitter comment within a week after Lincoln's death. And it was added that "the murder of the chief magistrate . . . was in their thoughts from the beginning before he had taken his seat in Washington or a single drop of blood was spilt." The assassination was played up as a result of a deliberate plot, involving the whole South, or at least its leaders. Surely people who could commit such crimes were not people to whom could be entrusted the rebuilding of state governments or the protection of the rights of the enfranchised Negroes. "Every ounce of what is called 'magnanimity' to a rebel counts as a pound of suffering to our loyal friends at the South, to the blacks in particular" (*Independent*, April 20 and October 26, 1865).

But this magnanimity was precisely the characteristic of Johnson's policy, as it would have been of Lincoln's; and the churches, jealous for their reputation for loyalty, were anxious to show that there was nothing weak or sentimental about religion. It had iron in it and could be fierce against the enemies of God.

The break came when Johnson, in February, 1868, for the second time removed Stanton as Secretary of War in spite of the Tenure of Office act. The *Independent*, now by far the most important religious paper in the country and with the largest circulation (75,000), published in full, with trumpetings of triumph, the speech of Thaddeus Stevens which the publisher, H. C. Bowen, had got from Stevens in advance and telegraphed from Washington. It was a notable scoop for religious journalism and vividly symbolized the interest which the churches took in the impeachment.

The New England conference of the Methodist Episcopal church, meeting in Boston, in March, 1868, approved the action taken for the impeachment, regretted the hostility of the President to the policies of Congress "which has compelled his impeachment for high crimes and misdemeanors," and requested the prayers of the churches "that the consummation of the conflict now going forward may be conformed to its previous steps and obtain for us as a nation the continued and crowning blessings of God." The Methodist General conference in session at Chicago in May set aside an hour for prayer that the impeachment of the President might not fail. It had not yet come to the point of admitting lay representation, but it did for the first time admit colored delegates to the general conference. The Baptists were equally favorable to a strong policy toward the South and the removal of its friend in the White House, believing that "the South is as fierce, as unscrupulous, as unrelenting as ever before, with no doubt a considerable accession of malignity in the consciousness of its own importance" (*Baptist Standard*, February 27, 1868).

In spite of the support of the churches, the impeachment proceedings failed by a narrow margin. The vote was 35 to 19, two-thirds being required for impeachment. Johnson did not live long enough to see his own vindication. As the years passed, it came to be conceded that he was at least honest, but no other virtue was allowed him. His return to Washington as a senator drew forth this comment on his former course: "What then could reasonably be expected from passionate, pig-headed, honest Andrew Johnson but just the self-asserting egotism and unmitigated mulishness with which he backed, balked and brayed from the beginning to the end of his administration"; and even his death a few months later was pronounced "not in any sense a public calamity" (*Independent*, February 18 and August 5, 1875).

The religious mind in reconstruction years was not sufficiently sensitive to the question of plain honesty in government to give it a rating of equal importance with such issues as amnesty and suffrage. At the time when an appeal for Negro suffrage was being made in the name of righteousness and justice, public extravagance and corruption reached the point where, according to the *New York Herald*, 250 million dollars of public funds had been stolen or squandered.

"If any respectable party will go into the next elections upon a platform of retrenchment and a thorough change of the present corrupt Congress, success will follow. Such a platform would beat all the Negro platforms the radicals could construct" (*New York Herald*, July 2, 1866). That this was not a wholly partisan estimate is confirmed by the terse summary of General Sherman, who wrote to his wife: "Washington is as corrupt as Hell." Though not all the radicals were involved in this corruption, Johnson's opposition to pork-barrel legislation won him many enemies who became the natural allies of those who, from whatever lofty motives, opposed his program of Reconstruction.

So much for the contribution of the northern churches to the bitterness of the period. What about those of the South? The attitude of the northern churches at the end of the war must be viewed in the light of equally extreme utterances on the other side, especially just before and during the conflict. The church in the South had not merely taken the other side in a political struggle and a war, but it had given the blessing of God to slavery and secession and had condemned its opponents as apostates and infidels. Abolitionism was described not merely as an economic error and an invasion of private rights but as "a crime against civilization and a sin against God." The religious sanctions for slavery and secession developed simultaneously with the religious sanctions for abolition and union. The South, indeed, was far more united in defending slavery on the ground that God wills it than the North was at first in claiming a divine command for emancipation. FitzHugh, the Virginia economist, lecturing at Yale before the war, had said that those who exalted liberty to the exclusion of slavery "are in effect committed to socialism and communism, to no private property, no church, no law, no government, free love, free lands, free women and free churches"—which sounds like a Chamber of Commerce description of Soviet Russia. (J. H. Denison: *Emotional Currents in American History*, p. 94.)

Southern pulpits proclaimed that abolition is infidelity. The duty of armed resistance was urged. "We are not only contending for our own rights but for the Bible itself. Abolition is infidel" (*Southern Presbyterian Herald*, December 2, 1860). It was proposed that the flag of the Confederacy include among its symbols an open Bible.

A sermon by a southern Baptist minister declared: "It is not simply a contest between different forms of civil polity or of civilizations. It is a conflict between divine revelation and human reason—between the Providence of God and the devices of man. Our institutions are scriptural, sanctioned by the practise of patriarchs and prophets and the precepts of the Savior. The fanaticism that assails us is the product of infidelity, of rebellion against God that presumes to be wiser than the scriptures and would substitute its disorganizing dogmas of liberty and equality for the conservative teachings of the New Testament. We southern ministers are the only preachers who proclaim an unmutilated Bible. Northern ministers have suppressed or perverted its teachings. . . . We are the champions of God's truth and he who falls in the contest will fall a blessed martyr" (*Charleston Mercury*, November 17, 1860).

The Alabama Methodist Episcopal conference in January, 1861, declared that "African slavery is a wise, humane and righteous institution approved of God." The Southern Baptist convention in 1861 formally approved the formation of the Confederacy and said that the northern churches were breathing out slaughter and clamoring for sanguinary hostilities. The Presbyterian Church in the Confederate States of America affirmed in 1862 that "the struggle is not alone for civil rights and property and home, but for religion, for the church, for the gospel."

Bishop Elliott, Episcopalian, in a Thanksgiving sermon delivered in Savannah, Georgia, September, 1862, after Confederate victories, gave utterance to a philosophy of history and a theory of God's part in it which won wide approval: "Presumptuous interference with the will and ways of God" (*i.e.*, with slavery) was the sin for which the nation was being punished. "When slavery was endangered by the scanty profits which were yielded to the planters by their old staples of indigo and rice, God permitted a new staple to be introduced—cotton. . . . When the border states which could not profitably grow this staple were calculating the value of the slave institution for themselves, and were actually debating in conventions its speedy extinction, a sudden and unexpected value was given to their old staples of wheat and tobacco; men again called it a happy accident, and the slave rose once again into importance, and God used self-interest to check the disposition toward emancipation."

The general assembly of the southern Presbyterian Church in 1864 declared: "We hesitate not to affirm that it is the peculiar mission of the southern church to conserve the institution of slavery and to make it a blessing to both master and slave."

These sentiments were expressed not once or twice but a thousand times in the pulpits and religious papers of the south. The clergy took a prominent part not only in defending the institution of slavery as an ordinance of God but in urging secession as a necessary means of protecting it. Some of their sermons were reprinted again and again and circulated as tracts. This was especially true of the sermons of Doctor Palmer and Doctor Furman. Many other conferences and conventions besides those mentioned unanimously adopted resolutions expressing the same sentiments, and many ministers were sent as delegates to the conventions of the seceding states. The North had every reason for believing, and indeed all the evidence in the world to prove, that the churches and their leaders in the South had identified the cause of religion absolutely with the cause of slavery and secession.

It is scarcely surprising, therefore, however regrettable it may be, that when the war was over those who had themselves been denounced by the southern pulpit as infidels and apostates should feel that the South was destitute of true religion and must necessarily remain so until and unless it was soundly converted by northern missionaries. The vehemence of the language in which this conviction is announced is, however, somewhat surprising. For example: "All eyes are turned upon the fair land that after fifty years of vital separation from the North is open to our civilization and Christianity. . . . The apostate (southern) church is buried beneath a flood of divine wrath; its hideous dogmas shine on its brow like flaming fiends; the whole world stands aghast at its wickedness and its ruin. The northern church beholds its mission. It sees these foes of our Lord and His Christ cast out from their sovereign seats. . . . We must occupy their places. Every church feels this; every late synod, conference or council arranges for it; every journal abounds in discussion concerning it" (*Independent*, July 27, 1865).

As a matter of fact, the projects actually attempted were by no means so impressive, nor were the terms in which they were expressed often as vicious, as those of the *Independent*. The fact that bulked largest in the thought of the northern churches was that there were four million Negroes in the South badly in need of both education and religion. The North greatly underestimated the desire of the southern churches to uplift the freedmen and grotesquely misconceived their spirit, but it could scarcely underestimate their financial resources. It was quite true that there was great need of help from the North.

The Congregational National Council, which met in Boston on June 14, 1865, promptly took up the challenge offered alike by the depleted state of the South and the inviting opportunities in the West. It "blew a trumpet of no uncertain sound on the state of the country, justice to the traitors, and suffrage to the freedmen," and planned to raise $750,000 for missionary work throughout the United States. A large part of this was intended to go and actually did go into the southern states. But the work done there under Congregational auspices had to do chiefly with the establishment of schools for Negroes and but little attention was given to converting the whites from their state of apostasy.

The Methodist missionary board in December of that year appropriated a million dollars for its foreign and home missionary work, of which amount $400,000 was designated for the southern field. The Methodist centenary in 1866 increased the denominational morale and helped in the promotion of the enterprise. The educational part of it was certainly badly needed. At a conference of Methodist Negro preachers in Mississippi at Christmas, 1865, a call for the election of a secretary was baulked by the discovery that not one of the preachers present could write. The Freedmen's Aid Society (Methodist) was organized in August, 1866, and within a year had five thousand pupils in fifty-nine schools. Industrial training was part of this plan.

The Presbyterians, like the Congregationalists, made no great efforts at evangelization among the Negroes and confined their work chiefly to the establishment of schools. The Methodists and Baptists with their more emotional appeal had great success in winning Negro converts. By 1871 there were twice as many Negro Methodists as white Methodists in the South. While the ideal of the northerners, with their rather doctrinaire notions of equality, had been to have Negroes and whites in the same churches, it did not work out that way. The great growth of Negro membership was in the separate Negro churches.

The emissaries of the northern churches who went into the South felt that the spiritual salvation of that area, the triumph of the Lord's cause and their own personal safety were tied up with the success of the radical branch of the Republican party and a strong and stern policy of reconstruction. In October, 1865, the editor of a Baptist paper wrote: "Let the military be withdrawn and the union men will be slaughtered like sheep by these unhung traitors." It was true enough that the northern missionaries and preachers who went into the South immediately after the war had to face difficulties and dangers. Most of them went with a very genuine zeal for the moral, spiritual and cultural uplift of the South's new citizens. There were others who used the Negroes' religion for political purposes.

Since the church had been so completely in alliance with the government in the effort to perpetuate the Union and put down slavery on one side and to perpetuate slavery by putting down the Union on the other, it was scarcely possible that political and religious considerations could be kept separate in the years of reconstruction. The Rev. Gilbert Haven, a man of high standing among the Methodists and the unanimous choice of the committee on publication for editor of *Zion's Herald,* summed up the attitude of the northern churches in an article published in January, 1867: "The southern church of all faiths has been of one heart and mind with the southern states in the devotion to that doctrine of devils—the ownership of man by man. . . . The diabolic unity of these churches is marvelous. Archbishop Lynch is their chief ally and guide and through his influence obtains recognition (of the Confederacy) by the Pope, the only one they ever received from a potentate. Bishop Polk lays down his life for the state and his senior bishop in his eulogy declares that his condition as a slave-holder especially fitted him for the episcopal office and puts him among the martyrs of the church. The Methodist bishops are equally fervent in their treason, as are also the leaders of the Presbyterian and Baptist orders. God saw the league and sin complete . . . the cup of iniquity was full. He must Himself come down and destroy these wicked husbandmen and give His vineyard unto those who will bring forth the fruits thereof." The occupation of the vineyard by northerners therefore had full religious sanction. Civil reconstruction requires "the removal of traitors" and control by loyal men. "Religious reconstruction also must come from the north. No southern church has power to unite or uplift its community. It has sinned beyond the world it professed to guide and its weakness and wretchedness surpasses that of society and the state. No other southerners that I have conversed with equal her clergy in bitterness of rage and despair. They made an idol of what others made only a matter of business or of pride. They set this god in the temple of Christ and declare it to be the only god. They still cling to the iniquity; they still rave at the truth. They are ferocious haters of God and man."

Bitter as these words were, every line of them can be matched by equally bitter denunciations of emancipation and its advocates by the southern clergy. But since the North had the power after the war, it was northern bitterness and bigotry which found opportunity for the most odious expression in actual policies and for the support of harsh political measures in the name of religion.

The Negroes themselves had gained legal freedom but had entered upon a condition of extreme confusion in mind, body and estate. Many assumed that freedom from slavery meant freedom from work. Many changed their names and started on migrations with no more definite purpose than to demonstrate their freedom to go. With the breaking of the ties which had held them to bondage, there was also in many cases the breaking of all other ties. Families were abandoned and there was a great and aimless shifting of population. The relaxation of the old restraints of compulsion left many with no restraints at all. While some sundered families took advantage of their new freedom to reunite and many informal unions of slave days received a legal sanction that was long overdue, many found a more alluring opportunity to break off old marital relationships and start all over. The disciplines of slavery had evidently been a poor school of domestic virtue. Colonel Watterson has told how the grant of the "elective franchise" was received with bewildered enthusiasm, since many of the recipients did not know what it was, and how the beneficiaries streamed into town expecting to carry it home in all sorts of receptacles from wheelbarrows to jugs.

The development of industry among the Negroes was hampered by the persistent rumor, kept alive by interested politicians, that the estates of the former masters were to be divided among the former slaves and that every freedman was to have "forty acres and a mule." In general, these free farms remained only a mirage and the phantom mules could never be hitched to a plow. Gradually the disillusioned Negroes who remained on the land settled down to the dubious lot of tenant farmers. But there were right-thinking white men, both northern and southern, who saw that education and industry must form the foundation for the Negroes' welfare, and normal schools and industrial institutions began almost immediately to be established. General Armstrong's Hampton Normal and Agricultural Institute set a pattern later followed by Booker Washington's school at Tuskegee and many others.

No sooner had freedom been attained than the ambitions of the more alert were focused upon two objectives, classical education and public office. The desire for office came first, appealed to the larger number and was soonest gratified. During the time when ex-Confederates were disfranchised, all Federal and states offices in the South were in the hands of Negroes, carpet-baggers and scalawags. What this sudden projection of an unprepared race into positions of governmental responsibility did to the government concerns us less at the moment than what it did to the race. It vastly increased the difficulty of developing economic independence, emotional stability and a normal culture. The rate of mortality among the freedmen, especially among their children, was terrific. War had taken its toll from the whites, but famine and pestilence preyed by preference upon the blacks.

But the Negro's religion was something which he had no disposition to leave behind when he emerged from slavery. In the general relaxation of social control there was unprecedented opportunity for religious excitement, and revival meetings and baptizings were among the most popular outdoor sports. Unscrupulous white politicians and Negroes with the capacity for leadership took advantage of the general confusion of ideas for their own purposes and religion was put to political uses on a large scale. While northern equalitarians might protest against the organization of separate Negro churches and insist that blacks and whites should worship together, as a matter of fact that was what they had done in slave days (the Negroes in the gallery, of course) and it was exactly what they did not do when freedom came. Separate Negro churches had already been organized (the African M.E. in Philadelphia in 1816, the African M.E. Zion in New York in 1820), but they had made almost no headway in the South. Bishop Paine of the African M.E. Church went from New York to Charleston in May, 1865, to gather the Negroes into Negro Methodist churches. White Methodists and white Baptists in the South recommended the licensing of Negro preachers and the establishment of Negro Sunday schools, many of which promptly developed into churches. These organizations almost immediately experienced a tremendous increase which was stimulated by the new revivalism which reproduced with characteristic embellishments the most ecstatic scenes of the camp meetings half a century earlier.

Generally speaking, in spite of the fears expressed by radicals both in the pulpit and on the stump in early reconstruction days, the former owners soon proved to be the best friends of the free Negroes. The Ku Klux Klan ruthlessly eliminated them from governments which had been left a prey to corrupt whites and illiterate blacks under the radical reconstruction scheme adopted by Congress, but gradually the phenomena of hysteria induced by sudden freedom passed away, some sort of economic stability even though on a low level was restored, schools began to offer opportunities for the ambitious, and the churches, now freed from the debasing effect of their subservience to political passions, began to make their proper contribution toward sane and decent living.

At the end of the Civil War, the agrarian South with its slave and cotton economy had ceased to be an obstacle to the dominance of the capitalistic and industrial North. The triumph of the North cleared the way for the development of capitalism. The two opposing attitudes to slavery, both largely economic in origin, had been idealized and sanctified; so also had the two conceptions of government. Slavery was inhuman, barbarous, demoniacal; or slavery was a divine institution, an essential part of the Christian social order, a blessing to slave and master. Secession was treason and perfidy against which the help of God might be reasonably asked and confidently expected; or secession was a noble defense of liberty, honor, and the sanctity of home and property for which the help of God, *etc., etc.* These deep antipathies could not be resolved by a victory of arms. The war proved nothing, settled no right, convinced nobody, and the churches helped to embitter both the conflict and the subsequent period of readjustment. They did, however, perform immense services to individuals both during the war and after it, and the passing of the old issues left room for the rise of an American system to which the churches of both North and South came to give their support.

Chapter III

WESTWARD HO!

The westward movement of population immediately after the Civil War and the simultaneous expansion of the churches to keep up with the migrating people were but a revival and continuation of the movement which had had its first great impetus in the discovery of gold in California in 1848. The panic of 1857 had destroyed for many people in the East every reason for staying where they were and had quickened their ears to the call of the West.

Then gold and silver were discovered in 1858 in what is now Nevada, including the Comstock lode which produced $340,000,000 in silver in the next thirty years. Gold and silver were found in Colorado in 1859. Its nearness as compared with California compensated for the fact that there was perhaps less of it. But, anyway, no one then knew how much there was. "Pike's Peak or bust" was the slogan of this new generation of Argonauts. Some achieved one of these objectives and some the other; some both. But the pressure of poverty behind and the pull of gold ahead were mighty stimuli to a western migration that would have occurred anyway, but more slowly.

There were new gold discoveries in Arizona in 1862, following the reopening of the old Spanish mines, and the copper deposits found later proved more valuable than the gold. Idaho became the goal of the gold rush from 1860 to 1863.

The three factors in the development of the West were minerals, cattle, and agriculture. To some extent these interests indicate successive periods, but there was much overlapping. The flow of population into the mountain areas was primarily determined by mining interests and the dates of the organization first of territories and then of states is a record of achievements built on this foundation of gold and silver. The advance of the frontier was always by sudden leaps to the scene of new mineral bonanzas, followed by a subsequent gradual filling in of the intervals. Before this was accomplished a fairly substantial civilization had been built along the Pacific, so that the final disappearance of the frontier was, like the completion of the first transcontinental railroad, the result of a meeting of lines that were advancing from both sides.

Mining itself never supported a large population and only those states which later developed resources in animal husbandry or agriculture had a growth to match their expectations. Nevada, for example, with a population of 42,000 in 1870 when it was three years old as a state, has never much more than doubled that figure. California, on the other hand, with 92,000 in 1850 (already more than Delaware at that time) had run into the millions as a result of the development of its mines and its agriculture even before its climatic appeal began to draw the seekers for winter sunshine. Colorado, organized as the territory of Jefferson in 1859 and as the territory of Colorado in 1861, had ample population to justify its admission to statehood in 1876 and continuous growth thereafter. More accessible than the far western diggings, it had received nearly 100,000 gold seekers in the first year of the rush of the 'fifty-niners, though more than half of them did not stay long.

"The great American desert," discovered or at least first made generally known by miners in transit to the Golcondas that lay beyond it, was conquered first by the cowboy and then by the homesteader. Before 1866, Texas had been the one great cattle state. The beginning of the cattle industry on a large scale and over a wider area dates from the discovery about that time that cattle could live on the prairie grass of what was still an unbroken buffalo range between the Missouri River and the Rocky Mountains and could survive the winters without shelter. There followed an influx of cattle and cowboys, and for two decades the cattle men were lords of the plains. Dodge City, Kansas, Ogallala, Nebraska, and Miles City, Montana, became the three principal centers, and the opening of the transcontinental railways furnished the necessary means of shipment to market.

Within a very few years the possibilities of raising winter wheat in the less arid parts of this area were discovered and there ensued a struggle between the cattle men and the farmers. The Homestead Act, signed by Lincoln in 1862, and the Morrill Act of the same year providing for Federal subsidy to an agricultural college in every state, stimulated the western movement of the farmers who were destined to form the bone and sinew of the new commonwealths into which they had entered under difficulties imposed both by unfavorable climatic conditions and by competition and often the armed opposition of the cattle men. By 1880 the decision in this latter struggle was in favor of the farmers.

Upon the life of the mining camps religion made but little impression. Its representatives there were few and they labored against the handicap of an abnormal social structure, an almost complete absence of family life, and a degree of poverty in general cultural resources which usually seemed to be in direct proportion to the abundance of gold dust. The facts which determined the social characteristics of the mining camp were, first, the almost total absence of women (at least women of the sort who could lend any support to a religious enterprise); and second, the fact that nobody expected to stay. But even in the mining camps and in the towns which grew up around them there were in the aggregate not a few preachers who are worthy of remembrance and admiration. One remembers, for example, the street preaching of William Taylor in San Francisco in the 'fifties. Although deriving its wealth from the mines, San Francisco was never strictly a mining town. It had already become considerably more than that when Thomas Starr King went to California for his health in 1860.

Unitarianism already had a footing by the Golden Gate and its prestige was greatly increased by the arrival of King, who had been minister of the prominent Hollis Street Unitarian church in Boston for eleven years and was besides a lyceum orator of note. As minister of the Unitarian Church in San Francisco, his sermons and lectures had much to do with keeping California in the Union. In 1860, Lincoln received only 28 per cent. of the California vote and the brilliant and popular Albert Sidney Johnson, later a Confederate general, was in command of the Federal forces in San Francisco. In 1864, California gave Lincoln a majority of 30,000. King had died a few months before that election but he preached few sermons during the first three years of the war that were not in some fashion pleas for the Union cause. His figure in bronze by Daniel Chester French now stands in Golden Gate Park—no small tribute to the political influence of an eastern preacher who spent less than four years in the state. When he was still a young Boston preacher of twenty-nine, a clipper ship was named after him which plied around Cape Horn to San Francisco, so he came to the Golden Gate with some introduction. Whether or not he was the most popular preacher in Boston, he probably had the best name for a ship—Starr King. What happened in San Francisco was no criterion of what could happen in any other western town of the time, but in 1864 the pew rents of King's church amounted to $20,000 a year, with $5,000 more from Sunday collections.

In the cow country the churches had little chance to operate, for the population was both sparse and migrant except at the shipping centers, and the cowboys in general were not greatly addicted to the practises of religion even when opportunity was afforded. There is record, however, of at least one Methodist congregation in western Kansas composed almost wholly of cowboys (W. H. Sweet: *History of Methodism in Northwestern Kansas*) and I knew personally, somewhat later, of course, one woman who, every Sunday for twenty years drove eighteen miles and back to conduct, in a little Arizona cow town, a Sunday school whose clientele consisted almost entirely of cowboys.

But it was with the coming of the homesteader and the building of towns along the railroads which had penetrated this vast area that the churches began to exercise a significant influence and to build permanent organizations. The railroads were the arteries of the new western country. Railroad building had gone on only a little less rapidly during the war than in the years just before it, and the consolidation of lines and the increase of traffic greatly enhanced the profits of the enterprise. Now for the first time investment in railroads ceased to be considered a highly speculative matter which could be indulged in only by people who had money that they could afford to lose—as was the case with the automobile and airplane industries in their early stages. Railroads like the Erie and the Illinois Central which had never before paid dividends were paying 8 per cent. or more by the end of the war, and their stocks rose to spectacular heights—the Erie from 17 to 126½, the Illinois Central from 6½ to 132. In 1865, the transcontinental lines had been authorized but not yet constructed. The Union Pacific, chartered in 1862 to build westward from Nebraska, and the Central Pacific to build eastward from California to meet it, were to begin construction within a few months. The Atchison, Topeka & Santa Fe had been given a Federal land grant in 1863 and the Northern Pacific in 1864, but both were still in the throes of trying to finance actual construction.

The railroad mileage in the United States, which totaled about 35,000 miles in 1865, was doubled within the next seven years. But the increase in mileage was even less significant than the extension of the area served. The building of the transcontinental lines served many purposes. It gave opportunity for the investment of eastern capital. It furnished occupation for labor. It drew immigration, both by furnishing work during the days of construction and by making new lands accessible for settlement. It put an end to the threatened danger that the far western communities would develop a culture and a political life independent of the East, creating a new unity between East and West to take the place of the strained and shattered bonds between North and South. It tied the nation together not only with hoops of steel but with at least the beginnings of settlement and civilization throughout the great spaces between the Mississippi and the Pacific. The great empty areas which before had served only to separate the East from the communities in the far West now began to give promise of uniting them into one nation of truly transcontinental extent. The old stage coaches had been picturesque, and, within necessary limits, efficient, but travel by them had been both slow and costly. Benjamin Holladay, who sold out his equipment to the Wells, Fargo Company for $2,500,000, charged $175 for carrying a passenger from the Missouri River to Denver, $350 to Salt Lake City, and from $400 to $500 to California. When the Central Pacific building eastward and the Union Pacific building westward met at Promontory Point, fifty-three miles west of Ogden, Utah, on May 10,

1869, it was the end of an epoch. Transportation at once became faster, cheaper and safer, and the volume of travel increased correspondingly. The building of subsidiary lines as feeders to the transcontinental roads had proceeded simultaneously.

The railroads were a boon to the West and a necessary instrument in the development of the whole country, but they were also to a very great extent a gift from the country to the promoters, who took money with one hand from their stockholders and with the other from the government, built the roads with the proceeds of bond issues and bonuses—and pocketed part of that. The Federal government gave the Union Pacific 120 square miles of land for each mile of track, and, in addition, a loan of $32,000 in United States bonds for each mile. The building of the line was put into the hands of the Credit Mobilier, a corporation composed chiefly of the inner circle of those who controlled the railroad. The Union Pacific paid the Credit Mobilier $93,000,000; Credit Mobilier paid the contractors $50,000,000; leaving a net profit of $43,000,000 for the inner circle. The actual capital which they had invested amounted to $218,000. They all became millionaires. When the Thurman Act, in 1878, required a deposit of 25 per cent. of the net earnings and all receipts from the government for transportation in a sinking fund for the repayment of the loan, Jay Gould, who then had control of the road, defied the government (*New York Times*, August, 1884). The dishonest financing of the railroads in this period of the great westward expansion long remained a demoralizing factor in American life. It is not on record that the churches had much to say about it at the time. Occasionally, a bold minister or religious editor would give utterance to a criticism, but the councils of the churches were silent. The thing was too intimately tied up with politics—which was, in fact, one of the worst things about it—and the northern churches were still so busy being "patriotic" (that is, Republican) that they were indisposed to venture any criticisms of the existing order.

But, however expensively and dishonestly built, the railroads both served and stimulated the westward migration, and this sudden opening of vast new areas in the West was a fact as important for the East as for the West. The completion of the first transcontinental line in 1869 was first a nine-days' wonder, and then an accepted fact. "The

Pacific railroad is an every-day reality with us now. . . . One can hardly inquire for a friend without being told that he has 'gone to California,' and people take pleasure in saying it in such an off-hand way as to show you that it is not a matter of any special consequence" (Chicago correspondent in the *Independent*, August 12, 1869). And this within three months after the completion of the first through road to the coast!

Meanwhile, during the war years and immediately after, all the northern cities were enjoying building booms, although the cost of building had greatly increased. It was during the war that the Capitol at Washington was completed. The *Chicago Tribune*, on October 8, 1863, thus summarized conditions in that city: "On every street and avenue one sees new buildings going up. Immense stone, brick and iron business blocks, marble palaces and new residences; everywhere the grading of streets, the building of sewers, the laying of water and gas pipes, all in progress at the same time."

The economic depletion of the South, in violent contrast with the North's rather swaggering prosperity, was due even more to the grotesque corruption of reconstruction than to the waste of war. Arkansas, for example, increased its state debt almost five-fold between 1868 and 1875 and had little to show for it, while its counties, which had been practically debt-free, came to the verge of bankruptcy. Most of the other southern states fared no better, and some of them worse. The churches inevitably bore their share in this financial debacle, for the people who would normally have supported the churches were staggering under a load of inordinate taxation to meet the expenses of governments dishonestly and incompetently administered by carpet-baggers and newly enfranchised and wholly incompetent Negroes. Nevertheless, they took hold of their local problems with indomitable courage and with what resources they could muster.

The churches faced their new tasks badly divided by the issues of the war but with an energy comparable to that which was sweeping business and industry into new ventures and whole populations into hitherto unpeopled areas. Split and shattered as they were, the churches of the North had acquired a little experience in working together by coöperation in the Christian Commission, which was organized in November, 1861, on the initiative of Y. M. C. A. leaders to "attend to the spiritual wants" of the soldiers. It also did nursing, furnished food and clothing where needed, and distributed reading matter. Most of the reading matter was Bibles, tracts and hymn-books— 1,370,953 hymn-books! In some camps revivals were held. "It is estimated that in Camp Convalescent, near Alexandria, Virginia, more than 1,000 conversions occurred in a single year" (*Methodist Almanac*, 1865). The Christian Commission collected and spent over six million dollars. All its personnel, both clergy and lay, served without pay. All of this represented the coöperation of Christians of various denominations, rather than of the denominations themselves.

Efforts at reunion began almost as soon as the war was over, but about all that happened was that the Old School and New School Presbyterians in the North united, as those of the South had done during the war.

After the meeting of the New School assembly at which the report of the reunion committee had been received with enthusiasm, Theodore Cuyler wrote: "In the blessed, full-banked flood of Christian love, the ice-floes of controversy and prejudice were swept away in the irresistible torrent." That is to say, northern Presbyterians, both Old and New, found, as the southern Presbyterians already had, more to unite them in their common loyalty than to divide them in their theological differences. But as between North and South, the ice-floes of controversy still prevailed against whatever torrents of Christian love there were—as they did also with the Baptists and Methodists.

Nevertheless, the churches were quick to hear the call of the new opportunities. "Loyalty" and anti-slavery conviction might assure them that the South needed to be conquered by a northern gospel as certainly as it had needed to be conquered by northern armies, but as a matter of fact the idea of converting the apostate South was largely a matter of journalistic rhetoric. Northern Methodists did, to be sure, take possession of a good many southern Methodist churches, and it was one of President Johnson's offenses that he had restored these to their rightful owners as soon as the matter was brought to his attention. But after the first frantic days of reconstruction, northern missionary effort in the South increasingly took the form of education, especially for the Negroes.

But the compelling fact of history and geography was that there was a new West—a West into which population was pouring along the lines of the newly constructed railroads. Within a decade after the close of the war, the enormously increased facilities for travel and the effect of this increase on the movement of population had both set a new problem for the churches and given them a new instrument with which to meet it. It was, of course, only a new phase of an old problem. The church has always followed the frontier, and a period in which the frontier advanced with the speed of steam instead of the deliberation of ox-carts merely gave a more striking exhibition of this ancient and enduring characteristic.

In spite of the distractions of war, the churches had been increasing their resources, both personal and material. The growth in membership from the Revolution to the Civil War was more rapid than the growth of the population. At the outbreak of the Revolution, not more than one person out of twenty-five in the American colonies was a church member. The idea that our colonial and revolutionary ancestors were all God-fearing, church-going people is a persistent illusion. Between 1800 and 1850 the number of church members was multiplied by about twelve, the total population by four and one-half. From 1850 to 1870, church membership increased 84 per cent., from 6,000,000 to 11,000,000, while population increased 65 per cent., from 23,000,000 to 38,000,000. The value of church property was $87,000,000 in 1850, $171,000,000 in 1860, and $354,000,000 in 1870. In this rapid increase in tangible assets, the Roman Catholics had a little more than their proportionate share with $9,000,000, $26,000,000, $61,000,000 for the three years mentioned. Increase in the value of urban real estate contributed part of these gains. The church has always profited by the "unearned increment."

Until the completion of the first transcontinental railroad, there was relatively little concerted and organized action on the part of the churches to occupy the new territory, though it would be easy to cite exceptions to this statement. The Methodist Church Extension Society was founded in 1864, and the Congregational National Council in 1865 had raised money for the evangelization of the West as well as the education of the South. Other boards of home missions, of church extension and of education came into existence soon, after 1870, and the process of expansion proceeded with a quickened tempo. In gen-

eral, it may be said that up to about 1890 the dominant interest was
in the occupation of new territory. Then followed more intensive
efforts, frequently competitive. After the turn of the century there was
a more lively awareness of the new frontiers, which had indeed been
discovered by adventurous spirits some years earlier, in the problems
of urban life, immigrant populations, and industrial and international
relations.

But the obvious business of the churches in the late 'sixties and the
'seventies was to go West. Here was a Canaan, upon which Calebs and
Joshuas like Marcus Whitman and William Taylor had made favorable report, open to occupation, with a railroad running through the
center of it and not an Amalekite in the whole land. While individual
missionaries penetrated to remote spots and devoted laymen often
planted the seed of churches wherever they happened to be, the main
lines of church development followed the railroads. The enterprising
Baptist Home Missionary Society, for example, secured from the
Union Pacific and Central Pacific railroads the promise of a free
site for a church and a parsonage in every town along their lines.
Chaplain C. C. McCabe, assistant secretary of the Church Extension
Society of the Methodist Episcopal church from 1868 to 1884, plied up
and down the western railroads establishing, or overseeing the establishment of, churches at the boasted rate of "two a day." By 1890, the
loan fund of that society had aided in the building of 9,000 churches—
not all in the West, of course. The Congregationalists, who, in spite
of their long history, were just beginning to have a national organization, pressed vigorously westward, not founding churches in as many
communities as the Methodists were able to do by their system of
circuits and their utilization of lay class-leaders, but taking excellent
care of those that they did establish. Unitarianism was not without its
ambition for westward expansion, as the experience of Starr King in
San Francisco had proved, and the *Christian Register* is quoted as
saying that "the first church organized in Kansas was the Unitarian
Church in Lawrence." But by 1869 they had only two churches in
that state, while the Congregationalists had forty-nine (eight of them
less than a year old), the New School Presbyterians over twenty, and
the Methodists probably more than either.

The Disciples, born and bred on the frontier, were at home in this pioneering work but lacked the resources of both trained men and money which the older denominations were able to draw from their bases in the East. Their one missionary society was charged with the responsibility for both home and foreign work, but did little of either, until the organization of a foreign missionary society in 1875 operated as a spur to the older society whose energies were now released for work in the home field. By far the greater part of the planting of new churches in the West during the early period was done either by individual effort or by state organizations. The church extension board of the Disciples was not established until 1883, when it at once began to bring strong support to the beginnings that had already been made in all the prairie and mountain states. The Lutheran advance was largely a matter of keeping up with the German and Scandinavian immigrants who had brought their faith with them into new fields. Many, unfortunately, had left it behind; perhaps no larger a proportion than in other groups, but, since they came from countries where everybody was supposed to be Lutheran, the defection was the more conspicuous. Nevertheless, Lutheranism became an important factor in the religious development of the Northwest.

The Episcopalians began immediately after the war to build on the foundations which had been laid in the West during the preceding quarter-century by Bishop Kemper, who had begun with Indiana and Missouri as his diocese and had added Iowa, Minnesota and Wisconsin and parts of Kansas and Nebraska. Bishop Talbot created a diocese in Montana, Wyoming, Colorado and Utah where, at the time of his entrance, there had been not much but scenery and the brawling confusion of the mining camps. In a patient and orderly way, parishes were established, dioceses created and missionary work done among both whites and Indians, always with strong support from the eastern base of supplies. The names and work of Bishops Whipple, Hare and Tuttle are memorable.

The time of vigorous interdenominational work had not yet come. The Young Men's Christian Association, however, began even before the completion of the first transcontinental railroad to hold religious meetings at the railroad stations along the Union Pacific for the benefit of the crowds who were going West and for the workmen on the line. Services were held at all important points along the road and with the army of track-layers at the end of it. At Benton, Nebraska, when it was for the moment the last town reached by the rails, one series of services was being held on a street corner, another in an auction tent, and another in a gambling tent. Benton was, in fact, composed chiefly of tents. "Not since 1858," wrote the *Independent's* western correspondent, on April 9, 1868, "has there been such a year of religious interest in the West. Revivals have prevailed everywhere. One of the principal instrumentalities in promoting this work is the Christian Convention, which is now a well-established institution. The first one was held last October in Lawrence, Kansas. A Mass Christian Convention meets next week in Madison, Wisconsin."

But even in the 'sixties the religious activities in the West were not all of the street-corner and tent variety. These were the flush times before the panic of 1873, and as cities came to civic consciousness and began to build anything that was substantial and impressive, they built impressive and substantial churches. Des Moines in 1868, claiming a population of 12,000, "now is in its swift enterprise the antithesis of its name, 'of the monks'; depots, horse-railroads, river bridges and costly edifices are anxious to get themselves finished in a day. Among the novelties are a Baptist temple with cappings of many-colored sandstone, and a thirty thousand dollar New School (Presbyterian) sanctuary" (*Independent*, January 23, 1868).

Of the older denominations those which most successfully met the demands of the new frontier were the Methodist, Baptist and Presbyterian. These had no monopoly upon either energy or devotion but they had the most experience in pioneer work and the best developed technique for carrying it forward. The denominational consciousness had been dormant in Congregationalism until about 1837. Congregationalism had, in fact, up to that time never been in the position of one of a number of sects competing on an equal basis. Where it had been anything at all it had been nearly everything. With the disestablishment of the churches in New England it had to learn how to live under a new order and with the opening of the West it had to learn how to expand. The plan of union between Congregationalists and Presbyterians (1801) was a reflection of the fact that the two denominations were in substantial agreement on theology (at that time a rather unmodified Calvinism), found their differences in polity too great to permit merging but not important enough to prevent close coöperation, and saw the advantage of working together for expansion of their common faith into what was then the new West.

After a third of a century of cooperation with the Presbyterians under the plan of union, the Congregationalists became aware that, as a denomination, they were getting rather the worst of it. It was estimated that between the Alleghanies and the Mississippi Congregational missionaries had founded two thousand churches which became Presbyterian. Now a new consciousness of kind arose among the Congregationalists and new plans were adopted to make it promotionally effective. Oberlin College was established in 1832. Specifically Congregational associations began to be formed in Ohio, Illinois, Michigan and neighboring states. Illinois College at Jacksonville antedated Oberlin by two years and an Illinois band and an Iowa band of young preachers came out from eastern seminaries to plan Congregational churches. Iowa College and Beloit College were founded in 1847. In the decade immediately preceding the war there was a steady advance in Wisconsin and Minnesota. Marcus Whitman's journey to Oregon in 1835 was a foreign-missionary enterprise since his purpose was to Christianize the Indians and since the United States did not then have a clear title to the Oregon territory. Missouri was entered, rather tardily it seems, in 1852 by the establishment of a Congregational church in St. Louis. But the lines of migration to Missouri had been largely from Kentucky and southern Illinois and not from New England. The Presbyterians and the Congregationalists were neck and neck in the race for the Golden Gate and neither of them more than half a jump behind the gold seekers, for the Presbyterians established a church in May, 1849, and the Congregationalists one in July of the same year under the ministry of a Yale graduate.

The Albany convention of 1852—the first Congregational gathering of more than state proportions since the Cambridge synod in 1648—directed its attention especially toward the Middle West and began the raising of funds to aid in the erection of meetinghouses in the states of the Mississippi valley. It was as a part of this general movement for the evangelization and education of the West that the Chicago Theological Seminary was organized in 1854. Immediately after the war there was a new access of zeal for denominational organization and advancement. The national council which met in Boston in 1865 rejected a proposal to declare its adherence to the "system of truths which is commonly known as Calvinism," asserting in more general terms its acceptance of "the faith and order of the apostolic and primitive churches," and undertook the raising of $250,000 for missionary work in the South and West. During the next fifteen years Congregational activities included three items. The first was the establishment of a regular series of triennial national councils beginning at Oberlin in 1871. The second was the founding of educational institutions in the South, including Howard University at Washington, D. C., and Fisk University at Nashville, both in 1866, Hampton Normal and Agricultural Institute in Virginia in 1868, Atlanta University in 1869 and half a dozen others in other southern states. The effort to establish Negro churches met with little success, but the educational program was rich in results. The third was a steady wave of church building in the western states, so that year by year new territory was entered, evangelized and organized until by 1882 there was not a western state or territory in which Congregationalism was not represented. Nevertheless, Congregationalism continued to be for the most part a church of those somewhat above the average cultural level. Its strength was in the more rapidly growing cities rather than in the towns and villages and its influence and prestige were more than proportional to its numbers.

The Methodists in the years immediately after the war were concerned with problems of internal readjustment as well as with those of territorial expansion. It is evidence of an abounding vitality that they accomplished both so effectively at the same time. The separation between the northern and southern churches had been embittered by the experiences of war and the political and military activities of the churches on both sides, and the bitterness had been exacerbated by the occupation of southern Methodist church buildings by northern Methodist preachers by order of the Secretary of War in 1862. The missionary activities of the northern church led to the organization of conferences throughout the South and to the inclusion of Negroes among its membership. At the same time two Negro Methodist churches which had been organized much earlier in the North—the African Methodist Episcopal Church and the African Methodist Episcopal Church Zion—had a spectacular growth in the South. In 1870, the Negro members of the Methodist Episcopal Church South, upon the suggestion of the white members, formed a separate organization known as the Colored Methodist Episcopal Church. Thus four Methodist churches were seeking Negro membership, and a fifth was not unmindful of its obligation to give guidance and education to the black brother. Both white churches were building churches and schools in the South, and both soon took the long overdue step of admitting laymen to their general conferences, but only the northern church was in a position to undertake the winning of the West.

The Methodists had no need of any quickening of their denominational consciousness, as the Congregationalists had. They were born with it. The story of their westward expansion could be fully told only by the recital of a multiplicity of details separately insignificant but in the aggregate momentous. What happened in northwestern Kansas is a sample of what happened all over the West. In 1865, a Methodist layman took up a homestead in Clay county, and promptly organized a Sunday school. "There were no school houses in the country. Religious services were held in the cabins and dugouts of the settlers, or in the groves in warm weather. Indian raids were not uncommon" (W. H. Sweet: *History of Methodism in Northwest Kansas*). "Classes" were organized. An occasional homesteader served as local preacher. A circuit was formed; then divided into two, each with six or eight appointments. Quarterly meetings were held with the presence of a visiting presiding elder. Here was what we have since learned to call an "indigenous church," with no help from any society or board until presently the church extension society began to give help in the erection of buildings—a matter not so easy to take care of locally as it had been in the timbered states farther East, where it had always been a simple matter for the members of any community to chop down trees and build a log house.

The college-builders followed close upon the heels of the first wave of settlers. Before the beginning of the Civil War, the Methodists had already founded these colleges in the western states: McKendree College, Illinois, 1834; Lawrence University, Wisconsin, 1848; University of the Pacific, California, 1851; Willamette University, Oregon, 1854; Hamline University, Minnesota, 1854; Cornell College, Iowa, 1857;

Baker University, Kansas, 1858. This dry list of names and dates is eloquent when one considers the cultural and economic level of these states at the periods mentioned. Founded in 1858, Baker University in Kansas had over 200 students in 1865. Two years later it "is the oldest living working institution in the state and has more students than half of the other denominational schools." Kansas had become a state in 1861 with 107,000 inhabitants, so there was no great constituency for all these denominational colleges, especially since there were already three state institutions in Kansas, but colleges were considered indispensable to denominational self-respect. They were not large. Baker had only three teachers in 1872—but Yale never had more than four until it was nearly a century old. In 1873 came the general financial crash, and the next year the grasshoppers ate every green thing in Kansas except the prairie grass and the apples. In 1877, conditions were so far improved that the president of Baker received a salary of $526, and furnished his own house.

Nebraska furnishes an equally typical example of the building of churches with the building of a commonwealth. The political struggle over the slavery question after 1854 was one in which the church-members took an active part on the anti-slavery side. The Nebraska conference was organized in 1861, when the territory had a population of 28,000. The next year it resolved "that we hold in the deepest abhorrence the wicked and treasonable efforts of the southern states." Economic difficulties kept the churches near the starvation point through the decade of the 'sixties, but the population grew to 122,000 and the churches more than kept pace. In the 'seventies there was a four-fold increase in population, a rapid westward extension of the frontier of settlement, a multiplication of churches with little improvement in their material condition, and a scourge of grasshoppers. Circuits were the rule and one-church pastorates were rare exceptions. After 1880 came the period of more and better buildings, better organized churches, and settled pastorates. The churches and the state had suffered and matured together. And so they did all over the West.

In the same spirit, and with much the same results, the Baptists and Presbyterians were building churches and thereby helping to build commonwealths. In 1869, nine young men from an eastern seminary formed themselves into a Presbyterian Kansas band under the leadership of Timothy Hill. These and a hundred others who followed them in the next twenty years planted about three hundred Presbyterian churches in Kansas and the Indian Territory. It would be impossible accurately to estimate or evaluate the service which religion rendered in laying the foundations of civilization upon the western frontiers, but, apart from the value of the ethical and spiritual idealism which it contributed, account must be taken of the fact that the churches did much to make men feel at home under new and often austere conditions and to keep them there through the hard years.

But the new settlements, like the old colonies, contained not only their reasonable proportion of those who had never had any interest in religion but a considerable percentage of those who, though brought up in the nurture and admonition of the Lord, had said good-bye to God when they crossed the Missouri River. In the mining camps, the dominant mood was that of men who had no expectation of staying long. They were going to get rich quick and go back East. So long as that temper prevailed, there was great difficulty in building churches or any other kind of permanent institutions. In the agricultural centers —both those of the prairie states and the new irrigation communities which sprang up a little later and were multiplied when the Federal government took a hand through its reclamation service—the spirit was entirely different. There, as at the railroad junctions and trading centers, the boomers were confident that cities would rise, and these new cities must of course have all the appurtenances of the cities that they had known in the East, churches included. There the business man's association or the Chamber of Commerce was an active ally of the church-builder, though often enough it was quite indifferent as to what kind of church should be built. If the local boomers supported one denomination rather than another, it was because a church had to be run by somebody and there had not yet been developed any method of operating churches apart from the traditional denominational machinery. Protestant home missionary societies raised and spent an average of a little less than a million dollars a year in the decade of the 'fifties; two million a year in the 'sixties; three million a year in the 'seventies; four million a year in the 'eighties.

Meanwhile, it must be remembered, both the church and the country had other interests than the settlement of the West, though perhaps few so exotic and improbable as that reflected in the announcement concerning a certain Mr. Puncheon who delivered several addresses to packed audiences in Chicago in 1868. "On Sunday afternoon the Opera House would not hold a tenth of those who wanted to hear him; nor would it on Tuesday evening contain those who desired to hear him on 'Daniel in Babylon,' at an admission fee of one dollar" (*Independent*, May 28, 1868). One of those interests was education, and another was high finance. In regard to neither was the church very critical.

In *The Education of Henry Adams* we find this: "In essentials like religion, ethics, philosophy, history, literature, and art, in the concepts of all science except perhaps mathematics, the American boy of 1854 stood nearer the year one than the year 1900." And so far as the formal content of education was concerned, the boy of 1865 stood approximately with the boy of 1854. The changes which were already close at hand had not yet revealed their import. And since teachers cannot be reasonably expected to have the gift of prophecy, education was inevitably adjusted to the past rather than to the future—even though, as we now know, the then very near future was to witness radical transformations. In 1860, there were only 321 high schools and academies in the United States, and more than half of these were in Massachusetts, New York and Ohio. The number of public high schools was not more than 100. In spite of the multiplication of denominational colleges—many of which would have rated as junior colleges, or less, if the term had then been current—higher education was in its infancy. In 1873, there were only 23,000 college students in the whole country, most of them in the East and many of them below present college grade. Up to 1870 such departments as history, political science and sociology existed either in embryo or not at all. At Columbia University, for example, one professor taught all the mental and moral philosophy, logic, English literature, history and political economy that were taught. The modern period in higher education was ushered in with the administration of Eliot at Harvard, McCosh at Princeton, Gilman at Johns Hopkins, and White at Cornell.

The other important interest besides westward expansion and education was business, now for the first time showing signs of being about to become Big Business. The word "million" began to figure prominently in the popular vocabulary. Besides an enlarged domestic demand for all sorts of commodities, the manufacture of which behind a tariff wall became increasingly profitable, there were foreign wars from which American trade derived profit—the Austro-Prussian war of 1865–1866 and the South American war involving Brazil, Argentina, Uruguay and Paraguay. Steel was the great new industry. Following the invention of the Bessemer process in England in 1858 and its establishment in the United States in 1864, the industry grew tremendously with increasing profits and increasing centralization. The building of railroads furnished a steady demand for rails which took most of the product of the steel mills. The meat-packing industry was a product of these same years. The Union Stock Yards of Chicago was incorporated in 1865, and the great names still prominent in that connection are the ones which gained their eminence in those early years. As in the case of steel, concentration brought lower prices to the consumer. The development of milling followed the same pattern —concentration in a few centers and in the hands of a few men, with an accompanying improvement and cheapening of the product and the building of great fortunes. The industrial revolution so far seemed all to the good. The story of oil is almost too romantic to be included in a serious history, but it was a romance of reality. Few of the uses of petroleum were known. It was a lubricant, an illuminant and a patent medicine. But a few prophetic spirits already saw in it the making of one of the world's great industries, and thousands were rushing to this and that new oil field in Pennsylvania as to gold fields. In 1865 the first tank car was put on wheels and the first pipe line was built. John D. Rockefeller had made his first modest investment in oil three years before, and two years later he organized his first oil company. A score of other industries, formerly carried on by individuals and small concerns on a small scale, furnished fields for the development of great manufacturing corporations. Such were the making of shoes, clothing, watches, cotton goods, sewing machines, farm implements, pianos and organs. Mr. Pullman began to make his cars in 1867. The great brewing companies whose product was soon to make Milwaukee famous multiplied the volume of their product by five within the eight years after the war.

While the occupied rural area was increased enormously by the opening of the West, the predominance of the cities in the total national economy also increased. This was necessarily so in a period of capitalistic development, for capital is collected in cities and directed from cities. The American people were living together in larger masses than ever before, but they had not yet learned how to do it with comfort or safety. Urban transportation was still a matter of horse-drawn cars and cabs. New York got its first elevated in 1870. Cities were built almost entirely of highly inflammable materials. While the Chicago fire of 1871 was the greatest, it was by no means the only notable conflagration of the period. Concrete was first used in construction in 1870. Passenger elevators began to be introduced only a little before that time when the height of the newest hotels and office-buildings reached six or even eight stories. Telephones and typewriters did not come into use until the 'seventies.

The business of making and selling things on a grand scale and building the material foundation of a new civilization brought with it new and startling developments in the business of finance. Then as now there were all kinds of big business men, from Jim Fisk and Daniel Drew, stock market pirates and railroad wreckers, to Peter Cooper, Abiel A. Low, father of Seth Low, and Theodore Roosevelt the elder, father of President Theodore Roosevelt, all successful men of affairs who were also idealistic and public-spirited citizens. But the general level of business ethics was low, and the church, perhaps confused by the complexity of new moral issues or blinded by the generosity of those who spent piously the money that they gained in devious ways, had little to say about it. The new financial sins had not yet acquired the odium which had long been attached to the sins of the flesh. Daniel Drew, scuttling the Erie Railroad and escaping across the Hudson River to the sheltering shore of New Jersey one jump ahead of the sheriff, was founding a theological seminary and attending prayer meeting when he was not printing bogus shares or devising and practising the technique of watering stock. Commodore Vanderbilt found no inconsistency between extending his patronage to the adventuresses Woodhull and Claflin and founding Vanderbilt University. ("The Commodore's great wealth would alone make him a notoriety, but it is on the score of his personal character . . . that we have given him a niche in our gallery of live Americans," *Independent*,

October 15, 1868.) And Jay Cooke, who had no scruple about corrupting legislatures in the interest of the Northern Pacific Railroad, was president of the Evangelical Education Society of the Protestant Episcopal Church. ("We need all the Jay Cookes we have and a thousand more. We want them because they are a help to the present age; because they use their money for noble, patriotic, benevolent, and Christian purposes," *Independent*, November 5, 1868.)

It was, in short, not only the age of the great westward advance and of post-war prosperity, it was also the Gilded Age. There was much gold at the heart of it, but the gilt on its surface was glittering and thin.

Chapter IV

THE GILDED AGE

The decade immediately after the Civil War had other characteristics not directly related to the advancing frontier. It was a period of imported culture rather superficially apprehended; a time of Victorian elegance and mansard roofs; a period of high regard for the conventions of personal conduct, loose ideas of integrity in government and business, and bad taste in art. Mumford speaks of the springtime of American culture, from 1830 to 1850, after which the Civil War, like an unseasonable killing frost, ushered in an untimely autumn, 1865 to 1895. (Lewis Mumford: *The Brown Decades*, New York, 1931.) This is, I think, too harsh a judgment.

America had leaped to its new work with great gusto. Only a little later it also began to learn to play, but not at first with a very good conscience. Respectability laid a rather heavy hand on manners and morals. It was a gilded age in business, but a period of dark domestic interiors, of walnut in place of the earlier rosewood and mahogany, and of black haircloth for chintz. E. C. Stedman, the broker-poet, compared America mourning for Lincoln to a vulgar woman who looks like a lady because she is dressed in black. The combination of financial and patriotic interests and the gainful aspects of the war are reflected in these quotations (cited by Mumford) from the diary of a poet, perhaps Stedman himself:

Nov. 8, 1864. Stood two hours in the rain and voted for old Abe. Realized on stocks and made $1,375.
Nov. 9. Yesterday a great triumph for the national cause. Thank God! The future of America is now secure.
Nov. 10. Fall in gold. I make on everything I manage for myself.

The blaring and blatant qualities of the culture of the age were exemplified in the gigantic music festivals held ostensibly in the celebration of peace and thereafter as expressions of civic pride. The crowning glory was attained in the Boston festival of 1872, directed by P. S. Gilmore, with 20,000 singers and an orchestra of two thousand pieces reinforced by military bands, both foreign and domestic, with an obligato of anvils and artillery. This was not, to be sure, an episode in the history of religion, but it is part of the picture of the national mood within which and against which religion had to make its way.

"Analyze the most talked-of men of the age," says Parrington, "and one is likely to find a splendid audacity coupled with an immense wastefulness. A note of tough-mindedness marks them. They had stout nippers. They fought their way encased in rhinoceros hides. There was the Wall Street crowd—Daniel Drew, Commodore Vanderbilt, Jim Fisk, Jay Gould, Russell Sage—blackguards for the most part, railway wreckers, cheaters and swindlers, but picturesque in their rascality. There was the numerous tribe of politicians—Boss Tweed, Fernando Wood, G. Oakley Hall, Senator Pomeroy, Senator Cameron, Roscoe Conkling, James G. Blaine—blackguards also for the most part, looting city treasuries, buying and selling legislative votes like railway stock, but picturesque in their audacity. There were the professional keepers of the public morals—Anthony Comstock, John B. Gough, Dwight L. Moody, Henry Ward Beecher, T. De Witt Talmage—ardent proselyters, unintellectual, men of one idea but fiery in zeal and eloquent in description of the particular heaven each wanted to people with his fellow Americans. And springing up like mushrooms after a rain was the goodly company of cranks—Virginia Woodhull and Tennessee Claflin, 'Citizen' George Francis Train, Henry Bergh, Ben Butler, Ignatius Donnelly, Bob Ingersoll, Henry George—picturesque figures with a flair for publicity who tilled their special fields with splendid gestures. And finally, there was Barnum the Showman, growing rich on the profession of humbuggery, a vulgar greasy genius, pure brass without any gilding, yet in picturesqueness and capable effrontery the very embodiment of the age. A marvelous company, vital with the untamed energy of a new land. In the presence of such men one begins to understand what Walt

Whitman meant by his talk about the elemental." (V. L. Parrington: *The Beginnings of Critical Realism in America*, p. 12, Harcourt, Brace & Co., 1930.)

Among the epithets that have been applied to the years immediately after the Civil War are The Gilded Age, The Tragic Era, The Dreadful Decade and The Pragmatic Acquiescence. The first of these terms has special reference to the rapid increase in wealth and the spirit of hope and adventure which accompanied it; the second, to the political malfeasance of the reconstruction program; the third, to a certain philistinism, the depraved state of public taste and the grotesque incongruity between the pretensions of Victorian morality and the lusty and robustious unrestraint with which the leaders of the period pursued their chosen ends; the fourth, to a lapse from the idealisms of the preceding generation to the mood of getting what you want and getting it quick regardless of methods. The prophets of the first were the railroad builders and the masters of the budding and burgeoning million-dollar industries; of the second, Thaddeus Stevens and Ben Wade; of the third, P. T. Barnum and all the lesser but more serious men who applied claptrap and tawdry methods to the achievement of worthy ends. The fourth was perhaps too widely diffused and too vague to warrant attaching to it specific names. None of these descriptive terms tells the whole story but each has its special appropriateness, though all of them ignore the worthier aspects of the period.

There was sharp contrast between the undisciplined idealisms of the 'thirties and 'forties and the practical-minded enterprises of the Gilded Age. William Miller could persuade thousands that the end of the world was coming in 1842. He would have had a harder time in 1868. In that halcyon day of hope and progress, people could easily believe anything about the world, especially the western world, except that it was coming to an end. That thought would have been intolerable. What!—the world come to an end before the Union Pacific was built through to the coast and when all those vast resources of the mountains and the plains were on the verge of development? A sensible God would never think of such a thing, and sensible men would have none of it.

Yet this enhanced confidence in the inevitability of progress and the certainty of cash returns from adventurous enterprise was bought with the price. There was a "pragmatic aquiescence" in whatever methods seemed most promising of quick profits and most consonant with the prevailing mood of expansion and enrichment. Nobody knew much about evolution yet, but everybody believed in the inevitability of progress and the infinite perfectability of America. The war was over. The social order had been vindicated. Business was good and getting better, and a terrestrial millennium was just over the brow of the hill. (I speak, of course, of the mood of the North.) There were few now who cared to build little Utopias of their own as models of the way in which society should be revolutionized. Why revolutionize anything that was already so nearly right? Fourierism, which in one form or another had motivated a score of idealistic communities a generation earlier, was about dead. Though Horace Greeley kept the faith and encouraged the establishment of a colony which was named after him in Colorado, the actual development of even that community was wholly along other lines. People were not interested in the radical reconstruction of society but in the development of the natural resources of this good world and in getting rich in the process. There was a wave of hysteria that was half carnality, corruption and avarice, and half faith and hope in and for the country. The historian of the Adams family says of this period: "As the nation turned aside from whatever idealism there had been in the war, it was to throw itself into an insane rush for power—money, land, mines, politics, railroads, any form of control that would lead to power for the individual. No one appeared to have any idea what he was going to do with wealth or power when he got it. There was merely a mad rush to get it. There was no time to think or someone would get it first." (James Truslow Adams: *The Adams Family*.)

The decade following the Civil War witnessed what has been called "a moral collapse without precedent." Congress and state legislatures were corrupted to secure grants to the railroads. The promoters enriched themselves at the expense of the stockholders and the government. The Tweed ring, which got its full grip on New York City in 1868, had within the next three years looted the treasury of an amount which may have been as little as fifty million dollars and may have been as much as two hundred million. The adventures

of Jay Gould, Daniel Drew, Jim Fisk and Commodore Vanderbilt
with the Erie Railroad are classic. When the first three got control and
issued ten million dollars of fraudulent stock certificates, the fight
shifted to Albany for the legalization of the issue. Gould bought
the votes of legislators at an average price of fifteen thousand dollars.
One state senator took seventy-five thousand from Vanderbilt, then
a hundred thousand from Gould and voted for the latter. The effort
of Fisk and Gould to corner gold led to Black Friday, September 4,
1869. President Grant, doubtless technically innocent, emerged with
a badly smirched reputation. What was happening on a large scale
in high places was happening on a smaller scale almost everywhere
else. The general level of business morality has perhaps never been
so low.

The South was to a great extent exempt by reason of its own
limitations and misfortunes from this carnival of corruption, except
as it was imported in the process of reconstruction. The immediate
effect of the war had been to bring prosperity to the North and ruin
to the South. The North was already rapidly becoming industrial,
and the war and the subsequent surge of activity made it more so.
The South was and long remained mainly agricultural. Its labor
system was convulsed and its working capital annihilated. It was
not only impoverished but left in a position where it got small benefit
from the general national revival of manufacture and trade. But it
escaped also the demoralizing concomitants of the prosperity that
passed it by.

The national wealth increased from fourteen billion to forty-four
billion between 1860 and 1880; so Blaine said in accepting the
Republican nomination in the latter year. The tendency was already
toward the concentration of wealth in a few hands. In 1867 a magazine, the *Galaxy*, said that ten men owned one-tenth of all the taxable
property in New York City, and it named them and listed their
holdings. From time to time there were protests in the name of
religion, though these for the most part came later. "We dissent from
Mr. Blaine and the tendencies he represents," said the *Christian Union*
(October 16, 1884). "We do not estimate the wealth of the community by its aggregate values but by its distributed comforts."

The rapidity with which the material instruments of civilization were being improved is indicated by a partial list of inventions: 1865 saw the first web printing press, the first tank car and the first oil pipe line; 1866, the trans-Atlantic cable; 1867, the combined reaper and binder, and the Pullman car; 1868, the first typewriter; 1869, the Westinghouse air-brake; 1875, the refrigerator car for shipping meat; 1876, the first telephone; 1877, the first phonograph. Business was exuberant under the stimulus of the new opportunities for investment and the new wants which these and other inventions both satisfied and stimulated. Instead of the hoped-for spiritual awakening, which is always expected after a war and never comes, there was a rank growth of that practical materialism which expresses itself both in an inordinate eagerness to acquire wealth and in an undisciplined use of it, and which, infecting even religion, creates a disproportionate interest in external expansion and the building of visible institutions.

But this same eagerness for wealth and this exultation in the visible prosperity of the nation as a whole rendered the leaders, both secular and religious, relatively blind to the condition of the workers. Wages were low and living conditions almost uniformly bad. An occasional humanitarian critic pointed out the disgraceful state of the tenements and the outrageous conditions under which women and small children worked for wages only a little removed from absolute zero. But for the most part the moral as well as the financial leadership of the country was hypnotized by the idea that the country as a whole was booming.

And so for the time it was. The financial crash of 1873 checked expansion, ruined thousands and chilled the buoyant spirit of optimism. Pulpits moralized on the sinfulness of the former luxury and the medicinal qualities of the depression. Beecher, however, rebuked the shallow humility that saw in ruin the salutary road back to the sweet and godly simplicities. The crisis of 1873 brought various interesting consequences: the first real flood of hoboes the country had ever seen, as a result of unemployment; the first selling on the installment plan, especially of pianos and organs; and reductions in preachers' salaries. Inevitably, also, it checked for a time both the building of expensive churches in the East and the planting of new ones in the West. Following it came the greenback agitation, the question of resumption of specie payment and an epidemic of repudiation of state and municipal bonds. In the panicky state of the public mind which continued after the real panic was over, fine points of honor were blurred and there was a tendency to escape from honest obligations.

Labor troubles naturally increased and sometimes led to breaches of the peace. Church sentiment, which had had long generations of training to respect law and order and almost no training at all to consider the human rights of the new industrial masses, was much more shocked by the riots of strikers than by the conditions which caused the strikers to riot. "Whenever a riot appears, the only thing to be done is to apply to it with unsparing severity the law of force. If the club of the policeman knocking out the brains of the rioter will answer, well and good; but if not, then bullets and bayonets, canister and grape, constitute the one remedy and the one duty of the hour" (*Independent,* August 2, 1877). The duty, perhaps, under some circumstances, but scarcely the remedy. But at that time it was orthodox doctrine that the sole duty of organized society with reference to labor was to keep it quiet. "The government cannot wisely undertake the task of regulating the relations of capital and labor beyond the simple duty of enforcing contracts" (*Independent,* July 26, 1877).

In the midst of the financial chaos of the mid-'seventies came the Centennial Exposition of 1876. It helped the national morale, and, strangely enough, it was a financial success. The Sunday closing question provoked discussion and the Exposition was closed on Sundays. The liquor question also was raised, and the privilege of selling liquor on the grounds was sold at auction. In the same year startling revelations of political corruption disturbed the pride which the achievements of a century as commemorated by the exposition had aroused. Belknap, Secretary of War, was impeached for accepting bribes. The Whiskey Ring was disclosed, together with Blaine's probable receipt of money from the railways for legislative favors. President Grant's financial indiscretions came to the public ear. The New York legislature was bribed by the street railway interests. A seat in the United States Senate was purchased outright on the floor of the Connecticut legislature. The Philadelphia gas ring was uncovered. And the Beecher-Tilton scandal, whatever may have been the real facts in the case, had only recently caused such a tremendous uproar that the church itself could not feel wholly free from the taint of corruption. All of this, however, was preliminary to an era of reform.

Reference has already been made to the rudimentary condition of secondary and higher education. The elementary public schools, which had been developed into a secular and tax-supported system apart from the control of the churches largely through the work of Horace Mann in the 'thirties and 'forties, had by this time developed into a broad, reasonably adequate and nation-wide foundation for the entire educational structure. In the older states the school systems had developed rapidly and the newer ones took pride in demonstrating their interest in the higher things by making prompt provision for the establishment of both common schools and state universities.

Elementary education, whatever else may be said of it, was thoroughly orthodox. Sectarian teaching was excluded from the public schools by constitutional provision in most of the states, but the tone and teaching of the public schools in most parts of the country was soundly evangelical. Ten states had excluded sectarian teaching from the public schools before 1865, either by amendment or by their original constitutions, and twenty-five more did the same between 1865 and the end of the century. This did not, however, necessarily exclude all religious teaching. In communities whose sentiment was relatively homogeneous, the religious atmosphere of the public schools continued for a time with relatively little change. In general, during the generation following the war these constitutional limitations meant little more than that the teachings of no important sect should be attacked and that denominational propaganda should not be permitted. The religious and Protestant tradition nevertheless ran strong.

It is to be remembered in this connection that the first tax-supported schools in the United States were distinctly religious schools. (See E. T. Cubberly: *Public Education in the United States.*) In colonial and immediately post-revolutionary days the main purpose of education had been frankly and avowedly religious and moral. In the South, public education was chiefly in the hands of the Anglican Society for the Propagation of the Gospel, and in New England the

Puritan control of the schools was complete and unquestioned. The New England primer contained this characteristic sentiment:

> The praises of my tongue
> I offer to the Lord,
> That I should learn so young
> To read his holy Word.

No less edifying were the collateral comments, if not the main current of teaching, in some of the text-books in common use during the quarter century after 1865. Steele's *Fourteen Weeks of Chemistry* (1873) opened with this: "Each tiny atom is watched by the Eternal Eye and guided by the Eternal Hand. When Christ declared the very hairs of our heads to be numbered, he intimated a chemical truth which we can now know in full to be that the very atoms of which our hair is composed are numbered by that same watchful providence." Roget—whose *Thesaurus* is still current—wrote an *Animal and Vegetable Physiology as Exhibiting the Power, Wisdom and Goodness of God*. And Asa Gray's *Botany for Young People in Common Schools* opened with a text of scripture and defined his science as a demonstration that "the wisdom and goodness of the Creator are plainly written in the vegetable kingdom." Geology had no quarrel with Genesis in the public schools, and the evil spirit of evolution had not yet troubled the placid waters of biology. The common school subject of geography, which included something of both geology and biology, gave opportunity for the assertion, in Cruikshank's *Primary Geography*, that "God made the world for man to live in and has fitted it for man's convenience and comfort." Colton's *Geography* asserted that the peculiarities of animals are to be ascribed to "a Being of superior wisdom and beneficence," rather than to variations of climate and other natural conditions, and exhorted the student to view all aspects of the earth's surface "as parts of a comprehensive whole created and governed by divine power."

So much was theism rather than sectarianism or even Christianity in any very specific sense. But since adherents of other faiths were few, it was considered no breach of the ban upon sectarian teaching to claim, as Colton's *Geography* did, that Mohammedanism "consists of a confused mixture of grossly false ideas and precepts," and that "Christianity is the only system which elevates man to a true sense of moral relations and adds to his importance." The ultimate triumph of Christianity, coupled with the present temporal advantages enjoyed by its adherents, was thus confidently forecast in Warren's *Common School Geography*: "Christian nations are more powerful and much more advanced in knowledge than any others. Their power also is continually increasing. . . . There is little doubt that in the course of a few generations the Christian religion will be spread over the greater part of the earth." Even Webster's "blue backed speller," which was eighty-two years old in 1865 and which still sold at the rate of a million copies a year for the next fifteen or twenty years, had a highly moral, not to say religious, tone; and the edifying nature of the mottoes in the penmanship copy books is famous.

The generation, therefore, which was in the public schools in the 'seventies and 'eighties, and even later in some places, was being taught a fundamentally religious view of the world, with a strongly Christian and sometimes a strongly Protestant coloring, and was given to understand that the rules of moral conduct, as well as the laws of nature, rested upon divine sanctions.

The question of Bible reading was differently decided in different places. The Cincinnati school board, for example, in 1870 repealed the regulation requiring Bible reading at the opening exercises of the public schools and instead prohibited such reading, but the courts sustained an injunction prohibiting the board from putting the new policy into effect. The New Haven school board, on the other hand, in 1878, first prohibited religious exercises in the schools and then, on the receipt of a petition of protest signed by 20 per cent. of the voters, reversed its decision. The Protestant press in general favored the retention of the Bible reading on the ground that it was not sectarian, but some of the more liberal organs argued that it amounted to making Christianity an established religion and that the schools would suffer more from the consequent sectarian dissension than they would be benefited by the Bible reading.

The frank inculcation of piety for the young is illustrated by a story in McGuffey's Fifth Reader of a boy who, having lost a "limb" (not leg; oh, dear no, for this was the Victorian as well as the Gilded Age), is being comforted by his mother with instances of great men who have triumphed over difficulties. But this was no American

Magazine success story. These men—deaf Beethoven and blind Huber
—"very soon found God's will to be wiser than their wishes. They
soon felt a new and delicious pleasure which none but the bitterly
disappointed can feel."

"What is that?" asked the boy.

"The pleasure of rousing the soul to bear pain, and of agreeing with
God silently. There is no pleasure like that of exercising one's soul
in bearing pain, and of finding one's heart glow with the hope that
one is pleasing God."

It was an age of modesty also, so far as avowed ideals and popular
teachings to the young were concerned. In Maria Edgeworth's *The
Parent's Assistant* occurs this edifying episode. Patty, aged six, had
fallen downstairs. "She did not cry but writhed in pain. 'Where are
you hurt, my love?' asked her father who came on hearing the noise
of the fall. 'There, papa,' said the little girl, touching her ankle which
she had decently covered with her gown." (This quotation, and some
of the others in this connection, are suggested by Mark Sullivan:
Our Times, New York, 1927.)

In practice, youthful piety perhaps scarcely kept pace with the
orthodoxy of its teachers and text-books. It seldom does. Governor
Chase Osborne of Michigan, writing of his experiences as a boy in
Indiana in the 'sixties and 'seventies, says: "We were tougher than
the boys and girl of today, but we did go to Sunday school and learned
'Now I Lay Me' and the Lord's Prayer."

So far as the manners and morals of adults were concerned, the
period was by no means unique in exhibiting a contrast between the
ideals and conduct professed by the godly and respectable and the
actual behavior that was in general observable; but perhaps the spread
between the two was rather wider than at most other times, and it was
all the more notable because the rather fastidious Victorian principles,
however much they might be ignored, were so infrequently challenged
by any one who could claim even a shred of respectability.

Surprisingly indifferent as they were to the financial and political
corruption of the period and brutally insensitive as they now seem to
have been to the rascalities of reconstruction, the religious were much
concerned about worldly amusements. Though the term "puritan"
has gained wide currency in the description of stern abstinence from

indulgence in all manner of doubtful gayeties, Methodism had much more influence than New England Puritanism in shaping the code of conservative evangelical ethics. The Y. M. C. A.'s first efforts to provide amusement for its constituency met vigorous objection. The activities of the institutional church and of settlement houses a little later drew similar criticism. Even semi-secular papers like the *Independent* published extended arguments on the moral perils of dancing. The stage was practically taboo. "*The School for Scandal* is a play the whole of which no woman could read to any man not her husband or other close relative without giving him cause to suspect her purity." (In 1792, the same play had been banned in Boston when the sheriff broke in upon a performance of it, closed the house and lodged the principal actor in jail.) When President McCosh had the temerity to put a billiard table into the students' club room at Princeton, a committee of the trustees in charge of the morals of the college ordered it removed. In 1872, the dominance of this attitude in regard to amusements led to writing into the Methodist book of discipine the law against dancing, card playing and theater-going. An occasional liberal spirit among the respectable decried the criticism of popular amusements and especially the emphasis which the church laid upon abstinence from them. Washington Gladden, in 1867, wrote at length in criticism of the prohibition of dancing, cards and billiards, said some kind words about these amusements, admitted the dangers, but thought that more harm was done by prohibiting them than by allowing each Christian to decide for himself. This, however, was a very bold attitude for a preacher to take.

Some of the stricter moralists in the churches thought that the reading of all fiction should be forbidden to Christians. However, it was not necessary to have recourse to avowed fiction to get exciting literature. The virtuous 'seventies did not have Ernest Hemingway or D. H. Lawrence but they had the edifying and no less stimulating confessions of escaped nuns and the experiences of *Wife Number 19*. "Brigham Young's rebellious wife divulges all the dark secrets of Mormonism and polygamy. Introduction by John B. Gough and Mrs. Livermore. Agents sell from ten to twenty every day. Hundreds are doing it and you can do it. Nothing like it. Two hundred illustrations." (Advertisement in *Independent*, November 18, 1875.) Litera-

ture with an erotic appeal under a pious jacket had great success in
an age when respectability and repression were practically synonymous.

The feminist movement was gaining strength slowly but it never
aroused much interest in the churches. Its more radical wing was led
by Elizabeth Cady Stanton, Susan B. Anthony and Lucy Stone, all of
whom had begun their battle for suffrage and other civil rights before
the war. More radical than these, because radical in so many other ways,
were the notorious sisters Woodhull and Claflin. The right wing of
the feminists consisted of those who were more interested in culture
than in caucuses and who began the organization of women's clubs
and encouraged the attendance of women at colleges. The Sorosis
Club, founded in New York in 1868, was the mother or the model of
countless other local clubs of women organized for the pursuit of
literary, musical and other cultural interests. The General Federation
of Women's Clubs was formed in 1889. Walter Damrosch has said
that the development of music in America has been chiefly in the
hands of women; more so than in any other country. The training
and the widening of outlook that the women received in both the
political and the cultural aspects of this whole movement had much
to do with making them the effective factor which they soon became
in the life of the churches. And on the other hand, their work in
church organizations gave prestige and a sort of spiritual sanction to
the movement as a whole even though the churches were hesitant
about putting themselves on record in favor of suffrage. But in 1877
a minister, a Mr. See, was brought to trial before the Newark Presbytery for allowing two women to speak in his church. The charges
were sustained and preaching by women in that presbytery was forbidden. Two months later the Methodist preachers' meeting of New
York City invited a Miss Oliver to preach before it but there was
so much protest that the invitation was rescinded. Rev. J. M. Buckley
quoted with approval the statement of President C. G. Finney that
"bringing out women as preachers and desiring to hear them preach
is an aberration of amativeness."

The temperance movement furnished the most important field for
the exercise of women's influence in public affairs. Before the war
the fight against alcohol had been partly religious and partly non-
religious, and from time to time there were sharp hostilities between

the two groups of temperance advocates. The old Washingtonian Societies, which made a virtue of completely divorcing the promotion of sobriety from religious motives, had gradually given place to a type of temperance evangelism best represented by John B. Gough. The consumption of liquor increased rapidly after the war and the high license which was adopted as a war measure—put over, perhaps, while the boys were at the front?—seemed to bring back to the business and the patronage of it a respectability which they had been rapidly losing. In the twenty years beginning with 1860 the capital investment in the liquor business increased from $29,000,000 to $190,-000,000. The National Prohibition Party was organized in 1869, but the effective fight began with the organization of the Women's Christian Temperance Union in 1874. From that time forward, and especially under the gracious leadership of Frances E. Willard, the war upon the saloon became, without any definite design to that end, the chief means by which women gained a place of dignity and power within the churches.

Two ministers more perhaps than any others gave prestige to the clergy—Beecher and a little later Phillips Brooks. Beecher's patriotic services during the war had gained him a secure place in the affections of the North. His oratorial ability, his urgency for righteousness in public affairs and his unconventionality and freedom of thought made him a national figure. Never a scholar in any technical sense, he was a temperamental and congenital liberal. The year when his father, Lyman Beecher, then president of Lane Theological Seminary at Cincinnati, was being tried for heresy was the year in which Henry Ward Beecher was graduated from the same institution. He was the first evangelical preacher of prominence to view evolution without alarm and in general he was in the front line of every advance of liberal thought within evangelical limits. He was editor of the *Independent* from 1861 to 1863 and was the founder of the *Christian Union* and its editor from 1870 to 1876.

The clergy in general, with some notable exceptions, like the church as a whole still showed little sign of making any immediate adjustment to the newer social and intellectual conditions. The packing together of urban industrial workers into slums, the pouring of millions of immigrants into the country and the development of new scientific and philosophic insights brought little immediate response from the church. Its patterns of thought were largely academic and authoritarian, and its habits of action were predominantly rural except where these had been rather thinly overlaid with a veneer of the mores of recently acquired wealth. In these respects the church did not differ from the country as a whole. It viewed population in terms of area rather than of density, and it saw opportunities in the opening West more clearly than responsibilities in the growing cities of the East. The spectacular development of the cities included a great increase in the wealth of the economic upper stratum, a large increase in the number of those who had the means of living in reasonable comfort, and a tremendous increase in both the extent and the depth of poverty. To this total situation the churches in general responded by erecting finer buildings, with higher steeples, to match the expanded wealth of their prosperous clientele. The economically secure worshiped in imposing structures built by the aid of the very rich, most of whom were church members. The churches had known for a long time what to do with and for the poor and the manual laborers in the country. Country and village churches had been and still were (and still are) made up of such people, and it was no problem at all. But the churches did not know what to do about the poor in the cities. For the most part they did nothing. America in the Gilded Age was expanding in the West and building fortunes in the East at an ever-accelerating tempo. Presto—crescendo—— Crash! The panic of 1873.

The one enterprise for the promotion of religious life in the cities which escaped the taint of this excessive preoccupation with respectability and catering to the well-to-do was the series of spectacular revivals carried on by Moody and Sankey and their contemporaries and successors. The method of the revival was old, and its theology was old, but in Moody's hands it was the means by which the church found a way of escape from the trammels of its own prosperity and respectability.

Chapter V

THE REVIVAL OF REVIVALISM

Religion had been relatively sluggish for two decades before the Civil War. The most notable exception was the period of revival which began in 1857 and had pretty well run its course even before the outbreak of hostilities put a final stop to it. It was an extraordinary movement in that it had almost no conspicuous clerical leadership and was both originated and carried on very largely by laymen. It had every appearance of being a spontaneous outburst of piety and zeal rather than a planned campaign. There was not much preaching in connection with it, practically none at all of the usual revivalistic sort, but there were prayer meetings by thousands. It had its greatest success in the eastern cities where the number of converts was very large. A report to the Presbyterian general assembly in May, 1858, stated that fifty thousand persons had been converted in a single week.

After the war the churches were confronted with a multitude of new problems, but were slow in making adjustment to any of the new conditions except the demand for western expansion. The denominational organizations had little energy to spare for anything but that and the keeping up of their own fences. The most definite efforts to meet the new religious needs of the cities and to stem the tide of post-war demoralization in faith and morals came from undenominational sources. The Young Men's Christian Association, which was multiplying and enlarging its local organizations and housing them as rapidly as possible with a view to meeting the concrete needs of youth in the cities, and the great evangelistic movement, of which Moody's was the prophetic and Sankey's the lyric voice, became the most conspicuous religious phenomena of the time, aside from strictly denominational enterprises. These two were not unrelated, for Moody had been a Y. M. C. A. man before he became an independent evangelist. The Association, however, was his instrument for a time rather than his inspiration. Born a Unitarian in Massachusetts, he came as a very young man to Chicago, then a very young city, became a Congregationalist, and began to do mission and Sunday school work in his characteristically energetic fashion even before he became connected with the Y. M. C. A. When he did join it, he was the chief factor in the erection of its first building in Chicago and when that burned down a few weeks after its completion, he immediately raised money for another.

Moody was and remained a layman. He got his early training not in a theological seminary but in a shoe store. Having passed through the stages of Sunday school teacher and superintendent, religious worker among young men, slum worker and sidewalk evangelist— not preaching but buttonholing pedestrians to ask them whether they were saved—and all of this while earning a living and working up to a very good income in the shoe business—he began his work on a larger scale not by "entering the ministry" or by any conscious deter- mination to become a revivalist, but simply by deciding that, since he was going to talk to people about the salvation of their souls, he might as well talk to a good many of them at once. While he was willing to take desperate chances so far as his own private affairs were concerned—as when he gave up an income of $5,000 a year to engage in unpaid city missionary work when he was just about to be married—he always impressed his hearers as a business man of sound common sense who had got religion and was holding them by the coat-lapel while he talked to them about it, rather than as a professional prophet making a speech to a crowd. He never lost sight of the individual in the multitude, and no audience was large enough to generate in him the oratorial complex.

Such theology as he had was extremely simple—naïve, one might say. All men are naturally bad; even the good are bad. Hell yawns for them and only the blood of Christ can save them. They must be converted, they must believe—and they can. Anybody can believe.

Unbelief is sin and the mother of all other sins. Christ died for all. God loves all men and desires their salvation. Everything apart from the salvation of souls is trivial and unimportant.

The theological basis of evangelism changes from one period to another. The great awakening of the eighteenth century had been built upon the strictest Calvinism and the fear of Hell. The western revival of the years just before and after 1800 had swept together all kinds of theologies into its maelstrom of emotionalism. Finney rejected Edwardian Calvinism and emphasized the responsibility of man. Moody lacked the foundation of scholarship on which the Edwardian revival was based but he was also free from the fantastic and exaggerated emotionalism of the camp-meeting era and from the fanatical perfectionism which had characterized much of the evangelism of the 'thirties and 'forties. His message had the personal and lay quality of the revival of 1857, plus the dynamic of a powerful personality. Moody believed in Hell and that belief furnished the basic motive for all his preaching, but he did not thrust it into the foreground. He was as orthodox as any man could be, but his appeal was almost wholly to love rather than to fear, and he stressed the love of God as it had not been done before and as it has scarcely been done since. He explicitly rejected feeling as a guide to action. "Feeling! Feeling! Feeling! I wish that word were banished from the inquiry room. I thank God I have a better foundation for my faith than feeling." The Bible, the infallible Word of God, was his ground of certainty, though he preached to the feelings of men with fervor and with unfailing success. He had an intolerant theology, though he did not know that he had any, but he had a tolerant spirit.

In his later years he resented the disturbance which modern science was making in the familiar patterns of religious thought, but he did not go out of his way to seek quarrels in this field. When Henry Drummond, the first great evangelical evolutionist, came to America, Moody joined forces with him and they spoke from the same platform. A more thoughtful conservative would have seen that Drummond's science had implications which were hostile to his theology. But Moody was not interested in implications or in theology, only in the fact that Drummond was warmly, evangelically and evangelistically Christian. Higher criticism had scarcely come into the field of popular knowledge in Moody's prime. So far as he knew anything about it, he was hostile but not excited. He declared that he was less disturbed about the alleged discovery of scholars that there were two Isaiahs than about the fact that so few of his auditors knew there was even one.

In comparison with the majestic simplicity of Moody's personality and of his appeal, many of his successors appear very small indeed. Whatever may have been his intellectual limitations, he had no disposition to make the success of Christianity contingent upon the defeat of science or upon the disavowal of the findings of scholarship, and he used no cheap tricks to secure popularity. Least of all did he make any effort at self-enrichment. Whatever money he collected, and it was a good deal, was at once poured back into the support of his work. He put a million and a half dollars—largely the proceeds of royalties on the Moody and Sankey hymn-books, for Sankey was equally unmercenary—into his school at Northfield, Massachusetts, and into the institute and church in Chicago, and at his death his estate consisted of $500 which he did not know he had.

Moody arrived on the scene at a favorable moment, for the spirit of revival was already abroad in the land. The *Independent*, not greatly given to exaggeration in such matters, reported (April 23, 1868) "8,000 accessions by revivals last week," 3,700 among Methodists, 1,300 among Baptists, 1,200 among Presbyterians. Plymouth, Massachusetts, had 200 (not all in one week), and at East Weymouth "300 hopeful conversions" are reported in connection with the Methodist and Congregational churches. At Texas, New York, religious interest rose so high that "the village bar is almost deserted and the dancing hall for sale." And this was before Moody had started. In the same year, Finney, who continued to be an evangelist after he became president of Oberlin College, reported that the revival there had been an unqualified success, though "under adverse circumstances or in the absence of a healthy religious influence, I should fear for the results."

The panic of 1873 stimulated rather than checked the revivalistic movement and the great period of Moody's success began while the country was still in the throes of financial disaster, though there was less of a tendency than there had been in the revival of 1857 to make religious capital of the assertion that the financial calamity was the direct consequence of the country's lack of religion. In 1876, after campaigns in Philadelphia, where the largest available hall was crowded and where the secretary of the meetings gave out "magnificent but offensive statistics," and at Brooklyn, he moved on to New York where his preaching and Sankey's singing packed the Hippodrome and made such an impression on the whole city that all the theaters suffered a serious loss in patronage. Moody's sermons, which were printed regularly in the *Independent* through this year, are very thin reading, but their effect with Moody behind them was tremendous. The following year, revival services were held in lower New York for the benefit of Wall Street business men. "The meetings appear to be well attended, though not by many Wall Street men."

Moody's life and work continued until the end of 1899, but in his later years he was much more interested in the educational institutions which he had planted than in revival campaigns. The decade from 1870 to 1880 was the one which saw the greatest percentage of growth in church membership and is generally reputed to be that of the greatest "spirituality."

After about 1880 new types of evangelism began to appear. One of them was a revival of the camp-meeting of earlier days. In the minds of many ministers who were by no means unfriendly to evangelism, the camp-meeting became a public nuisance. Three Pennsylvania Methodist preachers published their reasons for refusing to attend one: the camp-meetings had become largely a matter of recreation if not of dissipation; they kept open on Sunday; and many of them were conducted by irresponsible men of any or no church "who obtained money by collusion with railroad companies in Sabbath breaking." They were not altogether wrong in holding that these camp-meetings ought at least to be closed on Sunday to avoid the desecration of the day. Bizarre episodes and pious publicity stunts did nothing to raise the reputation of this type of revivalism. One "Evangelist Barnes," for example, converted thirty-three convicts in the Kentucky State prison at Frankfort and had them marched to the river under armed guard for baptism (*Christian Union*, August 17 and September 7, 1882).

But setting aside such odious extremes, revivalism developed in various forms during the last two decades of the century and even later. B. Fay Mills, Sam Jones, R. A. Torrey, Gypsy Smith, J. Wilbur Chapman, Charles Reign Scoville and Billy Sunday are illustrations of widely different types. Evangelism not only revived the methods which had been effective in pioneer days but freely adopted new methods to catch the public ear; but it stood fast against any invasion of modern thought into the area of Christian doctrine. The churches, as represented by their settled ministry, on the other hand, exhibited increasing hospitality toward modern thought but generally stood pat on conventional methods of procedure. In general, the evangelists have resisted "the new view of the Bible" and emphasized individual salvation by obedience to its commands and have belittled and often denounced the newer stress upon the social gospel. "The modern evangelist takes every opportunity to excoriate the social worker and the churchman interested in the social welfare of the community." (Charles Stelzle: *The Passing of the Old Evangelism,* p. 202.) The methods and the emphasis, though not necessarily the central message, of the most prominent revivalists and their great influence upon the rank and file of church members must bear some of the responsibility for the church's slowness in realizing and accepting its social responsibilities.

Whether or not the revivalistic method is as well adapted to urban conditions as to the rural and frontier environment in which it originated is a question. As an appeal to crowd psychology it might reasonably be expected to have the most success where there are the most people. As an appeal to the uncritical and rural mind, it would be at no special disadvantage in the cities, for American cities in the nineteenth century were populated chiefly by people who had moved there from the country or from other countries, and the boasted superiority of urban culture could be established only by selecting the more favored classes in the city for comparison. As furnishing needed excitement and opportunity for assembly to persons whose lives were otherwise dull and isolated, the revival or camp-meeting had something to offer to the frontier which the city dweller does not need. Nevertheless, the fact is that Moody and his successors packed the largest halls in the largest cities and won converts by thousands.

With the rising interest in child psychology and the problems of education, the hope of the church came to be placed in Christian nurture rather than in those short cuts to glory which revivalism had held out to hardened sinners. This substitution of growth in grace as a normal aspect of human development in place of a cataclysmic conversion was not in itself an absolutely new discovery. Horace Bushnell had stated it in his *Christian Nurture* in 1857, a volume almost as revolutionary in its implications so far as the popular churches were concerned as the *Origin of Species* which appeared two years later. By the beginning of the twentieth century the cult of the child acquired new popularity, the index of which was the growing interest in religious education and the diminishing reliance of the churches upon revivalism.

While the churches were occupied with the weighty matter of saving souls and saving the church itself from the onsloughts of modern thought upon its cherished doctrines, there were groups which focused their attention upon other matters. The Dunkards, assembled in convention "in a large barn belonging to Obadiah Over," at New Enterprise, Pennsylvania, discussed the keeping of musical instruments in the homes of the brethren, decided that the sisters must not wear hats, debated the technique of foot-washing and recommended that the brethren abstain from voting lest participation in politics should lead to a surrender of their principle of non-resistance. Even those who are inclined to smile at some of the items in this list of agenda will recognize that this company of rural saints was wrestling seriously with at least one problem which more sophisticated Christians did not discover until nearly half a century later.

Opposition to secret societies and fraternal orders also had a revival at this period when the orders themselves were enjoying a notable growth. C. G. Finney wrote, in 1868: "It is high time that the church of Christ was awake to the character and tendency of Freemasonry. Forty years ago we supposed it was dead and had no idea it would ever revive. But strange to tell, while we were busy in getting rid of slavery, Freemasonry has revived and extended its bounds most alarmingly." Probably it was the prestige of Finney rather than any wide-spread alarm about Masonry which gave him entré to the *Independent* for a series of articles on the subject. But no general excitement could be stirred in the East, though in some denominations in the Middle West, all secret societies were either explicitly or implicitly condemned. There were occasional reports of Methodist churches having the corner stones of new buildings laid with Masonic ceremonies. A national Christian convention against secret societies was held at Pittsburgh in May, 1868. Many of the Disciples, following the teaching of Alexander Campbell on the subject, were strenuously opposed to all secret orders. So also were the United Brethren and the Wesleyan Methodists and many individuals in other denominations. In 1877, it was stated that "about half of all Christian communicants in the United States belong to denominations which are opposed to secret societies"; but this was true only because nearly half of the Christian communicants belonged to the Roman Catholic church whose opposition to such societies had been of long standing.

The Third Plenary Council of Baltimore, in 1884, gave specific warning against Freemasonry and held that the papal prohibition applied against all secret societies. At the same time it encouraged the organization of strictly Catholic societies including the following classes: religious confraternities such as those of the Sacred Heart, of the Blessed Sacrament and of the Blessed Virgin; those for Christian charity; those designed to check immorality, especially temperance societies; social organizations to guard Catholic young men against dangerous influences; and Catholic beneficial societies and associations of Catholic working men. The Knights of Labor, whose condemnation in Canada by the Holy See had been secured by the Canadian bishops, were championed by Cardinal Gibbons who won the American bishops to his view and successfully presented their case in Rome in 1887.

The period of national prosperity immediately after the war had led to a great expansion in church building and the crash of 1873 left behind it a heavy burden of debts. At the end of 1877 there was a general movement toward the paying off of these debts, except in cases where the property had already been lost, and there was evidence of a chastened realization that there had been too much recklessness in the erection of expensive and showy buildings.

Beecher still was, and continued to be as long as he lived, the most prominent preacher in the country. It is impossible not to recur to him again and again in almost every connection. Evangelists might come and go, but Beecher's beacon burned with a steady and brilliant flame from the pulpit of Plymouth church, Brooklyn, for forty years. Through the almost continuous publication of his sermons and midweek lecture-room talks, at first in the *Independent*, then in the *Christian Union*, and in pamphlets as well as in collected volumes, he preached to the whole country as completely as any man could before the coming of radio. The great Beecher-Tilton scandal and the indecisive lawsuits which grew out of it (in 1875 and later) furnished the most sensational news even of a decade that was rich in scandals, but it could only color and not obscure his influence. A few weeks after a sermon by Mr. Beecher in November, 1875, had virtually announced a policy of silence in regard to the charges against him, the editor of the *Independent*, H. C. Bowen, wrote: "Mr. Beecher and his friends ought to consider that it is nothing but an almost un-paralleled exhibition of partiality for him that he was not long ago driven out of the ministry and out of respectable society by the indig-nation of the Christian public. We do not say that this ought to have been done; but we do say that there are not a dozen men in the country who, in the face of such damning evidence as stands against Mr. Beecher, could have maintained themselves for a month." (*Inde-pendent,* February 10, 1876.) The time has long since passed when it is either possible or profitable to determine the question or the degree of Beecher's guilt, if any. The fact that he could survive the charge in view of such evidence as there was is not an indication of the indifference of the church but a measure of his personality and in-fluence.

Greatest among the popular preachers after Beecher, and one whose attractive rhetoric made him seem modern while his ideas were those of an earlier time, was T. DeWitt Talmage. He moved serenely upon his eloquent way untouched by any currents of modern thought and reflecting brilliantly from the facets of his vocabulary the mind of the average church member in the 'eighties and 'nineties. He had little to say about the social implications of religion and devoted himself chiefly to presenting the Gospel as a means of salvation in Paradise. He was the supreme exponent of the religion of Mother, Home, and Heaven. One feature of his homiletical method which acquired a devastating popularity among his imitators was the use of bizarre texts in a sense related distantly if at all to the thought of the writer. The search for Talmage-like trick texts became an important Monday occupation for half the younger preachers in the country. Moody, in 1899, the last year of his life, said to a group of preachers: "I am sick and tired of this essay preaching. I am nauseated with this silver-tongued orator preaching. I like to hear preachers, not windmills." Perhaps he was not thinking of Talmage; but he might have been.

Chapter VI

BROKEN RAMPARTS OF CUSTOM AND CREED

When the Congregational National Council met in Boston on June 14, 1865, it listened, we are told, "with profound attention for two full hours" to an opening sermon from the text: "Ask for the old paths." The discourse was "an able and fearless exposition of the influence of the Congregational Church order in originating and forming our national character and institutions." To the approval of this council also was submitted a statement of Christian faith intended as a bulwark "for the defense of the Word of God now assailed by multiform and dangerous errors which strike at the foundations of our religion." Strengthened and enlarged, this statement was adopted as a "Declaration of Apostolic and Primitive Faith and Order."

This episode at the very beginning of our period and having to do with a denomination which stood at the forefront in education and culture fairly represents the status of Christian thought in 1865. A large part even of New England conservatism had, to be sure, departed far enough from Edwardian Calvinism to be viewed as heretical by the right wing, but as we look back upon them now, the two seemed to constitute one almost solid body of conservative orthodoxy for the defense of the Gospel against the dangerous heresies of Unitarianism and Universalism.

But there were already at work certain influences which soon became much more potent than hitherto for the modification both of faith and of conduct. To begin with a bare mention of some of these influences, the first perhaps was the back-wash from the war. In spite of all the work of the Christian commission and the chaplains, in spite of the evangelistic services that had been held in the camps

and the part that the churches had played in sanctifying the cause
of both contending parties, religion had lost a good deal of its grip
on the country and a good deal of its control over manners and morals
as well as over thought.

The increase of immigration was a social phenomenon which had
its effects on the moral codes and on religion as well as its economic
consequences. Steam transportation across the Atlantic had been inaugurated some years earlier but not until now had the volume of
trans-Atlantic travel by steam become impressive. The number of
immigrants entering the country in 1865 was less than 250,000. By
1873, the number had almost doubled and it was to double again
before the tide reached its full flood. In the decade following the war,
the immigrants were still largely English, Irish and German. The
vast majority of the Irish and perhaps a third of the Germans were
Roman Catholics. While a large per cent. of the earlier immigrants
had passed on through the ports of entry to points west, as the Scandinavians still continued to do, increased opportunities for employment
as industrial workers in the new industries now held a larger proportion in the cities. A considerable fraction of the German immigrants,
perhaps another third, were Freethinkers who, under the influence of
the liberal social and political movements and the Hegelian and post-
Hegelian philosophies, had cast off religion as an outgrown super-
stition.

At the same time the influence of liberal German thought was
making itself felt through the return of American students from their
studies abroad. The migration of American students to German universities had already begun before the war, though the stream was a
very thin trickle. But before any American university had developed
a graduate school of any importance, hundreds of young Americans
had gone to Germany and brought back both the methods and the
results of German scholarship. The influence of German thought on
philosophy and theology soon far surpassed that of either England or
France.

Most notable of all, perhaps, was the new position which science
began to occupy in the minds of non-scientists. Darwin's *Origin of
Species* was published in 1859 and the Duke of Argyle's *Reign of Law*

was a new book in 1867. Not less significant than the new ideas which these gave to scientists was the new place that they gave to science in the minds of philosophers and theologians and all who were attempting to construct a religious view of the world. Taking these influences altogether, there was enough dynamite in them to blow up the bulwarks of the old order. Not that the old order was necessarily wrong at all points, but its historic position of dominance was challenged, first among the intelligentsia and then in wider circles.

Perhaps Christians of the evangelical tradition were as much shocked by the tendency to give up the old-fashioned observance of Sunday as by anything. The coming of the "continental Sunday" in place of the Puritan Sabbath was viewed with alarm. The influence of immigrants, the increase of Roman Catholic populations in the cities and the general loosening of standards after the war, all contributed to the breakdown of the Puritan practice, and the increase in drinking tended to make this breakdown the more odious to many, though the Puritan mind had always been more sensitive about Sunday than about liquor. The spectacle of German communities spending their Sunday evenings in beer gardens—which were often, in fact, pretty respectable places of family resort according to present standards—served as a symbol of moral degeneracy.

Throughout the 'seventies the churches generally were much concerned about this matter of Sabbath observance. The Presbyterian General Assembly had passed a resolution condemning members of that church who were the "responsible" owners or managers of concerns that worked on Sunday. A Mr. Levin, a member of a Presbyterian church in Sewickley, Pennsylvania, chief proprietor of a Pittsburgh paper, was disciplined by the session of his church at the order of the Allegheny presbytery for desecrating the Sabbath. Another Presbyterian, a certain Mr. Groff, who owned a large but not controlling interest in the *Chicago Tribune*, got by on the ground that since he owned only a minority interest, he was not "responsible." A critic asserted, probably untruly, that that word had been inserted in the Assembly's resolution to protect Deacon Groff and others like him who owned less than a controlling interest in companies which made a profit on the Sabbath. In the 'eighties and thereafter the interest of the church as a whole in this particular item of Christian morality diminished and it tended to become the concern chiefly of one or two minor denominations and of a few reformers who specialized on guarding the Sabbath, but the whole church could be aroused from time to time when the issue became conspicuous, as in the question about keeping the Chicago Exposition open on Sundays in 1893. The decision in that case was that the Exposition grounds might be kept open as a park but that the machinery must not run. The changed method of Sunday observance has come to be seen as a phenomenon of urbanization rather more than as a conflict between American and European cultures or between Christian and pagan ideals.

Immigration had another effect besides introducing the continental Sunday and besides reinforcing the Catholic, Lutheran and Free-thinking constituencies, while adding little to the strength of Protestantism of the Anglo-Saxon tradition. Liquor began to be a potent factor in politics and the foreign vote was one thing that helped to make it so. In 1873, a brewers' journal said that the foreign element, especially the German, was large enough to hold the balance of power between the political parties. "The future is ours. The enormous influx of immigration will in a few years over-reach the puritanical element in every state in the Union." The seven million immigrants who came between 1865 and 1884 went far toward bringing this prophecy to realization.

It was not until some years later, in the last two decades of the nineteenth century and the first of the twentieth, that the liquor interests, grown now to great proportions and combined into immense corporations and closely knit associations, became a really powerful and sinister force in politics. By that time, the foreign element involved had been materially changed and the gentle German and the hilarious Irish were no longer the principal factors. (See Ernest Gordon: *When the Brewer Had the Strangle-Hold*, New York, 1930.)

There were other forms of iniquity so unsavory that not many nice people cared to soil their hands even by trying to curb them. Nice people, including church people, were willing to have laws passed declaring certain vicious practices to be misdemeanors and to take it for granted that the laws would somehow enforce themselves. But neither these nor the laws for Sunday closing and the regulation of saloons ever did enforce themselves.

Anthony Comstock, the "roundsman of the Lord," was probably the best example for all time of the volunteer agent for the suppression of immorality by legal process. In his youth a salesman for a drygoods house, he was pious with the untroubled devoutness of one who never knew that vexed questions of faith and morals existed. For him there was only white against black, purity versus sin, and down to old age no question vexed his mind except how to enforce the code about which he had no question. Sunday closing, the suppression of immoral literature, and the enforcement of the liquor laws were the fields in which he specialized. The three were closely inter-related. By 1868, at the age of twenty-four, he had had two sellers of erotic books arrested. In 1871, he was making charges against saloons that kept open on Sunday and against police officers who would not close them. No one ever doubted either his moral or his physical courage. He was a devout believer in the police power as an instrument of righteousness. Arthur Train, who as assistant district attorney in New York knew Comstock for many years, says of him: 'He was an enthusiastic smut-sleuth with a hound's nose for obscenity in either art or letters. I suspect that he enjoyed his calling, for he used gloatingly to exhibit with both pride and gusto to myself and other assistants of the district attorney peculiarly atrocious trophys of his various raids in the form of nasty photographs and obscene articles. Quantitatively, his career was a huge success, for he caused to be destroyed 15,000 pounds of [no matter what], over 60,000 ——, 5,500 ——, 3,000 ——, 194,000 ——, 134,000 ——, and jailed enough sinners to have filled a train of sixty-one coaches, allowing sixty to each coach" (Train, *Puritan's Progress*, p. 286).

The changes in religious thought which within the next half century amounted to nothing less than a revolution were the resultant of several influences, some of which have been mentioned above. For a good many years the official declarations of the churches, the utterances of a vast majority of the pulpits and the teachings of practically all the Sunday School teachers showed little deviation from the accepted patterns of orthodoxy. Nevertheless, the old bulwarks were shaken and cracked, not only by attacks from without, but by risings from within. Among the results were a mitigation of the rigors of Calvinism and the complete abandonment of the system by many within churches that had been traditionally Calvinistic; the acceptance of universalism, or quasi-universalism, or some moral equivalent of it, by so many outside of the Universalist denomination that the denomination itself reaped little benefit from the diminished prestige of Hell; the application of scientific methods to the study of the history of religion with an accompanying decrease of emphasis upon the supernatural; the acceptance of the concept of evolution and its application in the field of religion; a changed view of religious authority growing out of the view of the Bible resulting from critical methods of study; and the substitution of educational for revivalistic methods by the church in dealing with its own young people.

Horace Bushnell, of Hartford, Connecticut, had started a new trend of thought with his *Christian Nurture*, revised and re-published in 1861. Unitarianism had, to be sure, long ago challenged the conception of original sin, human depravity, and miraculous regeneration, but it had challenged so many other things besides that its arguments carried little weight in orthodox circles. Bushnell was a Congregational minister of high repute, working in the very center of orthodoxy, for Hartford Seminary had been established in 1834 because Yale was not orthodox enough. Revivalism in the period before the Civil War, as well as in the period immediately after, and to a great extent down to now, was based on the assumption that the normal process of conversion involves a violent internal revolution and a sudden change in the nature, status, and character of the convert. The gist of Bushnell's teaching was that the child in a Christian community and a Christian home ought to develop naturally into a Christian without realizing that he has ever been anything else, and without any shattering emotional experience of conversion. The implications of this humane idea were these: First, it laid stress upon the responsibility of the church and the home for Christian education, and gave a rational basis for that work of religious education which had already been started in the Sunday School movement. Second, it intensified and rationalized the opposition to the revivalistic method of conversion, especially as applied to the young. While the great revivalists like Finney and Moody had had their most spectacular success in winning sinners who obviously were sinners, the popular churches had come to rely very largely upon revivals as a means of harvesting the young who grew up within them and never became prodigals. The tendency was to treat all persons, young and old, who were not formally enrolled in the church as though they were prodigal sons. And third, it affected theological thought by stressing the moral in contrast to the substitutionary theory of the atonement, and by introducing a certain naturalism into the whole religious process. The fact that Bushnell was rated by many as a heretic and that his own church, in standing by him, was finally moved to withdraw from the Congregational consociation to which it had belonged, probably increased rather than diminished his influence in the long run, and he continued until 1876 to be a potent and beneficent influence upon the thinking and practice of the church. The views held by Bushnell and delivered by him to a local congregation and to the ministers who read his book were popularized by Beecher, who had the nation for his audience, and by other liberal-minded thinkers and writers who commanded smaller constituencies.

Through the 'seventies there was a good deal of preaching about future punishment, both *pro* and *con,* but mostly *pro.* "The question of future punishment has been a favorite topic in the New York and Brooklyn pulpits for two or three Sundays past" (*Independent,* January 17, 1878). Doctor Talmage was strong for hell. Rev. E. C. Sweetzer, Universalist, was naturally against it. Rev. Carlos Martyn, Dutch Reformed, Dr. R. S. MacArthur and Halsey W. Knapp, Baptists, and Doctors Hatfield and Finn, Methodists, all expressed faith in the orthodox view of eternal punishment.

In 1879, the *Congregationalist* (Boston) "does not see how one can honestly belong to the denomination and not believe in eternal punishment." The editor of the *Independent* (undenominational by this time) believes in the doctrine but does not consider it an essential of Christian faith. Lyman Abbott, in the *Christian Union,* argues for conditional immortality. "Man is mortal and must put on immortality"—but he does not dogmatize. He considers that hell has ceased to be a live issue. Later he adds: "Belief in future punishment is growing more universal" with the understanding of the inexorable operation of law, but "belief in any definition of future punishment less so." The term, "the new theology," though it really meant much more, was sometimes used in a specific sense to refer to such views about punishment—that the only real hell is the one which a man creates for himself as the natural consequence of his evil deeds. While the great body of the ministry was still untouched by this idea, it had to be recognized as a form of Christian belief within the church and not as a form of infidelity. There were some who saw that, while the question of the future state occupied the center of the theological stage at the moment, another more important would soon take its place—that of the canon and inspiration of scripture. But even before the existence of a new view of the Bible became a matter of common knowledge, evolution began to make its impress upon religious thinkers and soon the welkin rang with the sound of the battle for and against it.

Darwin's *Origin of Species*, published in 1859, made little immediate impression upon the American mind outside of scientific circles—though I find a record that young John Thomas Gulick, son of a missionary in Hawaii and himself later almost equally eminent as a missionary in Japan and as a contributor to scientific evolution through his own studies in zoology, read *The Origin of Species* in the year of its publication, while he was a student in Union Theological Seminary in New York. An American edition was soon published. Evolution came more vividly to the knowledge of Americans through the medium of Herbert Spencer's writings, which circulated even more widely in the United States than in England. In 1865, E. L. Youmans raised $7,000 to assist in financing the publication of Spencer's *Synthetic Philosophy*. Darwin's *Descent of Man*, published in 1871, made clear even to the non-scientific mind the implications of his earlier work. John Fiske delivered, in 1869 and 1871, the lectures which, later published as *Outlines of Cosmic Philosophy*, attained a popularity which even that heavy title could not prevent. Conservative Boston would not allow the "agnostic Fiske"—who later turned out to be a rather ardent Christian evolutionist—to deliver the Lowell lectures until many years later.

A new phase in the long warfare of science with theology began promptly and vigorously. Harvard and Cornell were almost the only institutions of learning in which the new idea got even a fair hearing, and Presidents Eliot and White became targets for the orthodox. Tyndall made a lecture tour in America in 1872 and 1873; Spencer in 1872; Huxley in 1876. By that time the more popular and theistic

interpretation of evolution by John Fiske had done much to assure
the more liberal Christians that evolution was not incompatible with
theism. When Drummond came a little later and toured the country
with Moody, he seemed to demonstrate that it was compatible also
with fervent evangelical Christianity. But meanwhile, also, J. W.
Draper, a chemist by profession, who had already written a history
of the intellectual development of Europe exhibiting the clergy to
rather poor advantage, published in 1874 his *Warfare of Science and
Religion*, which served as a standard text on that subject from the
standpoint of the left wing until Andrew D. White's work in the
same field in 1896.

The last quarter of the nineteenth century produced many and
varied interpretations of evolution in its relation to a philosophy of
life and of the world, many types of anti-theistic theories based upon
it, and many modes of reconciling evolution and Christianity. The
extremes were occupied by the persistently skeptical Huxley and the
persistently evangelical evolutionist Drummond. Huxley's visit was
especially disturbing to the conservatives, and the more so since it
appeared that he furnished much of the material out of which the
famous infidel Robert G. Ingersoll forged the weapons for his attack
upon Christianity, very much as Voltaire had furnished material for
Tom Paine.

It began to be suggested that Christian students might profitably
suspend their studies of the dead languages for a time and concentrate
upon the living sciences so that they might be able to meet the unbe-
lievers on their own ground; and also that the scientists who rejected
Christianity as incompatible with evolution might be reasonably asked
to familiarize themselves with the rudiments of the system which
they attacked. Charles Hodge, whose reputation and prestige were
great, but whose work soon ceased to be read outside of a limited
circle of students in the most conservative theological seminaries,
declared that "a more absolutely incredible theory (than evolution)
was never propounded for acceptance among men." Mark Hopkins,
ex-president of Williams—and ex-occupant of that famous pedagogical
position on one end of a log with the youthful Garfield on the other
—delivered a course of lectures at Princeton Seminary, the first of
which was devoted to denouncing evolution as "essentially atheistic."

But James McCosh, the president of Princeton, found it possible to think of evolution as God's method of continuing his creative work. Dr. William Hayes Ward published the discovery that Dr. Taylor Lewis, anticipating Darwin, had declared, in 1855, that the "Miltonic theory" of the sudden creation of each separate species was not scriptural and therefore not true. "Species grow out of species as individuals out of individuals."

Beecher's powerful influence was on the side of the modernists. After preaching a liberal sermon in Chicago he received many anxious inquiries as to whether he really meant what he seemed to mean. In reply, he wrote: "I am a cordial Christian evolutionist" (*Christian Union*, August 2, 1883). Lyman Abbott, Beecher's great successor both in the pulpit and in the editorial chair, was early added to the list of Christian evolutionists, and his actual direct influence on Christian thought was perhaps greater than that of any of the others. Henry Drummond's *The Natural Law in the Spiritual World* (1883), pointed out one line of reconciliation with persuasive simplicity. Not only the more liberal theologians, but many of the scientists, insisted upon the compatibility of the new findings of science with all that was valuable in the old faith. Christian members of the American Association for the Advancement of Science, interviewed at the 1884 meeting of the Association, declared their faith increased; and the reporter refers to a young infidel who began the study of geology to get arguments against God and the Bible, but found that "the agreement between Genesis and geology demonstrated the divine origin of the Bible" (*Christian Union*, September 18, 1884)—an episode which illustrates a transitional stage in the wrestle of religion with scientific truth before the processes and results of Biblical criticism had become widely known. The Genesis-and-geology discussion, of course, preceded the evolution controversy. Hugh Miller, who was a stone-mason before he became a geologist, had attempted to bring that to an orthodox conclusion with his *Footprints of the Creator* (1849), and *Testimony of the Rocks* (1857), but the question refused to stay closed.

If evolution did not win all the theologians, neither did it at once win all the scientists. Agassiz opposed it to the end of his life, and it was only as a new generation of scientists came on, trained under the influence of the new doctrine, that opposition came to be found almost exclusively in the ranks of the conservative theologians and the untutored laity. Through the 'eighties there was an almost constant discussion in liberal pulpits and papers of "the old and the new"—the new meaning, for the most part, evolution and the more recent discoveries in geology. The great names among the religious leaders who championed the "new" must not be allowed to conceal the fact that the vast body both of the ministry and of the working church members stood fast by the "old." The net result, however, was that the more intelligent, whether in the churches or out of them, found it generally impossible to maintain the simple cosmology and anthropology of Milton, and Christians with any pretensions to scholarship found it unnecessary to try to do so.

The first stage in the new era of science put the Christian apologists in the somewhat difficult position of having to defend religious concepts which were themselves about to undergo change through the application of scientific methods to the study of the documents upon which they were based. The results of the work of German Biblical scholarship began slowly to filter in and the study of the Bible by new methods, which treated it as a collection of literature whose date, authorship, and character were to be investigated critically, rather than as a book known in advance to be the inerrant product of inspiration, presently found a place in the more liberal seminaries and a lodgment in the minds of many of the ministry. As good a statement as can be found anywhere of the entire course of the changing attitude towards the Bible is that given by William Newton Clarke in his *Sixty Years with the Bible*, in which he narrates autobiographically the development of his own views through six decades.

At the beginning of our period, such a statement as the following is fairly typical of what was considered a sound position: "We could say beforehand, if we have a revelation at all, it must be infallible; for if not, the lie will ruin us before the truth can save us" (Rev. George B. Cheever, in the *Independent*, January 6, 1870). But in 1876, a minister of the Reformed Church could write in *Scribner's Magazine* on what he called "Protestant Vaticanism," inveighing against the suicidal folly of those church leaders who would suppress the doubts and queries of advanced Christian thinkers, urging that the creed should be revised, and arguing that the new creed should not require faith in the whole Bible. Two years later, Professor Toy writes in the *Sunday School Times* of Deuteronomy as a late compilation. A Scottish professor was at that very moment on trial for heresy for saying no more than that, but the American churches did not yet know enough about higher criticism to be sensitive on the point. It should be noted that the important works of Wellhausen, who did more than any other German scholar to make the concept of higher criticism familiar to the American mind, and its very name a household word, were published in 1876 and 1878.

There were struggles over orthodoxy on Biblical interpretations at Andover Seminary (Congregational) in 1881 and at Newton Seminary (Baptist) in 1882. At Newton the conservative president, Hovey, undertook to oust the professor of New Testament Greek, Gould, a Biblical scholar of the new school—and did, by a trustees' vote of thirteen to nine. The publication of Professor Charles A. Briggs' *Biblical Study: Its Principles, Methods, and History,* in 1883, was the most important landmark in American Biblical scholarship for this period. It covered the whole field and stated the whole case for the liberal side, but the conservative leaders were too busy fighting evolution just then to make an issue of Professor Briggs' views on the Bible, and he was not seriously molested until 1893, when he was made the defendent in a great heresy trial, the inevitable result of which he avoided by leaving the Presbyterian church for the Episcopalian.

Among the great liberalizing personalities in the pulpit in this period, and outside of the ranks of technical scholarship, four were perhaps preëminent. They were Henry Ward Beecher, Washington Gladden, Phillips Brooks, and George A. Gordon. Of these, Beecher was the most popular, the least scholarly, and the most pronounced in his advocacy of the new positions. He was a temperamental liberal before he was a theological liberal. In the *North American Review* for August, 1882, he summarized his view of the recent progress of religious thought and gave a comprehensive statement of his own views. The course of thought, he says, is not away from religion in America; religious sentiment was never so strong and active as now; but there is "a more diffused religion," less sectarian spirit, more liberty of thought. There is a transition in theology and a gradual substitution of a "theology of evolutionism" for Calvinism. Naturally, there is resistance from the old guard. These changes Beecher wholly approves. The *Watchman and Reflector* commented that with this article Beecher "has emphatically stepped down and out from any relation with Congregational orthodoxy. He definitely renounces the supreme authority of the Bible." At a meeting of the Congregational association of New York and Brooklyn on October 11, 1882, Beecher made a great affirmative statement of his faith and then resigned from the association. The association passed almost unanimously a resolution that his statement "indicates the propriety of his membership in this or any other Congregational association" and asked him to reconsider his resignation. But he did not. He continued for the remaining five years of his life, without personal denominational connection, though minister of a Congregational church (*Christian Union*, October 19, 1882).

Washington Gladden, born in 1836, one of the editors of the *Independent* from 1871 to 1875, did his great pastoral work with the First Congregational Church, Columbus, Ohio, but a greater work still as a leader in the new movement for the socialization of religion. Theological thought was not his primary interest, but his liberal tendencies coupled with his devotion to social enterprises as not merely humanitarian but as an essential function of religion did much to win followers of the newer views.

Phillips Brooks, born in 1835, was rector of Trinity Church, Boston, from 1869 until he became bishop of Massachusetts in 1891, less than two years before his death. He was a broad churchman whose influence in liberalizing religious thought grew not out of the fact that he accepted such new ideas as evolution and Biblical criticism, as he probably did, or that he preached or expounded them, as he certainly did not, but out of the fact that he refused to allow himself to be gravely concerned about them. His unbounded capacity for maintaining Christian fellowship with men whose opinions were other than his own was an immense contribution toward the creation of an atmosphere in which religious thought could be really free. Besides that, he advanced the prestige of religion by the fact that he was loved as perhaps no other American preacher has been loved by people in his own church, in other churches, and in no church.

George A. Gordon was installed as minister of the old South Church

(Congregational) in Boston in 1884. The *Christian Union* called it at the time "a significant installation," but no one could know then how significant it was to be. "He is neither old school nor new school, Calvinist nor Arminian, Bushnellite nor Parkite. He is equally ready to realize the possibility of verbal inspiration in one passage and to reject it in another; equally ready to admit the possibility of redemption after death and to refuse to assert it dogmatically." If this suggests that he was willing to teach that the earth is round or flat, as the trustees prefer, the impression is erroneous. He was a cautious liberal, but his influence was constantly on the side of more liberal positions than those of the majority.

Joseph Cook, of Boston, was a mighty champion, but it was sometimes hard to tell which side he was the champion of. Drawing immense audiences to his Monday lectures, which taxed the seating capacity of the largest hall in Boston, he first defended the old tenets by new methods; then, freed from the restraining influence of his old teacher, Professor Park, he moved forward so far that, while defending the Pentateuch against advanced German criticism, "he really goes farther in his abandonment of its Mosaic authorship than Professor Robertson Smith has done and farther than a careful literary criticism requires" (*Christian Union*, February 1, 1883). Again swinging into reverse, he attacked the proposed new Congregational creed and "constituted himself the champion of reactionism in theology." But whichever side of any question he was on, Joseph Cook was never anything less than oracular, and no one who knew Boston in the 'eighties can imagine a history of American Christianity which did not give him at least a page. Viewed in the perspective of the present, it seems that a short paragraph will do.

One of the results of the growth of more liberal theological ideas within the orthodox churches was a number of heresy trials. Nearly all of these were within the Presbyterian Church. The Congregationalists and Episcopalians developed a considerable degree of theological tolerance, the Methodists were more interested in administrative efficiency than in doctrinal uniformity, the Lutherans were practically unanimous in maintaining their old theology unmodified, the Baptists and Disciples had no ecclesiastical courts for dealing with heresy, and so threshed out the cases of their heretics in their religious papers without decisive results. Two cases of not much more than local importance occurred among the Presbyterians in 1883. Rev. W. W. McLane of Steubenville, Ohio, was put out of his pulpit by the presbytery for writing a book on *The Cross in the Light of Today*, in which he maintained a theory other than that of the substitutionary atonement. Rev. J. W. White, of the presbytery of Huntington, Pennsylvania, was suspended from the ministry for lax views on the physical resurrection and on the atonement and in particular for saying that when Christ died "he was not smitten with the divine wrath, but filled with all the fulness of divine love." But the heresy cases which attained national publicity were those of Doctor Swing and Professors Briggs, H. P. Smith, A. C. McGiffert, Borden P. Bowne and Hinckley G. Mitchell.

David Swing was minister of the Fourth Presbyterian Church in Chicago. Francis L. Patton, later president of Princeton and always a pillar of orthodoxy, instigated the charge of a general departure from the Calvinistic system; more specifically, the teaching of salvation by works, a "modal Trinity," denial of plenary inspiration, and a leaning toward Unitarianism. Swing was acquitted by his presbytery but, to save his church from embarrassment and secure his own greater freedom, he resigned his pulpit before the appeal of his accusers to the synod was brought to trial. He founded the independent Central Church, housed first in McVicker's Theatre, then in Central Music Hall which was built for the purpose. The new church took on many social activities—charities, classes and industrial schools—and became an "institutional" church. Doctor Swing was a great soul but no theologian.

Charles A. Briggs was a professor in Union Theological Seminary. He had been under suspicion for a long time because of his advocacy of the higher criticism and his publications in this field. But the New York presbytery refused to bring him to trial until compelled to do so by the General Assembly. The trial was held in November, 1892, chiefly on the charge of denying the inerrancy of the Bible, even in the original document. The presbytery acquitted him, but on appeal to the Assembly he was convicted and suspended from the ministry "until he could give satisfactory evidence of repentance." He did not repent but joined the Episcopal church and kept his professorship at Union.

Professor Henry Preserved Smith of Lane Theological Seminary in Cincinnati was also found guilty of denying the inerrancy of the lost original manuscripts of the Scriptures and the sentence was confirmed by the synod and, in 1893, by the General Assembly.

The case of Dr. A. C. McGiffert, a professor in, and later president of, Union Theological Seminary, was recurrent from 1898 to 1900. It never came to a formal trial and the proceedings of the Assembly which called his views in question were confined to condemning some of his opinions, re-affirming the doctrine of the inerrancy of Scripture, and referring the matter to the New York presbytery. The defendant relieved the church of its embarrassment by withdrawing from its ministry.

The only heresy cases of importance outside of the Presbyterian Church were those of Professors Borden P. Bowne and Hinckley G. Mitchell, Methodists, of Boston University. These came to a head somewhat later, in 1904 and 1905, but the issues were those of the period under consideration. The explosion against Professor Bowne hung fire until the time had passed when it could do him any harm. As a matter of fact, it did a great deal of good. He was a philosopher and theologian supremely concerned to make a reasonable and persuasive statement of the personality of God against whatever mechanistic and pantheistic theories of the universe there might be, and to exalt the worth and freedom of human personality against all mechanistic interpretations of human nature. While he was neither a scientist nor a Semitic scholar, he believed in the principles of evolution and of Biblical criticism. Most of all, he believed in freedom of thought and of scholarship, and was sure that neither the discovery of the late date or composite authorship of any book in the Bible, nor doubt as to the historicity of any or all of the miracles, nor the denial of any particular theory of the atonement, touched the central matters of Christianity. (I speak feelingly of him as a defender of the faith, for his writings were, more than those of any other, an aid to my own faith in the days of my youthful quests and questionings.) Bowne first drew the fire of the conservatives by his spirited defense of his colleague, Professor H. G. Mitchell, who, after teaching without molestation for nearly fifteen years the modern views of the Old Testament which he had learned in Germany, was attacked as a heretic in 1895, again in 1900, and was finally removed in 1905. The trial of Professor Bowne before a "select number" of the New York East Conference resulted in his acquittal by unanimous vote. More than that, it served to clear the air and to make the Methodist Church reasonably safe for scholarship—after Mitchell had been flung to the lions. Some of the staunchest of the moderate conservatives, including most of the real leaders in that church, were on Bowne's side. Dr. J. M. Buckley, the leading Methodist editor and anything but a radical, was attorney for his defense. But the sacrifice of Mitchell by the bishops the next year made Bowne a sharp critic of the ecclesiastical machinery of his church, and especially of the power of its bishops, for the rest of his life. (See F. J. McConnell: *Borden P. Bowne,* and H. G. Mitchell: *For the Benefit of My Creditors.*)

Dr. Daniel Dorchester, himself reasonably conservative, summed the matter up in 1887 by saying: "There is a growing disbelief in the supernatural, and a revolutionary spirit has entered every department of thought and action." Yet—"Divested of the husk of scholasticism and delivered from the spirit of dogmatism, the spirituality of the American churches is many fold greater than one hundred years ago."

Chapter VII

EXPERIMENTS IN COÖPERATION

The one fact which always first commands the attention of any foreign observer of the church in America or any foreign student of its history is the multiplicity of sects into which it is divided. America has been the world's most fertile seedplot for the sprouting of new sects. The area which now constitutes the United States was first settled by persons of diverse religious beliefs and practices. The church in this country was born divided; or, more accurately, the religion that came over with the earliest groups of settlers was a religion already divided. However much credit may be due to the founders and framers of our Federal government for having arrived at wise and humane opinions as to the desirability of giving all sects full legal equality and establishing none, the determining fact was that a Federal establishment would have been impossible in a country where no one church was stronger than the two that ranked next to it in numbers and influence. This was the first nation to guarantee full religious equality because it was the first that, from the hour of its birth, was composed of religious minorities. Many of the older eastern states, which had been more or less homogeneous in religion in their earlier colonial days, retained for a time some remnants of their established churches and gave preferential treatment to the "established order." New Hampshire, for example, did not until 1877 remove the constitutional provision that the governor and every member of the legislature "shall be of the Protestant religion."

Pioneer conditions, the absence of legal restraints, and the fierce passion for individual liberty combined to promote the multiplication of religious parties. It was a bewildered Frenchman who exclaimed,

"Mon Dieu! A country with two hundred religions and only one sauce!" Allowing for a slight inaccuracy in the statistics, there was substantial truth in the description. Americans were more interested in theological than in culinary refinement. But a mere count of the two hundred or more divisions which have a place in a complete diagram of the churches in America greatly exaggerates the confusion. Most of these sects are very small, many of them microscopic. Some of them represent the different national origins of immigrants who have no quarrel with each other's religion. For practical purposes one may consider that the religious forces of the United States are organized in about ten important groups.

But the existence of ten groups so nearly equal in resources and influence and all filled with zeal for expansion has produced a degree of denominational competition which has been one of the characteristic features of American religion, and one of its main misfortunes. It has, however, had the effect not only of guaranteeing the continuance of religious liberty—since a society that is a collection of minorities can scarcely put any minority under its ban unless it develops what seem to be outrageously anti-social features—but also perhaps of encouraging the spirit of independence within the several denominations. While denominational conflict and rivalry tended to intensify loyalty, as a state of war always does, it also provided ready means of escape for any who found themselves cramped in their own groups. If a discontented Methodist could not change the Methodist church, he could walk across the street and join a Baptist or a Presbyterian church, or start a new one.

During the first third of the nineteenth century there had been much coöperation and good will among the denominations. The plan of union between Congregationalists and Presbyterians was in operation. Sunday school associations were from the start undenominational. There were missionary societies, Bible societies, tract societies, anti-slavery societies, temperance societies, all of which were conducted without regard to denominational lines; and the revivalistic movements, then as later, tended to ignore sectarian barriers. But the era of good will came to an end about 1837 and an era of acrimony and competition supervened. Yet even this period was not without its alleviating episodes, for it was then that Dr. S. S. Schmucker, the irenic Lutheran, issued his noble *Overture* (1846); and many far-sighted American religious thinkers participated in the international and interconfessional conferences sponsored by the British Evangelical Alliance. But all that made little impression on the American churches.

After the Civil War, the impulse to union revived. The very word sounded good, especially in the North, and churches began to be more keenly aware of the handicap under which the Christian enterprise labored by reason of its division in the presence of new and urgent problems. The denominations which had been split by slavery and the war made futile gestures in the direction of reunion—except the Episcopalians, who reunited as dispassionately as they had divided—but the fact that the Baptists, Methodists, and Presbyterians at least took the matter under consideration was worth something. Further consideration will be given to these efforts in another connection.

Occasional union services were held. A joint Sunday evening service of Presbyterian and Episcopal churches in Brooklyn was addressed by Bishop McIlvaine, who spoke on unity in much the same terms that an advocate of the community church might use today. Beecher, in addressing the American Congregational Union, spoke of the unimportance of the issues which divide the denominations and the necessity of compromise, and said: "I would consent, if the Baptists would, to baptize infant children as a form of dedication and then to make them all, when they came into the church in manhood, be immersed as a form of baptism" (*Independent*, May 21, 1868). The American Christian Commission held a series of state union conventions in the Middle West in 1867 and 1868, which stressed "the essential unity of all believers of whatever denominations." The Oswego, New York, Congregational Association received a new church, formed of members of the Presbyterian, Methodist, and Baptist churches, all of which were "pastorless and nearly spiritually dead." Desiring to combine, they compromised on Congregationalism. It was stated that before this movement there had not been a convert in the town for ten years.

The Sunday school movement afforded a field in which the union impulse could be safely exercised. There had been many local and state associations and conventions between 1820 and 1830. Three national conventions had been held before the Civil War. The uniform lessons were suggested by Bishop Vincent in 1866 and the international series, undenominationally planned and administered, was inaugurated in 1873. Chautauqua Assembly, organized by Bishop Vincent in 1874, was originally planned chiefly for the training of Sunday school teachers.

The Young Men's Christian Association, which originated in England in 1844, was introduced into the United States in 1851 with the organization of the Boston association and held its first national convention in 1854 at Buffalo, but its great period of growth began immediately after the war. At its eleventh annual convention in 1866, forty-eight local associations reported, though more were in existence. The discussions at that convention dealt chiefly with temperance and the best method of conducting devotional meetings for impenitent young men. A suggestion for the establishment of "systems of recreation, including with certain restrictions dancing and billiards" was met by a resolution of stern disapproval—after which a "sumptuous collation" was served to the delegates. But the period of exclusive devotion to devotional services and sumptuous collations soon passed. By 1874 there were nearly a thousand branches in the United States and Canada, many of them with buildings devoted to practical social service and even to recreation. It represented the coöperative work of Christians of many denominations, not of the denominations themselves, and it did what the divided churches could not do and did not even care to try to do. The Young Women's Christian Association, organized in 1866, soon began a similar work, especially in behalf of working girls.

The Evangelical Alliance had been organized in England in 1846 with delegates present from many countries, including the United States. The Oxford movement had given Protestantism deep concern and Newman had gone over to Rome the year before. The avowed purpose of the Alliance was "to concentrate the strength of an enlightened Protestantism against the encroachments of Popery and Puseyism." The Alliance was formally introduced to the United States in 1866 by Dr. James McCosh, then of Belfast, Ireland, who came as a visitor and, at a meeting in New York with Phillip Schaff, who later became an apostle of unity, as secretary, spoke on the benefits of

Protestant union in advancing religious liberty, opposing Romanism and meeting the advancing wave of skepticism and rationalism. The American branch of the Evangelical Alliance was formed in 1867, and the greatest convention in its history was the one held in New York in 1873.

An "American congress of churches" was organized and held its first meeting at New Haven in May, 1885, having for its avowed purpose "to promote Christian union and advance the Kingdom of God by the free discussion of the great religious, moral and social questions of the time." It had been projected by Rev. W. W. Newton of Pittsfield, Massachusetts, at a meeting held at that place to celebrate the four hundredth anniversary of Luther's birth, November 10, 1883. Dr. Howard Crosby spoke on "the relation of divided Christendom to aggressive Christianity," and F. D. Power on "the unifying effects of worship." The congress was attended by representative Episcopalians (bishops), Congregationalists, Baptists, Presbyterians, Disciples, Methodists, Unitarians, Universalists, Quakers, and Swedenborgians. But this also was an association of Christians, acting individually, rather than of denominations. It was agreed that the congress should meet regularly at intervals of two years, but it soon lapsed.

Groups of ministers of various denominations were formed all over the country, and "city ministers' meetings," often connected more or less directly with the Evangelical Alliance, became common. Foreign missionary societies, while still without any definite machinery of coöperation, began to take the location of each other's stations into account and to keep out of each other's way so far as possible. Avoiding competition was the first form of coöperation in the foreign field.

The Episcopal Church, then as now, was sincerely devoted to the concept of unity, but was more hampered than some others in coöperative effort. When a daily union meeting in Cincinnati was presided over by an Episcopal bishop, it was referred to as "a rare sight"—as indeed it was. But no advocate of unity was more ardent than the Episcopalian, Doctor Muhlenberg, the last years of whose life were spent in persistent and fearless effort to secure the establishment of a commission on Christian unity by his church (*Christian Union*, August 16, 1883). The Massachusetts diocesan convention recommended that the coming General Convention reconsider the Muhlenberg memorial. But the General Convention, which was the centennial convention of 1883, took no action on the request for a comity commission. The *Churchman* tells why: "The Episcopal Church is conscious of no disabilities. Her equipment, charter, creed, and mission are apostolic. She stands today rooted and grounded in the history, life, and faith of the Pentecostal Church. Evangelical faith and apostolic order are her parallel lines of defense. Their organic completeness can be reached within her fellowship. If there is any virtue in the divine plan and order, they must be communicated precisely as they have been received" (The *Churchman*, August 11, 1883). Of course, as long as the Episcopal Church felt that way about it, it could do nothing else.

However, the next Episcopal general convention, that of 1886, took a step which became a landmark in the history of Christian unity—though it could scarcely be called a milestone, for it marked no real progress—when it adopted the "quadrilateral basis" for unity. Its four points were: the Scriptures of the Old and New Testaments as the revealed word of God, the Nicene Creed as a sufficient statement of faith, the two sacraments "administered with an unfailing use of the Lord's words," and "the historic episcopate locally adapted." It was pointed out by non-Episcopalians that this was little more than a polite way of inviting the world to accept the well-known position of the Episcopal Church, just as the invitation to Protestants to attend the Vatican Council in 1870 with a prior acceptance of the papal claims, and Leo XIII's later encyclical, *Praeclara gratulationis* in 1894 urging a "return to unity," were calls for a surrender rather than invitations to a meeting for parley on neutral ground.

The Disciples of Christ also were ardent advocates of union. That had been the primary purpose for which they came into existence. But, like the Episcopalians, since they knew so exactly what was the apostolic faith and order upon which the church must unite, and already occupied that position, their appeals for unity sounded to others suspiciously like an invitation to unconditional surrender.

The churches, divided as they were in theology and polity, found an important field for practical coöperation in the cause of temperance and prohibition. Liquor was recognized as producing a moral and social problem long before the churches took a definite stand on it.

The eighteenth century was notoriously a period of heavy drinking. After the Revolutionary War there was a notable increase in the manufacture and use of distilled beverages. The Methodist conferences at Baltimore in 1780 and 1783, following the precept of John Wesley, took a definite stand against liquor, but this was reversed a few years later and the general conference of 1812 refused to require a minister who sold liquor to lose his ministerial standing. It was not until 1848 that the "old rule" was put into the discipline. Lyman Beecher states in his autobiography that the bill for expenses in connection with "raising the frame" of a new church at Webster, New Hampshire, in 1823, included the following items:

7¾ gallons West India Rum	$8.62
4¾ gallons New England Rum.	2.37
3 lbs. sugar	.90
209 lemons	8.71

(This is not offered as a formula.) The religious revivals between 1800 and 1830 on the whole stimulated temperance reform, though the whiskey jug was not a stranger at camp-meetings. The Baptists and Methodists, in spite of the limitation mentioned, contributed most to the advocacy of temperance. The Presbyterians had a Scotch tradition that was not at once overcome, and New England puritanism was not fanatical for abstinence.

State temperance societies were formed and in 1826 the American Society for Promotion of Temperance. Its object was not to suppress the traffic or to make total abstainers, but rather to encourage the substitution of milder beverages for hard liquor and to change the social customs so that drinking should not be an imperative feature on almost every occasion. Dr. Leonard Bacon testified in 1830 to the great change that had been produced in five years—"An intelligent people rising up as it were with one consent, without law, without any attempt at legislation, to put down by mere force of public opinion expressing itself in voluntary associations a great social evil which no despot on earth could have put down among his subjects by any system of effort." He notes the admiration with which Great Britain and continental Europe viewed America's achievement of temperance, but contemporary records fail to substantiate this observation. On the whole his picture was unwarrantably rosy. Nevertheless, something had been accomplished. Social drinking had diminished, but the saloon was born.

The total abstinence campaign began about 1836, and 1840 saw the organization of the first Washingtonian society, an explicitly non-religious movement led by six men who had been hard drinkers. It became a sort of ex-drunkards' society. John B. Gough, who was fully qualified both by past experience and by oratorical power, worked with it for several years. It did great good, but too many of its star witnesses relapsed and it encouraged a morbid type of testimony. Gough said that he never knew a drinker to be thoroughly and permanently reformed unless he was also converted. The failure and final disappearance of the Washingtonian societies produced two results. One was that the churches got into temperance reform more actively and unitedly. The other was that emphasis began to be laid upon the restriction of the traffic by law—that is, prohibition. For a time the two types of anti-liquor propaganda ran parallel: the temperance campaigns, generally in revivalistic form with emotional appeals, testimonies of the saved, and pledge-signing; and efforts to secure state laws to curb or prohibit the business. The latter began about 1838, but in this as in the other the impulse was not wholly religious. P. T. Barnum was one of the active colleagues of Neal Dow to whose work was chiefly due the enactment of the first state prohibition law, that of Maine in 1851. A dozen or more other states had total or partial prohibition within the next ten years and in most cases the churches, acting together, played an active part in building the sentiment on which the laws were based.

The federal liquor license bill, signed by Lincoln in 1862 as a wartime revenue measure, was bitterly opposed by the temperance forces, by this time nearly identical with the religious forces, which foresaw its effect in "making liquor respectable." This war, like every other, was accompanied and followed by a general increase in drinking and it had scarcely closed when the legal battle over liquor began. It may clarify the process by which the fight for temperance became a fight for prohibition to cite and number some specific events:

1. A month after the death of Lincoln a National Temperance Convention was called. It met at Saratoga Springs, New York, in August, 1865, and the seeds of the prohibition party were planted.

2. The brewers' convention in 1866 urged its members to support only those candidates for public office who were "liberal and willing to give all beverages an equal chance," regardless of party.

3. Later in the same year the New Hampshire temperance convention called for the nomination of independent candidates when the regular candidates were not for prohibition.

4. In 1867 the president of the "brewers' congress" said to his colleagues: "We must raise ourselves to be a large and widespread political power." And the congress voted "to sustain no candidate of any party in any election who is in any way disposed toward the total abstinence cause."

5. Immediately after this congress, the Good Templars of Pennsylvania took up this challenge by declaring that it would "vote for no man who countenances the liquor traffic or uses liquor."

6. In 1868 the brewers announced that they had picked candidates who would work for their interests. "Neither men nor money were spared. The entire German population was enlisted." The race question began then and continued to be a primary factor in the temperance and anti-temperance fight so far as it concerned beer. The great brewers were practically all Germans and the contest was felt on both sides to be one between the tradition of English-speaking Protestantism (popularly called Puritan) and that of the continental peoples who had more recently come to America. This feeling continued as long as liquor continued to be legal. The *Brewers' Journal*, February, 1913, summed up the conflict by assuring its constituents that "the Anglo-Saxon element in this country is gradually receding before the enormous flood of European immigration and its prolific propagation of its kind. The few remnants of Puritanism are facing total extinction."

7. The National Good Templars convention at Cleveland, Ohio, 1868, resolved, "We accept the issue and will meet them at the polls."

8. The National Prohibition Party was organized in 1869.

The churches, though not unanimous for prohibition, furnished the bulk of the support for it. In 1865 Horace Greeley, favoring prohibition, and Rev. Leonard Bacon, a very honored Congregational minister in New Haven who took the opposite view, had an extended argument on the subject in the pages of the *Independent*. Doctor Bacon thought the Maine law had been a failure and that the teaching of moderation was better than total abstinence. Greeley said, "Having been convinced that alcohol is a poison, I hold that the law should treat it as a poison and regulate its procurement and sale accordingly. But my more serious difference with Doctor Bacon is based on his assumption that a law generally disobeyed is necessarily invalid and useless. Is he prepared to see lewdness and gambling restrained by license laws? Nothing could be plainer than the truth that all present legislation against these vices is at once essentially prohibitory and very generally defied." In 1868, the *Congregationalist and Recorder* (the *Congregationalist* having recently absorbed the *Recorder*) alarmed some of its constituency by its failure to support the cause. The *Recorder* had been "faithful to prohibition," but the *Congregationalist* was criticized in resolutions passed by three Massachusetts associations. State prohibition had just been voted down in Massachusetts.

But in spite of isolated instances, even notable ones, in which prominent churchmen opposed prohibition, the churches very generally united in support of both local option and proposals for state prohibition when these were offered. Supporting a third party movement was another matter. The number of votes for third party prohibition candidates in the presidential elections was always well below 10 per cent. of the number of adult male members of Protestant churches.

It was the relative indifference of these male members to the organized temperance movement that led to the organization of the Women's Christian Temperance Union in 1874. In the decade following the Civil War the need of temperance reform was greater and the activity in its behalf was less than it had been before. When the tide of moral and religious energy began to rise in opposition to liquor, it took the form first of efforts to pray the saloon out of business. As other methods were adopted—first the organization of the Prohibition Party, then the W. C. T. U., then in 1895 the Anti-Saloon League to work in all parties—the church still furnished most of the personnel and the support for the enterprise. Even Carrie Nation's militant outbreak in Kansas was rationalized if not motivated by a religious appeal; for photographic purposes, if not in action, she carried a Bible in one hand and a hatchet in the other.

The story of the Women's Christian Temperance Union for its first thirty years was virtually the story of Frances E. Willard. This remarkable woman was so much of a non-conformist that, though reared in Oberlin in the days of Finney, she long refused to join the church because of intellectual doubts, and so little submissive to discipline that she resigned a position as head of the women's college of Northwestern University, at Evanston, Ill., because she could not subordinate herself to the university authorities. In 1873, at Hillsboro, Ohio, she came under the influence of Dr. Diocletian Lewis, a physician who gained wide publicity through his advocacy of various reforms, dietary and other, and who was then urging the women to use direct methods in putting the saloons out of business. A large company of them marched to the saloons, prayed, sang hymns and induced patrons to sign the pledge. Men were taken out of the gutter and liquor was poured into it. Many of the women suffered violence and indignities and some of them were put in jail, where they continued to sing and pray. Miss Willard entered a saloon in Pittsburgh in 1874 and prayed on the sawdust-covered floor. A week later she was president of the local W. C. T. U. Having served her apprenticeship in the brief fanatical stage of the movement, she quickly directed it into other channels. The women's temperance movement now began to attack the saloon instead of addressing itself to the individual drinker. Miss Willard's acceptance of an unsalaried position as a worker for the W. C. T. U. instead of the lucrative teaching post that was offered to her was a decisive event in American social history, for to her was chiefly due the change in tactics which eventually eliminated the fantastic element from the serious campaign for temperance and prohibition. She persuaded the W. C. T. U. to advocate suffrage for women and to support the prohibition party. In 1879 she was elected president of the W. C. T. U.

With all of this, the denominations as such had little to do. But women of all denominations constituted the membership of the organization, and churches of all denominations were open to Miss Willard and its other representatives. Within a year after the formation of the first local society, it was reported that there was scarcely a

city or town from Bangor to San Francisco that did not have at least
the nucleus of a Women's Christian Temperance Union, the national
organization had been formed, the sentiment of the evangelical
churches was fully enlisted in its support, and a petition signed by
hundreds of thousands of women had been presented to Congress asking for the federal prohibition of the sale of intoxicants.

The Women's Christian Temperance Union warmly espoused the
cause of equal suffrage, but in this it did not at once carry with it
the bulk of male opinion within the churches, though probably the
percentage of supporters was much larger in the churches than outside of them. In 1880, it endorsed the candidacy of Garfield, chiefly
because he was a preacher, but he gave it no great encouragement.
Four years later, when both old parties refused to adopt a prohibition
plank, the W. C. T. U. gave its support to the Prohibition Party and
contributed to the first defeat which the Republicans had suffered in
a presidential election since 1856. The churches never gave any solid
support to the third party movement, but gradually they became, with
some exceptions, fairly united in their advocacy of the principle of
prohibition. On the whole, the fight for temperance and prohibition
gave the churches their most important field of common interest and
helped them to develop the sense of a common responsibility for the
betterment of social conditions.

Interdenominational organizations of young people were another
instrument through which the urge toward unity found both expression and development. Of these, the most important was the Young
People's Society of Christian Endeavor which began as a purely local
organization in a Congregational Church at Williston, Maine, in 1881,
under the leadership of Rev. Francis E. Clark, and swept across the
country like a prairie fire. In less than five years it had found such
wide acceptance that scarcely a respectable church in most of the
major denominations was without its Endeavor Society. But in spite
of the commitment to denominational loyalty, which was part of its
pledge, a few important denominations feared its unionistic tendency.
The Methodists organized their own Epworth League in 1889, the
Baptists their Baptist Young People's Union in 1891, and the Lutherans
their Luther League in 1895. The Methodist youth movement had a
long and somewhat complicated history, which will be traced in its

proper place. But even these serious withdrawals from the common current did not prevent Christian Endeavor from being a powerful unifying influence. It may have been somewhat overly pietistic and, with its insistence upon "taking some part in every meeting" may have tended to overvalue the conventional prayer-meeting aspect of religion and to elevate glibness to the dignity of a cardinal virtue; but it would be impossible to estimate the weight of its contribution in developing non-sectarian mindedness in the middle-aged Christians of today who were Christian Endeavorers thirty and forty years ago.

Religious journalism was, like most other religious enterprises, predominantly denominational. The religious papers which acknowl-edged no narrow allegiance were few but important. First among them was the *Independent*, which definitely ceased to be Congrega-tional in 1867. Even before that, whether edited by Beecher (1861-1863) or by Tilton, its attitude had fully justified its name. The *Christian Union*, founded in 1870 by Beecher, who edited it alone until 1876 and with Lyman Abbott for five years more, was also accurately named. In 1883, there was a project to establish an unde-nominational Christian weekly for New England, but the impressive committee which had the plan under consideration decided instead to recommend the *Christian Union*, which thereafter had a sense of wider mission and a stronger following. Both of these papers were theologically liberal, within evangelical limits; that is to say, they favored evolution and Biblical criticism and were not alarmed by new developments in theology. The *Christian Herald*, edited by Talmage, like Talmage's sermons, made its appeal to the popular mind rather than to the intellectuals and adhered faithfully to the older orthodoxy.

Theological education, prior to the end of the nineteenth century, was almost entirely conducted with a view to perpetuating distinctive denominational views. The development of the divinity schools con-nected with the larger universities and some of the independent schools into virtually undenominational institutions came later. Even Union Theological Seminary, New York, was not originally so com-prehensive as its name seems to indicate. Founded in 1836, it was so called because it was designed to train men to work under the "plan of union" between the Presbyterians and Congregationalists. Until 1905 the members of its faculty were required to subscribe to the Westminster confession. The growth of unifying tendencies in the theological schools has been largely a by-product of the modern scholarship which has liberalized their teaching. Changes in the formal requirements made upon instructors or trustees, or changes in the official designation of a school as belonging to this or that denomination, have come, if at all, as tardy recognitions of changes that have already occurred both in the type of teaching and in the personnel of the student bodies. Several of the more important eastern seminaries exercised a strong though indirect unionizing influence by drawing together students from many different denominations years before there was any explicit avowal that they were anything but denominational schools.

A significant episode not only in the history of Christian scholarship but also in the growth of the coöperative spirit was the preparation of the Revised Version of the English Bible. In 1611 the Church of England would not have welcomed the participation of dissenters in the preparation of the King James version. The Revised Version of the New Testament, made by a representative committee of English and American scholars of several denominations, was published in 1881. When James Gordon Bennett had the whole New Testament in this translation cabled from London for publication in the *New York Herald*, it was rightly considered not only a brilliant journalistic coup but an evidence of the great popular interest in the enterprise. The Revised Old Testament appeared in 1885. The American Committee continued its work and published the American Standard revision in 1901. Since that time there have been several private translations based on the principle of using a diction bearing the same relation to the current speech that the original documents bore to the common language of the people for whom they were written. The most prominent of these have been the Modern Speech New Testament, by Richard Francis Weymouth, 1902; the Moffatt translation, 1922–1926; and the American Translation by Edgar J. Goodspeed and J. M. Powis Smith, 1923–1931.

By the end of the nineteenth century there had been little progress toward the organic unity of the churches, but there had been an immense increase in the spirit of coöperation among them and their divisive differences in doctrines had ceased to occupy a central place in their thought. This was due largely to two causes: the rise of social and practical issues to a new importance, and the development of a new scholarship which gave prominence to issues which cut across denominational lines and, while introducing new planes of cleavage, rendered the old ones relatively unimportant.

Chapter VIII

THE ERA OF THE BROWNSTONE FRONT

The period is roughly from 1873 to 1893. Looking at the East, we may call it the Era of the Brownstone Front. The reverse gold rush— that is, from the gold fields back to New York to spend the money —was over. The crudity and chaos and the worst of the corruption had given place to something better. Boss Tweed had been put in jail (but not to stay). The Credit Mobilier had been exposed. Jim Fisk was dead (shot). Daniel Drew was gone (broke before he died). Woodhull and Claflin became respectable and virtuous Victorian matrons. Beecher lived down the unproved scandal. Respectability came back into fashion. Of all of which inward grace the brownstone front was the outward sign.

The panic of 1873 was a landmark in the financial history of the country, but manners and customs and cultural characteristics flowed on in an unbroken current with only gradual modification, as doubtless they had through such crises as the fall of Rome and the winning of American independence. Italian villas with cupolas and with castiron deer in the yards were still in vogue, and the brownstone front was the acme of urban elegance. Zinc-lined bath tubs were used once a week. Rogers groups represented the level of popular taste in art and afforded an easily attainable evidence of culture and modest affluence. Tidies on chair backs and tassled lambrequins were essential features of interior decoration and there was crocheted work on everything from match-holders to dog-muzzles, for ladies were ladies and did fancy work to prove it, even while some hundreds of thousands were getting interested in the W. C. T. U. and even more in the new women's missionary organizations. A few apartment houses were built, chiefly in New York, and boarding houses were viewed with alarm as enemies of the home and possible hot-beds of vice.

An 1883 estimate of the decadence of domesticity is contained in these words of Rev. Morgan Dix, rector of Trinity Church, New York: "The sins of the women of today are largely: lack of a serious view of life; desecration of the ideal of matrimony; deliberate determination of some married women to defeat the object for which marriage was instituted; to have no real home; to avoid first the pains and next the cares and duties of maternity; the habit, where a home exists, of neglecting it by spending most of the time away from it; growing indifference to the chief of all social abominations, divorce, and the toleration of lax notions about it" (*Christian Union*, March 15, 1883). Already there was alarm about the loose divorce laws which had originated in the West; but "now Maine and Connecticut rival Indiana and even Utah in the facilities which they afford for the disruption of the family." The number of divorces in the United States had doubled from 1867 to 1878. Doctor Dix, resting the whole case for indissoluble marriage on textual and ecclesiastical grounds, thinks that divorce is "an outcome of Protestantism, of the habit of interpreting the Bible according to man's private judgment, and is the dark stigma on Protestant Christianity." He was also the leading antifeminist among the Columbia University trustees who rejected a petition signed by 1,400 men and women for the admission of women to the university. The trustees considered the education of the two sexes in the same classrooms "unwise and inexpedient" and proposed instead a three-year reading course for young women, upon which the faculty might give an examination and award a certificate. But the feminist cause was further advanced than the Columbia trustees realized. Oberlin had had co-education for fifty years, though with some cautious limitations, as witness the case of Lucy Stone, who was allowed to take the classical course instead of the "ladies' course" and was even permitted to write a speech for commencement but was not allowed to deliver it in person.

The question of opening new occupations to women gave rise to frequent discussion. Much publicity attended the case of a woman who applied for a license as a steamboat pilot on the Mississippi. She had lived on the river with her husband, had piloted with him and for him, and her competence was unquestioned. The solicitor of the Treasury Department admitted that there was no impediment in the law, but refused to grant the application on the ground that woman is "unsexed" by such employment or by her employment in any field ordinarily occupied by men, and that Christian civilization was in danger. It illustrated the familiar process of giving religious sanction to a custom based largely on economic considerations. Christian civilization was not supposed to be imperiled or the home put in jeopardy or women unsexed by her employment in any sort of ill-paid job that men did not want. Most women workers at that time were factory workers and their average pay was from three to four dollars a week. Women workers in offices did not become numerous until the typewriter came into general use, and that was late in the 'eighties.

Women who did not work were carefully guarded. Social codes in polite society varied. In Philadelphia, says James Huneker in *Steeplejack*, a girl who allowed even her fiancé to take her to a theater or a ball without a chaperon found her reputation ruined. Elsewhere, the requirements were somewhat less strict. Sunday observance was still rather rigid, as has already been indicated, except among the Germans and some other groups of immigrants.

The rising interest in sport and recreation was, on the whole, one of the wholesome aspects of the time. The habit of summer-resorting might almost be said to have come into existence after the Civil War, and Long Branch, Newport and the White Mountains became favorite resorts. The cog road up Mt. Washington was finished in 1869, and Florida was discovered as a resort about 1870, though few cared to go any farther south than Jacksonville. Baseball began to be a national sport when A. G. Spaulding's club from Rockford, Illinois, made a trip through the East in 1870. The players were at first amateurs and the profit came through betting, which was generally crooked. The first professional game was played in 1869 and the National League was formed in 1876. Intercollegiate sport began about the same time with the Yale-Harvard football game of 1875 and the Yale-Harvard boat race of 1878. The Y. M. C. A. was beginning to build gymnasiums. International sport was chiefly confined to yachting. Popular sport started with croquet, which swept the country like a pestilence in 1866 and held its vogue to such an extent that in 1883 "the new art of dry plate photography" is recommended to amateurs as having "even more charm than croquet." The first tennis tournament was held at Yale in 1872. The bicycle became popular with the appearance of the high wheel in the 'seventies, fell out of fashion in the 'eighties and was revived in 1895 with the improvement and standardization of the "safety."

P. T. Barnum and Buffalo Bill cannot be left out of the picture of the American mind in the 'seventies and 'eighties. Beginning much earlier with a museum of freaks, curiosities and relics, Barnum became in 1871 the proprietor of the "Greatest Show on Earth." If there had been radio in those days, he would undoubtedly have had station WGS. Using the railroad instead of wagons, as earlier and smaller shows had done, he covered the country and did more than any other man both to determine the public taste for entertainment and to supply the demand for it. It was a reflection of the character of the age as well as of the showman that he insisted always upon the moral and educational value of his show. Many churches rated the circus along with the theater as amusements under the ban, but Barnum prided himself upon giving "clean" entertainment, and he did. Not content with being the acknowledged master of the canvas big top and the sawdust ring, without being in the least apologetic for his clowns and elephants he aspired also to be a promoter of art and culture in higher fields, as when he became the impresario for Jenny Lind. And he not only showed his supreme skill as the first great publicity man, but broke into the most exalted social circles when he introduced Tom Thumb at Windsor Castle. Barnum was a sincerely religious man, but the time had not yet come for publicity experts to contribute to religious literature. One shudders to think what would have happened if Barnum had written a book about religion—say a life of Jesus.

Buffalo Bill, né William F. Cody, fortunate in having lived through the period of real western adventure and on into the period of romantic appreciation of it, started his first Wild West show in 1883. Aside from Bret Harte's *Luck of Roaring Camp* and other stories in similar vein and Mark Twain's *Roughing It* and *The Gilded Age* and the dime novels of the Nick Carter type, it was the first notable effort to capitalize the heroic frontier days for exploitation in the East. In understanding the vogue and the technique of the revivalism of the period, one can gain some light by considering that Barnum and Buffalo Bill were among the popular educators of the time.

Popular literature was made up principally of two elements: the sentimental and nice, as in the novels of E. P. Roe and Mrs. A. D. T. Whitney (either one of whom might be considered the Harold Bell Wright of the period); and the thrillers and dime novels which furnished the surreptitious literary nourishment of youth and were the prototypes of the western movies. The *New York Ledger* and *Hearth and Home*, story papers of enormous circulation, furnished a mixture of religion, sentiment and adventure. Redpath opened his lyceum system in 1867 and flooded the country with lectures which ranged from good to excellent. Among the greatest attractions in his list of talent were John B. Gough, the temperance advocate, Tom Nast, the cartoonist, and Henry Ward Beecher. The cream was skimmed from that business by 1875. The business itself went on in increasing volume, but with no such outstanding star performers. Ten years later, Gough could not have earned $40,000 in one season, as he did in 1871–1872.

Godkin called it a chromo civilization. But even aside from the fact that there were some real values even in the least lofty of the elements which have been mentioned, there was some culture upon which not even the editor of the *Nation* could cast scorn. The first five years after the war brought the publication of two American translations of Dante—those of Longfellow and Norton—to be placed beside the earlier one by Parsons, and Bayard Taylor's *Faust* and Bryant's *Homer*. Dickens, who long before had made a highly successful and profitable lecture tour and returned home to tell in his "American Notes" the insulting half truth about the crudity of the country that had cared so much to see and hear him, was again warmly received in 1870. It was a nation of some crudity, to be sure, and perhaps it was partly its own consciousness of that fact and what we have since learned to call an inferiority complex resulting from it which, on the one hand, produced the hospitable acceptance of European lectures and literature and those European ideas which laid the foundation for theological modernism, and on the other hand stimulated, by way of reaction, whatever of blatancy and brazenness there was in the American character of the time.

The material advance is partially indicated by the list of inventions: 1879, the Selden patent for gasoline engines; 1880, the electric car; 1886, the linotype; 1887, the vestibule Pullman; 1894, the first motion picture show; 1895, the Haines automobile. The telephone, "the latest American humbug" according to the *London Times*, came into use in 1877 and the following year New York City had fifteen residence phones. Since the panic of 1873, finance had been less frenzied and the great industrial and commercial enterprises had standardized their financial methods on less arrantly unethical lines. So far as the railroads were concerned, the urge was now for uniform rates, maximum rates and the compulsory introduction of safety devices such as the new block system. The perils of the new feudalism through private control of the essential arteries of the nation's life were recognized by many. The *Christian Union* (February 15, 1883) editorially advocated public ownership of track and private ownership and operation of trains. On the other side, any movement to control railroads or railroad finance was met with the cry of communism. The treasurer of the New York Central testified that that road had paid $205,000 one year and $60,000 another to obtain legislation and that it had been obtained. The volume of stock speculation increased, though checked somewhat by the failure of Grant and Ward, and of Fisk and Hatch, and the Wall Street panic of 1884. Such criticism as the churches directed at high finance was rather the protest of the middle class against the arrogance and malfeasance of wealth than a protest motivated by fundamental conceptions of ethics or religion.

In 1861, there were said to be only three millionaires in the United States. In 1897, there were 3,800 as estimated by the statistician Charles Fahr, who said that at that time one-tenth of the American people owned nine-tenths of its wealth. (For purposes of comparison, it may be remembered that before the slump of 1929 there were reported to be 43,184 millionaires.) Among the fashionable and luxurious rich there was not a large proportion of church members, or at least of those whose membership was more than nominal. But most of the responsible leaders in the land were not only members, but active members, of Protestant churches. Jay Cooke, John D. Rockefeller, Jay

Gould, William H. Vanderbilt, C. P. Huntington, J. Pierpont Morgan, James J. Hill, Cyrus McCormick, P. D. Armour, Gustavus F. Swift, John Wanamaker—all were prominent men in their churches and some of them were Sunday school teachers or were otherwise active in religious enterprises. The same may be said of a considerable proportion of the political leaders in national affairs, including some who must be rated as sinister influences. Tom Platt, of New York, for example, was a member of Doctor Parkhurst's church.

The bitter partisan controversy growing out of the Hayes-Tilden conflict in 1876 was followed by a wave of political corruption, complicated by a fierce national struggle within the Republican Party. The rivalry of Platt and Conkling was followed by their coalition against Hayes—"the first President to claim that he was better than his party." As a matter of fact, he was, as Cleveland was better than his. The Blaine-Conkling feud in 1880 led to the nomination of Garfield, who was not only an active member but a preacher among the Disciples of Christ. The brevity of his administration gave little opportunity for any test of the effect of a preacher in the White House upon the ethical tone of national politics. The demand for reform in national, state, and municipal affairs became urgent. There were enough anti-Tammany Democrats to cause the election of a Republican governor in New York in 1879, and of Theodore Roosevelt to the legislature in 1881. He leaped into prominence in the following year by introducing a resolution to investigate a shady transaction in which a State Supreme Court justice and the Attorney General of New York were involved with Cyrus W. Field and Jay Gould in obtaining control of the Manhattan Elevated Railroad. Following his election as a delegate at large from New York to the national Republican Convention, the most influential organ of Protestant opinion said: "The rise of such a man as Mr. Roosevelt in New York politics shows how thoroughly the old régime has passed away. In Mr. Conkling's time such a man would have been singled out and crushed; there would have been no room for him inside the party; but in the freer air of today he becomes a recognized leader" (*Christian Union*, May 1, 1884). But after opposing Blaine's nomination in the convention, Roosevelt made his peace with the "plumed knight" of Colonel Ingersoll's impassioned and exaggerated eulogy and campaigned for him. That Roosevelt should support Blaine was an evidence that the era of united and effective action for reform had not yet come. That Blaine was defeated was an evidence that it was on the way.

In December, 1883, the *Christian Union*, while opposing the Prohibition Party, had demanded the formation of a new reform party and had outlined what it should stand for and what it conceived that both of the old parties stood for. The new party: a free ballot and a fair count; national aid for internal improvements; the Mississippi unobstructed to the sea; control of great corporations by the government; reduction of taxation; control of liquor traffic by local legislation; administration of government of business men; government of, by, and for the people. The old parties: shot-gun politics; Mormonism, Romanism, and slave-ocracy; niggardly appropriation for internal improvements; control of government by great corporations; high tariff, high taxes, high prices; free rum; "to the victors belong the spoils"; "bossism." The proposed third party of reform did not materialize. The forces of idealism found some expression and some satisfaction in the election of Grover Cleveland and in civil service reform.

A part, but not a large part, of the churches' interest in the attainment of a better social order through political action found expression in giving the Prohibition Party such support as it had and in carrying on many fights against liquor locally and in the various states. These efforts met a certain degree of success, but those forces within the church which make for social righteousness were not effectively organized and the entanglement of a large proportion of the leading "good people" with big business and partisan politics acted as a brake on the wheels of reform. The Kansas prohibition amendment was adopted in 1880, but prohibition was not yet *de fide*, and while most religious people were at least in favor of local option, there were many who were opposed to putting prohibition into State constitutions on the ground that this was a matter for legislation rather than for constitutions (*Christian Union*, August 30, 1883). The older type of temperance campaign conducted on evangelistic lines still continued. Francis Murphy was the Moody of temperance revivalism. In 1884 he conducted meetings under the auspices of various churches in Chicago for seven weeks, and it was reported that eleven thousand persons signed the pledge, including some notorious drinkers. But in spite of all the moral suasion that was applied by the temperance evangelists and the W. C. T. U., there was an increase of 15 per cent. in the per capita consumption of distilled liquors and an increase of 55 per cent. in malt beverages between the first and the second decade after 1865. It was evident that the moral suasion method was not producing the desired results.

Late in the 'seventies Doctor Talmage, then the most notable minister in Brooklyn except Beecher, and, with perhaps the same exception, the most popular preacher in the country, anticipated Doctor Parkhurst by visiting the slums, saloons, and dens of vice in New York with a police guard and reporting his findings from the pulpit. There is no ground for suspecting the sincerity of his motive but he was too little the effective crusader and too much the word-merchant to bring anything to pass. His pulpit report of the sins of New York and of the corrupt alliance between politics and vice created a sensation, but it all blew over in a storm of rhetoric.

Arthur Train described the period which we have under consideration rather cynically by saying: "It was an age of conventionality, euphemism, and prudery, of church going, sabbatarianism, and uplift, of Moody and Sankey, of Christian Endeavor and comstockery, of national self-satisfaction—in short, the brownstone era" (*Puritan's Progress*, p. 320). But however much conventionality and prudery there may have been, Puritanism had become pretty well a thing of the past. John Fiske said, in 1900, that "there is more Puritanism surviving in the South than in New England." Unitarianism had long since undermined Puritanism among the older population of New England. Immigration, especially the Irish, had swamped what was left. Modern religious thought and the increased dominance of secular interests did the rest. Puritanism never was a code of conduct but a principle—the idea of a holy state. Even those of most austere morals were by this time thoroughly convinced that the state was not holy.

The churches themselves gave evidence that they had participated in the general increase of prosperity. They had costly buildings, better music, with more pipe organs and finer choirs, more dignified services and a general air of culture and urbanity. The changes in all of these respects matched the mood of the prosperous bourgeoisie, but a large constituency was left behind, including, first, those who were capable neither of following a thoughtful sermon nor of appreciating a dignified and restrained service; and second, the less fortunate element among the industrial workers and those who were more concerned about the economic betterment of labor than about the promotion of the church and either the doctrines or the particular reforms to which the church gave its attention. Even as reasonably prosperous institutions for the reasonably prosperous, the city churches had their difficulties. Many churches had been built that were too costly for the people who had to pay for them and many where there was no good reason for building a church at all. "Every denomination is suffering from attempts to establish church organizations where they are not needed and cannot be supported and to contract debts for buildings where congregations cannot be obtained to fill them. Pastors turn themselves into financial agents and travel thousands of miles to obtain five hundred dollars for a needy church in Tennessee or Texas. New congregations formed in cities and in communities already amply churched tax the financial resources of their denominations" (*Independent*, January 14, 1878). It was suggested that the denominations establish joint advisory committees to be consulted before new churches were erected—a thing that was actually done forty years later.

Recognizing the general interest in church debts, the *New York Times* collected and published information about the value of church property in that city and the indebtedness upon it. The total value of church property in New York in 1878 was fifty-six million dollars. Of this the Protestant Episcopal Church owned nearly half. The Roman Catholic Church had by far the largest debt. Only one denomination, that of the Friends, was entirely free from debt. In the same year, foreclosure proceedings were brought against Doctor Talmage's tabernacle and a professional money raiser, Mr. Kimball, was called in to get subscriptions and save the property. Doctor Tyng's congregation, also assisted by Mr. Kimball, had to raise $200,000 to save its property. The Episcopal Church of the Intercession was sold under foreclosure. There followed a period of saner building and sounder financing.

The return of good will in and toward the South came gradually but steadily. It was assisted by the return of sanity to the North, which no longer thought of converting the former slave-holders from their apostate religion but took an interest in the promotion of southern education. It was assisted still more by the South's efforts for its own rehabilitation and the willingness of its best leaders both in and out of the churches to think more about future development than about past grievances. Such men as Joel Chandler Harris exercised a beneficent influence which, though not put forth in the name of religion, was religious at its core. Harris was for many years the editor of the *Atlanta Constitution.* To him, "harping on the old prejudices" seemed the sin against the Holy Ghost, for southern editors. He wrote: "The southern people have made other political mistakes since, but this was altogether the most disastrous. In a manner, we held the poor blacks responsible for the shock that their emancipation gave to our social organism. This was human nature, perhaps, but it was the most deplorable blunder that southern human nature ever made. Looking back over it all, the solution of the problem seems so simple that reflecting people are inclined to go off into some quiet place and beat their heads against the wall in sheer vexation." When Jefferson Davis declared in a speech in 1882 that "the cause (of secession) is not lost but only sleeping," Harris editorially denounced his "restless petulance and ridiculous rhetoric." "We have no doubt Mr. Davis believes the South is in chains, but everybody else knows she is freer and more prosperous in all directions than when slavery was a part of her environment."

If we look to the West, it was a period of the growth of the prairie states, culminating in the passing of the old frontier. In 1872, the buffalo were so numerous on the Kansas plains that the soldiers at Fort Dodge complained that they spoiled the hunting for game animals. A year later there was not one left in the Arkansas valley. A million and a quarter buffalo robes were shipped east by the railroads in 1872 and 1873; and only a few years later, when the buffalo was not yet extinct in the Texas panhandle and eastern New Mexico, fifty thousand skins were stored at one time in one warehouse in Albuquerque. It is foolish to mourn the slaughter of the buffaloes, though the process was ruthless and wasteful. They took up too much room. Buffaloes live on the plains and the plains cannot be at the same time buffalo range and cattle range, much less farms. Something of the same inevitability marked the disappearance of the nomadic and hunting tribes of Indians. Here again the process was inexcusably ruthless but the result was unavoidable. It was a clash of cultures and when savage nomad and armed hunter dispute for the land with the farmer, the farmer wins—if it is good farming land. Again the triumph of the terrible meek.

The census report of 1890 stated that the frontier had at last disappeared. "The unsettled area has been so broken into by isolated bodies of settlement that there can hardly be said to be a frontier line." The western movement of population continued in increasing volume, but going west was no longer a mass movement into unoccupied territory but an individual adventure in search of better land, a better job, or a new place to open a store. Less and less could the American people escape from present and pressing problems by going west and starting over. The urgency and complexity of these problems increased and the country had now to settle down to the mature business of solving them where it found them. It was this fact which gave point to the new activities of religion in the fields in which they had shown but slight interest. It is no mere coincidence that the attention of the churches began to be directed toward social and economic problems soon after the date which was officially noted as marking the disappearance of the frontier. This new interest, however, was characteristic of the close of the period under immediate consideration.

The home missionary societies of the principal denominations and the church erection boards were now functioning actively in the West. The imaginations of far-seeing men were still captivated by the idea that here was an unprecedented opportunity for the churches to begin on the ground floor in the building of new civilizations. There were, to be sure, occasional checks and notes of discouragement, as when Dr. Charles F. Thwing stated in 1882 that the Congregational Church was not growing in the West, that Iowa and Kansas showed a loss for the preceding year and Illinois and Minnesota an almost invisible gain, and that "in a single town of Nebraska are seven ministers who have abandoned the ministry and entered business." But the following year, the meeting of the Congregational Home Missionary Society heard reports as thrilling as ever about the rapid development, if not of Congregationalism, at least of the West and the country as a whole. "From 3,000 to 5,000 are pouring into Dakota every day. Increase of wealth is incomprehensible. $500,000,000 were added to the wealth of the country last year. We have 100,000 miles of railroad and built 10,000 miles last year." The figures may not be exact, but the feeling about the situation is significant. Only one or two western states need be mentioned specifically by way of illustration.

Dakota had only a thin trickle of white population before 1868. There were three serious Indian uprisings, the last of which was that of Sitting Bull in 1875. Custer's exploring expedition into the Black Hills in the preceding year had led to the discovery of gold and the rapid inpouring of population. Meanwhile the railroad had come. The Sioux were induced to sign away their lands in the Black Hills in 1876, and about 11,000,000 acres more of Indian lands were opened to settlement in 1890. This was followed by the Ghost Dance War, stimulated partly by resentment at the loss of lands and partly by faith in an Indian Messiah. The churches made no special protest against the perfidious treatment of the Indians by the government, being far too much implicated in the glorious enterprise of establishing a Christian civilization on virgin soil. But besides planting churches in the white settlements, they did missionary and educational work among the Indians, chiefly upon the principle of developing among them the closest possible imitation of the Anglo-Saxon civilization. Statehood was attained in 1889, with prohibition in the constitution from the start. The absorption of Indian lands continued with the taking over of 400,000 acres (the Rosebud reservation) in 1904 and 800,000 more in 1908.

It may be remarked in passing that, parallel with the acquiescence of the churches in general with the ruthless treatment of the Indians, there was developing a more sympathetic and appreciative even if somewhat sentimental attitude. Helen Hunt Jackson's *Ramona*, which ran serially in the *Christian Union* in 1884, was significant of this new mood.

In Montana, mining and the cattle business flourished side by side until 1910, when the last of the big cattle outfits disbanded, owing to the inroads which homesteaders had made upon the range. While cattle occupied the western lands there was little hope of developing churches. The cowboys had been but indifferent patrons of the churches, and the wide distribution of population had prevented the formation of other than small and scattered settlements. But in connection with all three types of economic activity—mining, cattle and farming—settlements sprang up and churches were planted in them. Often the churches arrived at these new communities in advance of the railroads. When Thomas C. Iliff went to Montana in 1871, he made the last 800 miles of his journey by stage and organized the few settlers of his community for protection against the Indians. Having had West Point training, he could fill the rôle of fighting parson better than some who have assumed that title. Later he became western secretary of the Methodist Board of Home Missions.

Admiration for the heroic work done by missionaries in the West cannot obscure the fact that much energy was wasted because of denominational competition. A questionnaire study of thirty-two Kansas churches by Rev. W. C. McCune in 1879 led to the conclusion that there were three times as many churches as were needed (*Independent*, January 23, 1879). But this McCune was perhaps something of a heretic. He had been tried by his presbytery two years before for starting a union church in Cincinnati, and, though the charge that he was "disloyal to the Presbyterian Church" was not sustained, he had withdrawn from it. A more serious evidence of wasteful rivalry was found in the appointment of a committee by the Congregational Home Missionary convention in 1883 to coöperate with other boards to call a comity convention to curb sectarian competition in the West. "Anyone familiar with the state of things in the newer commonwealths knows that the over-planting of churches has resulted in jealousies and divisions which have brought Christianity into disrepute and made the various religious denominations as hostile to one another as though they had nothing whatever in common. We know of one western town with a population of 1,000, including Roman Catholics, where there are five evangelical churches having their edifices and drawing from their respective missionary boards an aggregate of $1,500 a year." Hope of the rapid development of each of these new settlements into a metropolis intensified the eagerness to get in on the ground floor. The churches might crowd each other now, but think of the future! Look at Chicago! Look at Kansas City! Look at St. Louis! But look also at Alton, once a rival of St. Louis, and a hundred other towns which either did not grow at all or grew slowly.

Chapter IX

RELIGION AND THE CULTURAL LIFE

Suspicion that education was weaning the young away from religion began to be felt almost as soon as public schools began to exist and long before the common schools had been reduced to even the semblance of an orderly state-supported system. In the Presbyterian General Assembly of 1799, it was stated that "a vain and pernicious philosophy has spread its infection from Europe to America," and elders were urged to serve as school trustees in order to keep check on the quality of teachers and instruction from the religious standpoint. The spread of secular elementary education, tax-supported and state-controlled, raised questions not easy to answer: Can any sort of religious instruction be included in the curriculum of such schools? How much, if any? Can a generalized Christianity or a neutral type of theism be taught? Shall the Bible be read? Is a vague and denatured Christianity, made colorless by excluding what is not held in common by all denominations, adequate as a basis for character training? Even if it is, is it adequate as a foundation for the training of those who are to be leaders and ministers in the churches? Can the religious deficiencies of secularized elementary schools be supplied by Sunday schools?

Infidels and Jews objected to the teaching of any sort of Christianity in schools supported by general taxation. Catholics objected to the teaching of a form of Christianity that always turned out to be some form of Protestantism and to the reading of the (Protestant) Bible. Many of the stricter Protestants felt the inadequacy of a vague religiosity that was little more than "natural religion." Almost everybody saw that the Sunday schools did not give a very substantial education in religion and did not reach a sufficient constituency. The Roman Catholic reaction to this problem will be considered in another connection. It will help in understanding the Catholic attitude on the "school question" when we get to it if we note the attitudes and policies of two of the most Protestant groups, namely, the Presbyterians and the Lutherans, though in doing so we must go back to the period before the Civil War.

In response to an overture from the Synod of Kentucky, a committee of the Presbyterian General Assembly of 1812 declared that education was "the legitimate business of the church rather than of the state," and urged that an elementary school be set up in every congregation, taught by a "catechist." Pre-theological education was also part of the problem; and "manual labor schools," in which candidates for the ministry could earn their way while getting academic and religious training preliminary to the theological course, were part of the answer. There was, however, little immediate response to these suggestions.

The Old School Presbyterian General Assembly—especially solicitous about "the maintenance of doctrinal purity" and the "lamentable dearth of candidates for the ministry" after its separation from the New School Presbyterians in 1837—adopted in 1841 a report calling for an elementary school in every congregation and an academy in every presbytery. By this time the secularization of public education had been much advanced by the work of Horace Mann, who became secretary of education for Massachusetts in 1837. His public school system, from which all denominational tenets were to be excluded, was attacked as undermining religion. The schools of New York still had a decidedly Protestant coloring. The Catholics, led by Bishop Hughes, fought for a division of the school funds. The Presbyterians, and the Protestants generally, opposed division of funds and favored the retention of the Bible in the schools. In 1845, the Synod of New Jersey, coming approximately to the Catholic position, declared in favor of church schools supported by taxation, every taxpayer to have the privilege of designating the school to which his money should go. The Old School General Assemblies of 1846 and 1847 came out clearly for parochial schools not supported by public funds, and the Presbyterian churches began to establish them in large numbers.

The growth of the public school system, however, and its rapidly increasing popularity, as well as the impracticability of maintaining separate denominational schools among the sparse and religiously diversified populations of the newer settlements, doomed them to an early demise. Of the 264 Presbyterian parochial schools, nearly all dating from 1846 or later, only twenty-three were still alive in 1865. A few others were born out of due time after the latter date, when the movement was already far in its decline, but most of these were short-lived. In 1870, there were still twenty-three in existence, mostly of recent origin, but sixteen of these died in that year. In 1929, only two survived, and these were really one school in two parts, for boys and for girls, connected with a Scotch Presbyterian Church in New York City.

The Lutherans are the only other Protestant body that has undertaken to carry on elementary education on any large scale. The churches of the Missouri Synod—a much more numerous and extended body than that abbreviated name would indicate—soon after their organization in 1847 began to set up day-schools for their children, and the policy has been consistently carried out. In 1922, they had nearly two thousand teachers engaged in elementary school work, including five hundred pastors who also served as teachers on week days. They had, in addition, a number of high schools and normal schools. Other denominations have established academies and preparatory schools which have survived and flourished even in an age of multiplying public high schools, but no other has made any serious effort to conduct parochial schools.

The number of public schools, the number of pupils in them, and the expenditures for both lower and higher education increased much more rapidly than population; more rapidly even than wealth. In 1860, there were only about 100 public high schools in the United States; in 1880, there were 800; in 1900, there were 6,000. The public grammar schools still retained a considerable flavor of piety, but virtually all children, except those in Catholic parochial schools were getting their early education in schools which were avowedly non-religious. Some thought that they were not only non-religious but anti-religious because the Bible was being increasingly excluded. Rev. W. W. Patton argued, on the other hand, that schools without Bibles were no more "Godless" than banks or stores without Bibles. That argument was fallacious, for stores and banks are not designed to train for citizenship or to be character-forming institutions; but other and more cogent arguments to the same end prevailed. Actual practice varied in different communities. For example, in the middle 'eighties the Bible was read and hymns were sung in the public schools in Boston, but not in St. Louis. (I speak of both from memory.) The secularizing tendency in secondary education was equally notable as the tremendous increase in the number of public high schools reduced the surviving academies and church-controlled preparatory schools to a small proportion of the whole.

Education on the collegiate level had been started by the churches, and conducted under their auspices through the colonial period and in the early years of the republic, though not without some state support. Prior to the year 1800, fifteen denominational colleges and six that rated as non-denominational had been founded. By 1830, there were thirty-five denominational and fourteen non-denominational colleges. After that the numbers increased rapidly. In 1884, they were 309 and 61 respectively. In 1916, there were 419 colleges which confessed a denominational connection and ninety-five classed as independent, the latter not including tax-supported institutions. (These 419 represented thirty different denominations. One hundred and seven were Methodist, ninety-two Presbyterian, seventy-nine Baptist, forty Lutheran, twenty-three Congregational, twenty belonged to the Disciples of Christ, ten to the Friends, ten to the Reformed churches, and three to the Episcopalians.)

But the increase in the number of colleges nominally under denominational control is no more significant than the gradual change by which most of them have become less denominational, many of them less specifically religious. The passing of "eight o'clock chapel" is only one symbol of a far-reaching process. The secularization of higher education has had two aspects, one of which is the enormous development of the state institutions, and the other is the putting aside of definitely denominational character by the church colleges. By the latter part of the century a Baptist college or university was no longer an institution in which Baptist students were taught Baptist views by Baptist professors elected by Baptist trustees and paid with Baptist money; nor was it customary at good church colleges to have an evangelistic meeting during the winter, to ease up on academic requirements while it was in progress, and to bring pressure to bear upon students to "reach a decision" at least by the time of their graduation. The great gifts made to some of these institutions which had been founded by the churches and which were still nominally under their control, and the marked increase in the resources of nearly all of them, furthered rather than retarded the evaporation of their distinctive character. No way has yet been discovered by which a university with an endowment of twenty million dollars can be kept on the leading strings of a denomination.

The movement for educational emancipation was manifest also in the smaller colleges, whose academic respectability was coming to depend upon having faculties trained in undenominational or state universities. The loosening of the hold of the churches upon their colleges was furthered also by the influence of the European training of many professors, and by the development of new types of scholarship in an age predominantly secular. The atmosphere of the colleges was inevitably changed as there came into existence a great body of teachers and investigators trained in rigorous methods of research and not only not professionally concerned with religion but in many cases standing entirely apart from its organized forms. The philosophers of the earlier period, for example, from Jonathan Edwards down through James McCosh and W. T. Ladd, had all been theologians and preachers before they were philosophers. With William T. Harris, Josiah Royce, William James and John Dewey there was established a class of philosophers who were neither limited nor guided by any specific ecclesiastical interest. That college presidents came increasingly to be drawn from other than clerical sources was both a result and an indication of the same general movement. A period which saw the rise of a new type of secular expert in higher education was necessarily a period in which the problem of keeping education Christian had a new meaning and presented a new difficulty.

The growth of the state universities, and especially of their undergraduate departments, gave cause for anxious thought to those who were concerned that college students should have instruction in religion, and who had been accustomed to believe that this could be realized only in denominational colleges. From this point of view there was much criticism of the "Godless state universities" as early as the 'eighties, and it tended to increase rather than diminish as the leaders of various denominations found more of their own young people attending state institutions than in all of their denominational colleges together.

The first specific suggestion of a plan for meeting this situation by anything except straight competition between the church colleges and the universities—a competition in which the colleges generally got the worst of it—was made by Dr. Leonard Woolsey Bacon. Deploring the criticism of state universities as "Godless" and urging coöperation to supply what they lack, he gave the prospectus for an imaginary "Mark Hopkins College" which he thought might well be established at the University of Michigan, to his mind the most favorable place for the experiment. The college was to have dormitories, boarding arrangements and a study hall, a president and two tutors to "devote themselves to promoting the success of the students in their university course." Instruction was to be offered in subjects in which the university curriculum was defective—that is, not sufficiently Christian—and a religious atmosphere was to be created in which university students might live (*Christian Union*, October 12, 1882). Doctor Bacon's scheme never got beyond the stage of a mere project, but about ten years later the Disciples of Christ did establish a "Bible chair" at the University of Michigan which became the forerunner of many similar Bible chairs and "foundations" established at other state universities, first by the Disciples and then by other bodies. Some of these suffered for a time from the confusion of two objectives—that of giving religious education to undergraduate students, and that of preparing men for the ministry. The introduction of the latter feature resulted from the discovery of the advantage of conducting ministerial preparation in connection with universities rather than at isolated theological seminaries.

The decade from 1820 to 1830 had seen the founding of more important theological seminaries than any other equal period before or after. There had been time to reveal their weakness as well as their strength when Edward Everett Hale gave this advice to a novitiate: "Do not waste your time at a theological school. Get to work as soon as possible in human causes. Follow Christ's example who knew no ancient learning or science but gave to his brother man the unstinted riches of his faith and sympathy, the ministry of his love and service." And this from Boston! Distrust of formal training was not limited to the frontier. Nevertheless, theological education continued. Nearly half of the theological seminaries now in existence were founded between 1865 and 1900, the same period that saw the most rapid multiplication of colleges. Less than half as many new ones have been started in the almost equal period since the turn of the century—perhaps because there were already plenty, because the newly settled West was already supplied, because higher standards of instruction and equipment and consequent higher costs made the planting of new institutions a matter not to be so lightly undertaken, and because more theological students felt free to attend schools other than those of their own denominations.

The modern religious education movement belongs to the twentieth century, not the nineteenth. It may be said to have begun with the discovery that education in religion is not merely a matter of imparting knowledge of the contents of the Christian classics, but involves the formation of religious attitudes and the development of ability to make judgments and to choose courses of action in life-situations. But even before these modern concepts began to take form, and before child-study and psychology and scientific pedagogy began to enter into the picture, the Sunday school became a great institution and did a great work. Its efficiency was vastly increased by the adoption of the system of "uniform lessons" by the International Sunday School Convention in 1872. Bishop Vincent served as secretary of the Sunday School Union for twenty years beginning in 1868. The "graded lessons" were adopted in 1908, after many defeats at the hands of those who were more pleased by the thought of "the whole Christian world keeping step" by studying the same lesson on the same day than interested in fitting the lessons to the pupils.

Then as now, and as always, there was alarm about the sins of youth and the decay of discipline. A discussion of "causes of failure in the training of children" refers to "the startling number of crimes committed by young men and boys. . . . It is not now as it was forty years ago." The reason why the young go wrong so much more easily and frequently is found in their tendency to "find friends in a lower social class than their own" (*Christian Union*, December 4, 1884).

A foreign observer once said that the most American thing in America was Chautauqua. The Chautauqua assembly, with all its ramifying activities, was a projection of the personality of Bishop John H. Vincent. But more than that, it was a mirror of the mind of the average Protestant American—hungry for culture but neither willing nor able to pay a high price for it, warmly evangelical in his faith but with only a conventional and somewhat pietistic vocabulary for the expression of it, and keen for summer vacations and sociability. The old camp-meeting had been a glorified combination of piety and picnic. Bishop Vincent started in 1874 with a two-weeks' assembly for Sunday school teachers in an unused camp-meeting ground on Fair Point, jutting into Lake Chautauqua. His own doubts about the success of such a project were overcome by the enthusiasm of his associate, Lewis Miller, and the immediate popularity and rapid growth of the project soon swept away all doubts. Started as a brief training course for Sunday school teachers—the uniform lessons being then a new thing—it developed into an all-summer assembly with lectures and courses on a wide variety of subjects. The four-year reading course of the Chautauqua Literary and Scientific Circle had eight thousand readers enrolled in its first year, and when fourteen hundred of them finished the course at its first commencement in 1882, it was acclaimed as a "Chautauqua university." Bishop Vincent found a practical suggestion in this term, which had been used in rather exaggerated compliment, and in this same year secured a charter for a Chautauqua University, "a non-resident institution with full university powers for promoting higher education, principally by correspondence." Within less than a year, the Chautauqua School of Theology was in full swing, giving correspondence courses for ministers. William R. Harper's correspondence courses in Hebrew became a part of this enterprise. The fame of Chautauqua and the popularity of its summer assembly led to the imitation of it in all parts of the country and to the rise, upon the ruins of the old lyceum system, of all the little chautauquas which gave to communities, especially in the Middle West, one-week sessions of concentrated culture, including a balanced ration of inspirational lectures, male quartets and other forms of entertainment and uplift.

It was easy, as it still is, for the super-sophisticates to smile tolerantly at Chautauqua as a dispenser of middle-class culture to middle-class people. After William James had lectured to the comfortable and complacent culture-seekers at Chautauqua, says Charles A. Beard, he "heaved an immense sigh of relief as he escaped into the freight-yards of Buffalo where the noise, grime, and jar of reality broke the monotony of moderation, purity and median lines of thought." Thus refreshed, however, by that bath of reality, Professor James returned happily to Cambridge where there was almost as little noise, grime, and jar as at Chautauqua. And it is to be admitted that it was this respectable middle class of the Chautauqua-minded that, continues Beard, "in the main sustained the churches, filled the colleges with sons and daughters, supported the clean press, kept alive foreign and domestic missions, supplied the sinews for the Anti-saloon movement, backed the W. C. T. U., and, according to Matthew Arnold, carried the burden of American civilization in the Gilded Age."

For those who wanted something more esoteric and transcendental, there was the Concord School of Philosophy and there was also the new Hegelian movement, ably led and strangely led, as it seemed to some, by a St. Louis schoolmaster, W. T. Harris, whose *Journal of Philosophy* was the first philosophical magazine to be published on this continent. But Chautauqua was, more than any other agency, an expression of the great popular desire to coördinate culture with religion and a means of giving to that desire of millions all the literary and scientific culture that they had time or training to receive. The reality of the spiritual quality of the assembly is suggested by the fact that two of the best loved modern hymns were specifically written for Chautauqua vesper services in 1877—"Day is Dying in the West," and "Break Thou the Bread of Life," the words by Mary A. Lathbury, the music by William F. Sherwin, director of the Chautauqua choruses.

The expression of religious ideas and attitudes in general literature and in the arts is a theme which would lend itself better to treatment in a volume than in a few paragraphs. In spite of a certain prejudice against fiction in some of the more conservative churches, the novel with a religious coloring or a moral purpose or a Biblical setting became an important avenue of approach to the popular mind. *Uncle Tom's Cabin,* by Harriet Beecher Stowe, a sister of Henry Ward Beecher, was a pioneer in this field. Beecher himself wrote *Norwood,* but that was frankly a romance. The popular magazines of the 'seventies such as *Hearth and Home,* edited by Edward Eggleston and his brother, contained about equal parts of religious stories and tales of adventure. Religion had little or no place in the better magazines until recent years, except for some important articles in the *North American Review* in the 'eighties. E. P. Roe and J. G. Holland poured forth a flood of fiction, always sweet and "wholesome" and generally also pietistic and sentimental. *Robert Elsmere* was the first and for a good while the only great novel dealing with the new intellectual problems of religion. James Lane Allen's *The Reign of Law* gave a picture of the struggle between the conventional faith and the newer order. Lew Wallace's *Ben Hur* exploited the romantic possibilities of Biblical material. Sheldon's *In His Steps* was rather a tract in the form of fiction than a novel, but its story form and its vivid presentation of the social aspects of Christianity which were already attracting wide attention gave it a circulation which, including translations into almost all the languages that are in print, has been estimated at the incredible figure of twenty-three million. At the time of its publication, the author did not think enough of it to have it copyrighted. The list of novelists who have dealt with social conditions with which the church has found itself deeply concerned in the last thirty or forty years would be too long to include, but among the names would be those of Frank Norris, Hamlin Garland, Robert Herrick, Edith Wharton, Winston Churchill, and William Allen White. Harold Bell Wright, beginning as a preacher, has written stories of enormous popularity, always presenting high moral ideals and dealing with rather simple problems of faith and conduct.

Poetry continued to make, as it always had, its contribution to the expression of religious ideas. The older New England poets lived well into our period. Longfellow died in 1882, Lowell in 1891, Whittier in 1892, Holmes in 1894. Walt Whitman, though a Quaker by birth, sang of the religion of democracy and nature and full-blooded life, the worth of the natural man and the omnipresence of the miraculous. Emily Dickinson was "the last pale Indian summer flower of puritanism"—but a pale flower with a vivid crimson heart. Riley, the genial fundamentalist, by glorifying old ways and simple manners, glorified also the old and simple patterns of religion. William Vaughn Moody expressed the modernistic valuation of "the boon of endless quest." Edwin Markham, a California school teacher, leaped to fame with *The Man with the Hoe*, which became, more than any other American poem has ever been, the symbol of the new religious interest. Vachel Lindsay was an unconventional apostle of beauty but never ceased to be an outspoken advocate of evangelical religion and its organized activities. A new group of Catholic poets gave expression to the romantic and mystical appeal and in some cases to the newer social consciousness.

The drama, though religious in its origins, long ago became a prodigal son. If the church set its face against the theater, it was only after the theater had turned away from everything that the church was interested in. Fortunately, after some changes on both sides, there has been some degree of rapprochement. During the period from 1865 to the end of the century, the evangelical churches were, for the most part, hostile to the theater. The Methodist discipline had a rule against theater-going, adopted in the middle of this period, and other churches which did not have printed codes had unwritten laws that were well understood. When Beecher was criticized by Baptist papers for not trying to prevent the dramatization of his *Norwood*, whereby it was alleged that he had "weakened the restraints upon theater-going," it was replied that this was an absurd charge to bring against a man "who had never seen a play at a theater in all his life." The *Christian Union* took what was considered very liberal ground when it said that it could not "counsel the Christian teacher either to leave the drama alone or to engage in a war of extermination against it." Its message was: "Read Shakespeare to your child. Keep him away from the Black Crook by taking him to see Hamlet. We do not counsel private theatricals of any description."

Until recent years there were few American plays that had any values that could be called religious even in the most elastic sense of the word, and not many that had much literary or cultural value. The three-volume edition of the *Cambridge History of American*

Literature devoted two chapters to drama, but in the one-volume edition these were omitted on the ground that among American playwrights there was not one of a stature commensurate with Emerson, Poe, or Whitman. The collection of *Representative American Dramas*, edited by M. J. Moses (1925), includes among its fifteen plays not one of the slightest religious significance. The drama has been a form of art, most of it very crude art, but for the most part it has been conceived by its promoters as a business, by its patrons as a form of amusement, and by the ministers and the stricter laity as a demoralizing form of amusement. The attitude of condemnation relaxed with the coming in of more tolerant attitudes toward other so-called "worldly" amusements and the discovery of hitherto unrecognized values in the whole category of amusement in the normal and wholesome life. Recent years have seen a much more rapid disappearance of the traditional hostility of the church toward the stage as the result of three causes. One of these was the presentation of plays combining fine religious sentiment with high artistic quality, such as *The Passing of the Third Floor Back* (an English play that had a wide hearing in America) and C. R. Kennedy's *The Servant in the House*. Another was the rise of a type of play dealing seriously with those social problems with which the churches had at last developed a serious concern. On this ground even a play so boisterously profane as *What Price Glory?* commanded the admiration and support of many religious people. The third is the growing use of drama in religious education, both in the form of Biblical dramatizations and in plays tending to develop religious attitudes in relation to practical situations in modern life. (See Fred Eastman: *Modern Religious Dramas*.)

The course of American literature as a whole, including drama with the rest, in the period from 1890 to 1920, has been described as one of "convention, revolt, and general chaos." (E. E. Leisy: *American Literature, an Interpretative Survey*, N. Y., 1929.) In so far as this generalization is correct to 1920, it would be truer still to 1932. But there is nothing new about the convention-revolt pattern. It has been repeated all over the diagram of human history, not only in literature but in everything else. But whether for the third term you get general chaos or a Hegelian "synthesis," a "becoming" which itself becomes the starting point for a new convention to be followed by a new revolt, depends upon how many revolts are going on at once, and what kind; also upon the point of view from which the result is judged. To some minds, any departure from convention is the prelude to general chaos; to others, it is the necessary condition of discovery and progress.

The fine arts have a two-fold relation to religion. In the first place, they refine and enrich the human spirit, cultivate a sensitiveness to beauty and minister to joy on a level above that of the more obvious and material pleasures; and whatever does that is an ally of religion. And in the second place, they may become, and sometimes do become, means for the expression and stimulation of religious senti- ments and furnish the accessories of worship.

The European influence, which became much stronger with the increase of wealth and travel after 1878, had an effect upon both the quantity and quality of production in the fine arts in America. The coincidence of home-made wealth and imported culture produced a market for art, and the market stimulated the supply. Not all of it was bad, though most of it was, but the dominant note was imitation rather than creation. The opening of the Boston Museum of Fine Arts in 1876 and the New York Metropolitan Art Gallery in 1879, followed by the establishment of art galleries in the principal American cities within the next few years, brought the European tradition to the knowledge of those culture-seeking Americans who could not make the grand tour of Europe. Among the great artists of the period were Sargent, La Farge, Abbey, Whistler and Winslow Homer. More American, though not so great, were Frederic Remington, who cele- brated and romanticized the passing frontier, and Joseph Pennell, who saw the esthetic possibilities of city streets and steel girders. Still more American and still less great according to the canons of high art— though great in their own field as popular interpreters of the con- temporary scene—were the cartoonists, Nast, Homer Davenport, and later McCutcheon. Meanwhile civic pride and the demand for portrait statues of statesmen, generals and leading citizens produced a transi- tion in sculpture from togas to trousers. However sad may have been the esthetic loss in the adoption of the tubular trouser for perpetuation in imperishable bronze, in place of flowing draperies, the change at least symbolized some approach to reality. Even the Rogers groups of blessed memory, the most sentimental of which now seem humorous and the funny ones even funnier than they were intended to be, had the merit of spreading widely among the middle class the doctrine that art was something that did not need to find its subject-matter exclusively in nymphs and fauns.

Of the arts accessory to religion, architecture was the most obvious and necessary. American church-building started well with the Georgian colonial style and its many modifications. With the advance of religion on the frontier, economic considerations necessarily took precedence over esthetic requirements, and the only thought was to get the congregation under a roof and within walls which would keep out the weather. Some denominations, moreover, made a virtue of abjuring the building of "fine meeting-houses—great cathedrals costing forty thousand dollars." In the young and growing cities of the Middle West, almost any brick or stone building with a steeple came to be regarded with pride and admiration as a handsome church. An improvement in taste came with the work of Richardson and the new Romanesque. Parallel with this was a revival of Gothic, which the Roman Catholic and Protestant Episcopal churches had already done their best to naturalize in America. Enlarging ideas of the varied functions of the church, and especially the increased emphasis on religious education, made it no longer sufficient to have an auditorium with a place for a Sunday school in the basement and a little room somewhere for the ladies' aid. The "workshop" idea, or the factory principle in church building, produced more serviceable but not necessarily more beautiful edifices. Mail-order architecture and standardized plans produced better buildings for the money but covered the country with a multitude of churches that looked as though they had all been cast in the same mold. Vast numbers of churches of the pulpit-in-the-corner type with sliding partitions were built. These were, as Protestant churches always tended to be, auditoriums rather than houses of worship. Following these came the "white temple" (generally either Baptist or Methodist) and other neo-classic forms, of which the county-court-house style and the Carnegie-library style were variations. Still later came the skyscraper church, generally Methodist, with its combination of office-building or apartment house or hotel with church. This generally involved financing by bond issues supported by the earning capacity of the income-producing part of the building, and sometimes led to embarrassments when, in a time of depression, the church found itself entangled in the same difficulties that beset all owners of rental property. This, however, is a matter of economics rather than of art. In recent years the Gothic tendency has reasserted itself in the grand manner.

Music has a relation to religion not less intimate than that of architecture. A characteristic of the whole period has been a "brightening up" of the old hymnology, not always to its improvement, and the subsequent return to more sober forms. Popular revivalism played an important part in the first of these tendencies. Sankey's hymns were a perfect translation of Moody's sermons into musical language. The influence of Stephen Foster and the sentimental ballad carried church music farther in the same direction. The discovery of the Negro spirituals added an element of real value to musical literature but not one that could easily be adopted into the churches generally, though perhaps their manifest sincerity suggested that white Christians had more to gain by producing hymns as perfectly representative of their own minds and moods as these were of the Negro mind than by imitating the specific form. The Salvation Army, with its drums and bands and its frank adoption of the tunes of the street, furnished a strident note which, for all its blare, sometimes afforded a welcome relief from a too sweet sentimentality. Modern jazz has had its effect, but possibly more by reaction than by direct influence. Unlike the sentimental ballad, it could not furnish patterns for religious music to follow except as its syncopated rhythm was adopted in some revival songs, and it is noteworthy that the period of jazz has also been the time of a much more general return to older and more stately forms.

In the matter of instrumental music, the progress has been from reed organs and melodeons to pipe organs. The introduction of instruments in the Middle West was not accomplished without a struggle and more than one church was divided over "the organ question." But one should recall that there had also been a "bass viol question" in the New England churches earlier. The development of choirs and choir music was perhaps first an outgrowth of the old singing school, to which the village church choir was first cousin, but the development of musical taste and urban fashions led to an increased use of professional singers. This also met with some resistance and it was not always a clear gain either spiritually or esthetically.

Increased attention to the art of worship was largely due to a general improvement in public taste. Liturgical forms of greater or less complexity have been introduced in the non-ritualistic churches and it is no longer a matter of surprise to see vestments, processionals, crosses and even candles in churches of denominations which, half a century ago, would have scorned all of these things as "the rags of Romanism."

Painting has had but a small place in the Protestant churches. In general, the interior decorator has taken the place of the mural painter. Stained glass windows were destroyed by some of the early reformers not because they hated beauty but because the figures of the saints in the windows were considered idolatrous, and even the Roman Catholic church has never hesitated to destroy idols regardless of any artistic value that they might possess. But modern Protestantism has developed tolerance for figure-painting on glass, while it is still generally averse to the enrichment of the walls by the painting of either Biblical or symbolical figures. When a new Congregational church in Brooklyn was embellished with stained glass windows illustrating Biblical incidents, the *Independent* raised the question, "How far can these externals of religion be employed without the encouragement of doctrinal error or spiritual sentimentality?" Its answer was that there is no harm in such representation so long as it does not do violence to the church's creed and its actual interpretation of scripture.

Sculpture has had an even smaller place than painting in Protestant churches. Practically its only use has been in an occasional memorial tablet in bas relief and very recently in the external use of architectural sculpture.

Chapter X

THE CHURCH DISCOVERS THE HUMAN RACE

A contemporary European student has said that the social movement in the churches is the distinguishing characteristic of American Christianity (Visser 't Hooft: *Backgrounds of the Social Gospel in America*). But in thinking of the social emphasis in the teachings and activities of the churches, one must avoid the error of supposing that a thing is new when it has only been forgotten for a while and then rediscovered and given fresh applications. The Middle Ages—not to go farther back, as one easily might—had a conception of religion which included all of life. It dominated the state, regulated public and private conduct, and gave laws to govern economic and political behavior. The medieval church, for example, condemned usury—which meant the taking of any interest upon money loaned—as definitely as the church of the third century condemned war. To be sure, usury was practised, but with either shame or defiance, not casually, and with the realization that it was forbidden by an authority which had a perfect right to forbid it. One reason why the Jews got even such limited toleration as they did get was because of the convenience of having a class of people who were willing to perform a sinful but seemingly necessary economic function. The Italian, Benvenuto da Imola, put the dilemma of the medieval Christian business man in a nutshell when he said, "He who takes interest goes to Hell; he who doesn't goes to the poorhouse." (This in his commentary on Dante. His crisp Latin was: *"Qui facit usuram vadit at inferum; qui non facit vadit ad inopiam."*)

Early Protestantism carried over the idea of giving religion control over all conduct. The Genevan state, for example, virtually destroyed the distinction between sacred and secular authority, and the basic idea of Puritanism was that of a "holy state" in which all laws should be expressions of the will of God as interpreted by the regenerate, and all conduct should be in accordance with a program determined by the members and ministers of the church and enforced by the police power of the state. With Lutheranism, the exigencies of the religious struggle led to giving the state much control over religion while leaving the church competent to give laws for private morality. But Protestantism recognized the rising tide of business and made adjustment to its necessities. With the waxing spirit of nationalism, the increase in the volume and variety of business, the growth of the secular spirit and the diversification of religions, the state became the inclusive category and the church merely one of the institutions which existed within its shelter—a unique one, to be sure, but only one among many.

By the middle of the seventeenth century, especially in England, political action no longer sought religious sanctions, and economic policies were judged as profitable or unprofitable rather than as right or wrong. The new science of political economy took the place of the church's moral authority as the guide for Christians in their economic transactions. John Wesley could simplify the rules of Christian economics to this: "Get all you can; save all you can; give all you can." But how should a Christian get? The church had little to say about that, so long as the more obvious forms of theft and fraud were avoided. And so it continued with only slight exception through the eighteenth century and the early part of the nineteenth. One of the important exceptions was the development of a strong moral and humanitarian opposition to the slave trade. The abolition of that profitable but nefarious traffic drew much of its support from evangelical sentiment. And this uprising of moral indignation, both among the evangelicals and among secular humanitarians, acquired such force that the English representatives went to the Congress of Vienna in 1815 with practically no other plank in their platform for the rehabilitation of Europe after Napoleon's downfall than that the slave trade must be abolished.

But the slave trade was such an open and nauseous scandal that

protest against it was scarcely a fair test of the interest of religion in
social problems and economic methods. The Industrial Revolution
soon produced, among the working classes in England, conditions
that were not much better than the horrors of the middle passage. But
religion was not immediately disposed to concern itself greatly with
these matters. It was in commenting upon some criticism of current
industrial practice from the standpoint of Christian morality that an
early nineteenth century British statesman said, with unconscious
humor: "Things have come to a pretty pass if religion is going to
interfere with private life." Froude asserted that the characteristic
impulse of the representatives of religion was "to leave the present
world to the men of business and the Devil." And it was after 1865
that an American theologian, prominent in the Middle West, said
(perhaps unconsciously echoing Wesley's dictum) that "men should
make money according to the laws of business and spend it according
to the laws of God."

It was the work of the latter part of the nineteenth century and still
more of the twentieth to break down this two-century-old wall which
fenced religion away from economic and political matters and to revive
the idea that religion has some relation to public as well as to private
morality and that the political and economic fields are not remote
from its concern.

So the church, after rediscovering its social responsibilities in connection with the slavery issue, extended its operation into the fields
of temperance and prohibition, and then to those of commercialized
vice in various forms; after that to economic questions and industrial
policies involving the welfare of the workers; and finally to international questions. In all of these, some can see nothing less than a
return to clericalism. This is especially likely to be the opinion of
those who oppose the specific attitudes which the churches have
taken on these questions. It is in one sense a return; but not to
clericalism. One reason why it cannot be that is that the Protestant
churches themselves are no longer clerical.

The influence of such churchmen as Kingsley and Maurice and
of Ruskin and Carlyle in England produced the beginnings of an
awakening to the problems of labor and industry and to the cultural
and religious needs of the less favored portion of society. Before the

Civil War, William Ellery Channing, Horace Bushnell and Theodore Parker had performed something of the same service in America. Bushnell's influence was very great not only on religious education, in which it has been generally recognized, but on the social movement. He stressed the importance of environment in the development of personality, and environment included not only the family but the general economic and social setting of the individual in the community and in the state.

In describing a movement which began in so many places at once and moved in so many different directions, it is impossible to reduce all the facts to any very orderly pattern. But we must at least distinguish between the teachings and activities of those individuals who were the prophets of the social gospel and the official actions of the churches which represent a wider popular acceptance of these same ideas.

It was not a theory but a condition which led the religious mind to become aware that it could not ignore the processes which were producing human misery. The church had never been indifferent to misery. Charity had been one of its cardinal virtues. Giving alms to the poor had almost sacramental value. But it presently began to be disturbed by the sight of new forms of poverty and new kinds of misery, and those, too, in a country which was notoriously rich in resources and exultant over its prosperity. The new poverty of the industrial classes seemed to be quite definitely a man-made thing. It was an obvious by-product of the very processes by which wealth was being created. It could not be dismissed with a tossed coin and the easy assumption that it was God's will that "the poor ye have always with you." The misery of the poor in a simpler state of society might be set down as part of some inescapable cosmic plan; but child-labor in factories and mines, sweatshop work by women at starvation wages, industrial accidents from unguarded machinery—these were kinds of things which were clearly the result of bad human arrangements in the processes of creating wealth. Man was responsible for them and Christian men ought to do something about remedying them.

So the rise of prophets of the social gospel, and then the beginning of new social sciences, and then the acceptance by the churches generally of their share of responsibility for the creation of a better social order, did not come about through any processes of abstract thought but by the observation of concrete conditions which cried aloud for correction. The development of factories and the massing of immigrant workers in the larger cities had already created the slums. As the slums arrived before the technique of urban sanitation had been discovered, except of the most elementary sort, the conditions were unspeakable. Epidemics of cholera, smallpox, yellow fever, typhoid, and scarlet fever ran wild. Public hygiene soon began to make some slight impression on this state of affairs. The health boards of the principal cities were established in the late 'sixties and in the 'seventies. In 1867, New York took the rather obvious step of removing its slaughter houses from the downtown district. There had been scores of them, and even then they were required only to move above 40th Street.

It was a gilded age for financiers and a period of unlimited opportunities for all promoters of new enterprises, but it was not a prosperous time for labor. Work was abundant, to be sure, and wages seemed high, but a government report at the end of 1866 showed that, while wages had increased on an average of 60 per cent. in the past six years, the cost of living had increased 90 per cent. The wage of ordinary skilled labor was $2.00 for a ten-hour day. Women workers in factories—there were not many women workers in offices yet—got $3.50 to $4.00 a week. Girls in dry-goods-stores in the larger cities had a working day from 7:30 in the morning until nine and sometimes ten o'clock at night, with a wage of not more than $5.00 a week, and with none of the facilities for comfort or even decency which are now universal. To combat these conditions of labor, eight-hour leagues were formed in several states and a congress was held in Baltimore in 1866 to promote this reform. Six state legislatures passed laws which made eight hours a legal day's work—unless otherwise agreed upon. Naturally it was usually otherwise agreed upon. The worker who must take what he can get agrees to anything. Not until labor unions became effective was there any sensible improvement in wages or in hours or in conditions of labor.

Labor unions were still both new and feeble. In the absence of effective and responsible organizations, strikes were infrequent, generally unsuccessful, and seldom commanded any support from respectable public opinion. The National Labor Union, organized in 1866, went to pieces five year later. One of the most successful of the early unions was the Knights of St. Crispen, organized in 1867 to protect the interests of labor in the rapidly expanding shoe industry, but after a few years it collapsed under the onslaughts of the employers. St. Crispen, you may or may not remember, was the patron saint of shoemakers, but the church contributed only the name, and no special support to this organization. The Knights of Labor, organized in 1869, did not achieve any immediate results.

For the most part, the good people of the middle class, whether in the church or out of it, felt a vague and tepid sympathy toward underpaid labor and a very hot and righteous indignation against any disturbances of the peace that might occur when labor undertook to better its condition. A religious editor expressed practically the whole mind of his constituency on the labor question when, commenting on a coal strike in Pennsylvania in 1875, he said: "Whatever may be the reason alleged, mobs are to be put down at once and effectually at the point of the bayonet if necessary" (*Independent*, April 8, 1875). The parallel with Luther's advice to shoot down the turbulent peasantry will be readily noted.

The increasing flood of immigration complicated the social and industrial problem, and it was a flood which did not occur without some artificial stimulation by those who were interested in it. The railroads needed track workers and they had land to sell. They, therefore, became both real estate and immigration agents on a large scale. Their representatives operated in Europe to enlist large companies of immigrants to be delivered at given points on their lines, either as laborers or as home seekers. Mr. Carnegie encouraged the importation of foreign labor for his steel mills to curb the dissatisfaction of American workmen who would not rest quiet with meager wages for long hours while the owner's profits were pyramiding and while the management's insistence upon an open-shop policy prohibited an efficient organization of labor in self-defense. After the bloody Homestead strike in 1892, the policy of employing foreign labor was pursued still more consistently. The coming of immigrants in such numbers for this and other reasons resulted in the creation of vast masses of unassimilated aliens with whose lives the Protestant churches had few points of contact and for whose interests they only tardily developed a concern. There were occasional lamentations about the church's failure in the cities and regretful observations about "the squalid dwellings of the poor," but little was done about it.

The church was not indifferent to poverty and need, but it had learned to comfort its conscience by giving charity; and if it went beyond that, it was to utter pious platitudes about "helping the poor to help themselves." It dealt in palliatives, and was reluctant to touch the social-economic-industrial machine or to get at the roots of poverty. Then, as now, it was easy for the prosperous to recommend, as a cure for the troubles of labor, "steady individual self-help"—to quote Theodore Roosevelt's phrase which was the equivalent of the "sturdy individualism" of our time. As the churches were made up for the most part of sturdy and fairly successful individuals, no radical remedies seemed called for. It is quite possible, also, that the tardiness of the church in entering aggressively the field of social reform was in some measure due to the persistence of the belief that misery is the result of the individual's sin and an expression of God's displeasure. The philosophy of Job's friends even now receives some following. On this theory, evangelism and the call to repentance was the most practical sort of relief work. It took a long while to arouse an acute realization that suffering may be the result of other people's sins or even of the collective sins of a society made up of good people.

Among the earliest and most eloquent exponents of the social aspects of Christianity was a group which called itself the Brotherhood of the Kingdom, including Washington Gladden and Walter Rauschenbusch. Before them, Edward Everett Hale had carried on the New England Unitarian tradition which was more humanitarian than humanistic. William Jewett Tucker, of Andover, was the first to introduce social studies into the curriculum of a theological seminary. Josiah Strong combined a social emphasis with a rather conservative theology and also with an appreciation of the religious values of the world's great poetry, and the religious significance of national development. His book, *Our Country*, had immense popularity in the imperialistic period. George D. Herron, as professor of applied Christianity in Grinell College, Iowa, taught a rather radical doctrine which was in some sense a religious parallel of populism. It is not to be forgotten that William Jennings Bryan, long before he became the champion of the old theology against evolution, had infused religious fervor into his appeal on behalf of the agrarian West and the debtor class generally, whom he considered to be the victims of the national sin of the demonetization of silver. Charles M. Sheldon's *In His Steps* was to the new appeal for social righteousness what *Uncle Tom's Cabin* had been to the anti-slavery movement, except that it did not precipitate a war, and Sheldon's experimental editing of the Topeka *Capitol* for one week as a religious daily paper focused the eyes of the country upon the fact that there were at least some Christian leaders who thought that religion required some definite attitude toward the events of the day.

Parallel with the activities of the middle generation of these leaders were the efforts of the "Christian Socialists," led by W. P. D. Bliss, who about 1889 discovered (what everybody knew) that "the control of business is rapidly concentrating in the hands of a dangerous plutocracy," and asserted (what few believed) that "the teachings of Jesus lead directly to some form of socialism." But for the most part the men who have been mentioned, although they were the spokesmen for a socialized Christianity, avoided the odious term socialism with the political and irreligious implications of its European form.

Simultaneously, the college settlement movement was developing. Vida D. Scudder (Episcopalian) of Wellesley played a leading part in this, as did also Stanton Coit (Society of Ethical Culture) whose Neighborhood Guild, started in New York in 1886, drew its inspiration from Toynbee Hall in London. Jane Addams opened Hull House in Chicago in 1889, and Graham Taylor became professor of social ethics in Chicago Theological Seminary and founded Chicago Commons. These settlement houses, religious in spirit if not always in name, became laboratories for the study of social questions, organizers of remedial agencies, and starting points for legislative investigation of conditions which needed to be remedied by law. They were also, whether under religious auspices or not, tremendous stimuli to the social consciousness of the churches.

Among the leaders of Christian thought in this field in our own time have been Shailer Mathews, who has applied social values to theological restatement as well as to the expression of the present duty of the church; S. J. Case, who has emphasized social factors in the interpretation of the history of Christianity; Harry Ward, who has specialized on the question of industrial relations; Sherwood Eddy and Kirby Page, who have dealt largely with international relations, have taken their stand as absolute pacifists and have not hesitated to align themselves with the socialist party; and Arthur E. Holt, who, though successor of Graham Taylor at Chicago, has been especially interested in rural economics and in securing justice for the farmer.

It would be interesting to meditate upon the influence of the wars which fall within our period upon the development of the social ideas and ideals of the churches. After the Civil War came a reaction, but only in the minds of a few of the more independent thinkers, against the church's absorption with individual salvation and institutional glorification; after the Spanish-American War, imperialism and an enhanced sense of world mission, but also a revolt against exploitation and capitalistic influence; after the World War, an awareness of the problems of industrial democracy, economic justice, and international and inter-racial relations.

Slow as the churches were to recognize the importance of the new social problems, the academic world was still slower. The Christian socialism movement was already in existence and such prophets as Washington Gladden and Josiah Strong were already preaching the social gospel—to a rather indifferent and suspicious constituency, to be sure—before the science of sociology came into existence. The term "social science" had been coined by Robert Owen about 1820 and an American Association for the Promotion of Social Science was formed during the 'sixties. At its annual meetings it discussed such questions as education, science, insanity, prisons, and state ownership of railroads. But Professor W. G. Sumner, at Yale, was one of the first, if not actually the first, to make the study of society an academic discipline, and the new science of sociology did not rise to the dignity of a separate department until Albion W. Small became the creator and head of such a department in the new University of Chicago in 1892. His chief colleague was Charles R. Henderson, who was a practitioner in the field of social improvement as well as a student of the science of society, and who, while he could speak to the church

with the voice of one who was both in it and of it, could also speak
to the city so persuasively that at the time of his death he could be
called, in no mere flattering eulogy, "the first citizen of Chicago."

There were economists also among the reformers and there was
need of them. It was one of the standing criticisms of the church,
when it began to propose specific policies for economic and social
betterment, that it did not know its economics. It did not, but neither
did anyone else. W. G. Sumner, bold critic of the social order in
many respects, followed the Manchester School of *laissez faire* and
thought that competitive capitalism would work its way out of the
wilderness well enough and give labor its substantial rights if free
trade were introduced. The Wharton School at the University of
Pennsylvania was founded in 1881 in the hope, if not with the promise,
that it would defend the *status quo* including a protective tariff.
Benjamin Andrews, president first of Brown University and then
of the University of Nebraska, gave scandal to the eastern conservatives
by becoming a partisan of the agrarian revolt and the free silver
movement in 1896. Richard T. Ely, first at Johns Hopkins and then at
the University of Wisconsin, evolved an attitude radical enough to
make the conservatives look upon it as socialism; but in reality Ely
considered Christianity as the remedy for socialism, the very worst
type of which he said was spreading to an alarming extent among
the laboring classes in America. John R. Commons defended, on
economic as well as humanitarian grounds, the development of labor
unionism as an essential part of a well-balanced capitalistic scheme.

The radical theories of Karl Marx found some following in America,
especially among the recent immigrants, but little in the "respectable"
classes and practically none in the churches. Henry George, whose
Progress and Poverty was published in 1879, found enough sympathy
for his diagnosis of the economic condition to win for him international
fame, though his proposed cure, the single tax, never won any great
following. In his campaign for mayor of New York he ran a good
second—ahead of Theodore Roosevelt who was on the regular Republican ticket—but not because he had won many converts to the
constructive part of his program. Henry D. Lloyd's *Wealth Against
Commonwealth* was a thrilling arraignment of the financial and economic system. Nearly everybody knew that the patient was sick,

especially when a series of extraordinarily serious strikes in the East and Middle West in the early 'nineties coincided with the outbreak of agrarian unrest in the West which sought relief in the populist movement. Everybody had a diagnosis. But nobody had a remedy which seemed safe and acceptable even to the well-meaning among the fairly comfortable middle classes who realized that something ought to be done.

The church people generally through the 'eighties and 'nineties were getting disturbed about the condition of the restless poor, but they were even more disturbed about the threat of socialism, and it was difficult for many of them to dissociate this from the threat of organized labor. After the Haymarket riot of 1886 in Chicago, Roosevelt, who was a good churchman as well as a politician, was rabid against the strikers—all strikers—and laid the bombing to "labor" without discrimination. Henry George he set down as a fanatic and a fool. (John Dewey in 1928 classed him as one of less than ten of the world's greatest social philosophers beginning with Plato.) Reverend Joseph Cook, lecturing in Boston in 1879 on "Are Trade Unions a Nursery for Socialism?", was inclined to say yes, especially if the unions are filled with ignorant men, and "compulsory socialism is the chief danger in the future of universal suffrage. From that peril, which means nothing less than spoliation and anarchy, may God and discussion in the church and state save us." While Henry George was far from being a socialist, his teaching seemed to many to serve as an entering wedge for socialism. Commenting adversely upon this and all other radical remedies, Lyman Abbott, a liberal in most respects, defined the duty of the church as "to preach the gospel to the poor and needy; to provide teachers and places of worship for all, and to make any seeker after God welcome in any Christian church; to show the most concern for those who are most in need." That is to say, courtesy, free pews and evangelization for the unfortunate, but not constructive social measures backed by Christian opinion.

An occasional minister or prominent layman took a bolder stand. Tom Johnson, reform mayor of Cleveland in the 'nineties, was a member of the Cedar Avenue Christian (Disciples) church of which Harris R. Cooley was pastor. Cooley, whose church had in its membership many persons who were socially minded and socially active, including prominent labor leaders, became a member of Tom Johnson's cabinet in charge of social and charitable activities for the city administration. But the distinguished contribution of this church and pastor in this field was not counted to them for righteousness when they adopted the practice of "open membership," and they fell into great disfavor in their own denomination. Similarly, when George Bellamy founded Hiram House in Cleveland in 1895, he soon discovered that denominational affiliations were of very little help and denominational limitations were a decided hindrance in the operation of a social settlement. The affiliation was broken and the house still continues under the same leadership with increasing scope and usefulness. While we are speaking of Cleveland and settlement houses, it may be interesting to remember that Starr Cadwallader was sent there by Jacob Riis to found Goodrich House, and that Newton D. Baker and Frederic C. Howe were among its early residents.

When it was a question not of reconstructing the social order but of combating vice and political corruption, the church was capable of an occasional magnificent gesture. Doctor Parkhurst's invasion of the Bowery in 1892 was the most spectacular onslaught that the church had made upon the alliance between corrupt municipal politics and commercialized vice. From his pulpit in the Madison Avenue Presbyterian Church, New York, Doctor Parkhurst had made a sweeping assertion that the leaders of Tammany Hall were in guilty complicity with the saloons and immoral resorts. The anti-Tammany press gave large publicity to these charges. A grand jury investigated—or professed to investigate—and reported that "the author of the charges had no evidence on which to base them except newspaper reports which had no foundation in fact," and it expressed its "disapproval and condemnation of unfounded charges of this character which could only serve to create a feeling of unwarranted distrust in the minds of the community with regard to the integrity of public officials." Thus challenged, Doctor Parkhurst realized that, in fact, he had only hearsay evidence, and he determined to get first-hand knowledge of the facts. Enlisting the services of a detective and an assistant, he made the rounds of the most disreputable places in New York with his companions in disguise. What he found was plenty, and he made public on Sunday mornings on Madison Avenue what he had seen and heard on his midnight explorations in the Bowery. The result was a stirring of public opinion which resulted in a temporary overthrow of Tammany's power. A secondary result was a nation-wide reputation for Doctor Parkhurst, and an increased feeling in the church generally that it really had some business to be concerned with some features of the social situation besides its now almost traditional, but for the most part purely verbal, attacks upon the saloon and its not altogether unsuccessful efforts to secure the passage of regulatory laws which were promptly ignored and evaded by the thoroughly aroused and organized liquor interests.

It is impossible to speak of the church's attitude toward social welfare and public morality without referring again to the question of temperance and prohibition, for it was in this field that the energy which had been generated by the consideration of slavery as a moral and religious issue soon began to expend itself. Liquor was a concrete evil against which the church could direct its attack without danger of seeming to be unduly radical. And besides, it was an easy transition from the preaching of temperance as a private virtue to demanding prohibition as a public policy. For many minds also it afforded a gratifying simplification of the whole social problem to consider that all other evils—poverty, crime, insanity, divorce, and whatever else marred the perfection of society—would automatically disappear with the removal of this one evil. The consumption of alcohol had indeed increased considerably since the close of the Civil War, and the habit had regained a degree of respectability which it had long since lost. The advocates of temperance and total abstinence, who were for the most part church people, soon undertook new campaigns, partly persuasive and partly prohibitory, and in this one field of social reform the Protestant churches in general were outspoken and influential. Except in a very few states, saloons flourished without let or hindrance and it is no slander of the dead to say that the saloon was very generally and very closely tied up with commercialized vice and with corrupt municipal politics. By 1880 there were 80,000 legal liquor shops in cities of 5,000 or more population, or perhaps 100,000 in the country as a whole—and most of these operated illegally part of the time. No more need be said than has already been said of the campaign for temperance by the technique of revivalism. It had its effect, no doubt, in thousands of individual cases, but while it was going on at its highest intensity, the per capita consumption of liquor was increasing. Something more, apparently, needed to be done. For a few years after its organization in 1869, the Prohibition Party was the chief instrument for the promotion of prohibition, whether state or national. In some denominations this received considerable support from the ministry but there was little or no official action in its favor by the churches and the laymen as a body were not interested. The Methodist Church, which was later to become the most conspicuous advocate of prohibition, was in the North completely wedded to the Republican Party. It happened, however, to be a Presbyterian minister who coined the phrase "Rum, Romanism and Rebellion," the back-kick of which defeated Blaine in 1884.

The Women's Christian Temperance Union, organized in 1874, symbolized by its personnel as well as by its name the religious motive in this enterprise. It was effective in mobilizing Protestant sentiment, masculine as well as feminine, against the saloon, especially in local option fights, and it threw such influence as an organization of the defranchised could exercise on the side of the Prohibition Party. But it was through the Anti-Saloon League, which first appeared locally at Oberlin, Ohio, and which became a national organization in 1895, that the energies of the churches were organized in favor of prohibition, both state and national. With Wayne B. Wheeler, the dry-boss, as its leader, a type of "pressure politics" came into existence which, if not a new thing, was certainly new on the side of reform. While this was in some measure, as was generally declared, an attempt to enforce a puritanical standard of morals—but paradoxically in reference to a matter upon which the Puritans themselves had not been in the least puritanical—it derived its power chiefly from the fact that the saloon had been a demoralizing factor in social and political life, and from the further fact that in a machine age the drinking habits of an individual were seen, even by persons who had no moral or religious presuppositions about alcohol, to be a matter of social significance. The anti-saloon league became, to a very considerable extent, what Wayne Wheeler said it was—the churches organized against the saloon.

It might be argued that the church's general sense of its social responsibilities was checked rather than developed by directing so much of its attention to this one enterprise, if it were not for the fact

that at the very time when the anti-saloon league was most active the
churches themselves—not merely individuals with exceptional insight,
but representative church assemblies—were facing the still more
difficult and delicate social problems with more frankness than ever
before.

Reserving for a later chapter the consideration of the united action
of the churches on social questions through the Federal Council,
some attention may be given here to the denominational activities
both voluntary and official in this field, and first of all to those in the
Protestant Episcopal Church which, perhaps because of the Christian
Social movement in the Anglican Church of which Frederick D.
Maurice was the Moses and Charles Kingsley the Aaron, had a definite
precedent and tradition to follow.

The Church Association for the Advancement of the Interests of
Labor (C.A.I.L.) was organized in 1887. It included both Anglo-
catholics and low churchmen. Father Huntington of the Order of
the Holy Cross was active in organizing and conducting the association. So also was Professor John P. Peters, eminent archeologist and
Semitic scholar. Bishop F. D. Huntington was president from its
organization in 1887 until his death in 1904. The inclusion of men
of such different types in this and other social organizations may have
had something to do with preserving the unity of spirit in the Episcopal Church in spite of diversities of churchmanship. Its activities
soon came to include definite efforts to compose disputes between
capital and labor, as when Father Huntington, who had the advantage
of being a Knight of Labor as well as a member of the Order of the
Holy Cross, was influential in settling a coal strike in Illinois. The
miners, desirous of expressing their appreciation by a gift, were at a
loss as to what they could give to one who came so near to being a
monk. They settled it by giving him a pair of shoes, which they observed he badly needed. Bishop Potter, whom nobody ever mistook for
a monk, became chairman of the New York Council of Mediation and
Conciliation, with prominent representatives of capital, labor and the
public, which settled many strikes. Sweatshops and tenement-house
conditions also engaged the attention of the C. A. I. L. It was an
ardent supporter of the union principle. It secured a resolution from
the Episcopal General Convention that all printing and stationery used

in the church should be secured from firms that paid the union scale; and its magazine, *Hammer and Pen,* published white lists of firms employing only union labor. It was influential in the organization of the Actors' Church Alliance. It was one of the chief forces in securing the appointment of a commission on the relations of capital and labor by the Convention of 1901, which was the first step toward the taking over of the functions of this and other voluntary organizations by a body officially representing the church. By that time it had gained such wide acceptance within the church that it had seventy-five bishops as vice-presidents. Bishop Potter succeeded Bishop Huntington as president of C. A. I. L. in 1904, to be succeeded in turn by Bishop Greer and Bishop Manning.

The Christian Social Union, organized in 1892 on the pattern of the English society of the same name, took for its special field the study rather than the actual treatment of industrial conditions. Bishop Huntington was president of this as well as of C. A. I. L. and Prof. Richard T. Ely was secretary. Its roster included some of the most prominent names in the church. It sponsored lectures on social topics at theological seminaries and published an important series of monographs on industrial questions. It went out of existence in 1911, bequeathing its functions to the commission on social service which had by that time been appointed by the Convention.

The Companions of the Holy Cross was an organization of Church-women originating in Boston in 1884 and gradually broadening its membership to cover this country and others. It was particularly interested in working girls' societies and in the college settlement movement. Miss Vida D. Scudder, the first president of the College Settlement Association, was one of the active leaders of this movement.

The Church Socialist League originated in 1911 at a meeting called in Chicago by Rev. Bernard Iddings Bell. Its first two presidents were Bishop Spaulding and Bishop Paul Jones, successive bishops of Utah. The league has suffered in influence through being more radical than its constituency. Its open opposition to the war in 1917 ranked it among the unpatriotic, and Bishop Paul Jones, who was an outspoken resister, has been without a diocese from that day to this. In the past-war swerve toward conservatism, the very name socialism became a red flag and the league was disbanded in 1924.

The Church League for Social and Industrial Democracy was organized in 1919 to meet post-war conditions, encourage the substitution of "fraternal coöperation for mastery in industry and life" and "to give moral and practical support to those who shall clearly be seen to have incurred persecution through advocacy of social change." Less outspokenly radical than the Church Socialist League, it was more so than any of the other organizations mentioned. Nevertheless, it included a number of bishops and many members of faculties of theological seminaries. It took a hand in the investigation and ultimately in the settlement of the silk workers' strike at Paterson, N. J., in 1924, and the textile workers' strike at Passaic, N. J., in 1926. It still continues as an independent organization within the church, stressing the right of labor to organize and to protect itself by collective bargaining.

The General Convention of 1901 authorized the appointment of a standing commission on relations of capital and labor. This was later developed into a joint commission on social service which was given a full-time field secretary in 1911. One after another the organizations already mentioned have been taken over. When the National Council was organized in 1919 (at first under the name of "The Presiding Bishop and Council") the formation of a department of Christian Social Service was authorized. At this time industrial relations were more chaotic than they had been for many years and the commission found plenty to do. It is still in existence as an active agency for the promotion of the idea that industrial problems are at bottom moral problems and that the whole range of social and economic conditions is a field in which the church has a legitimate concern.

The Methodists have been no less sensitive to these problems, but they have been less fertile in producing organizations to cope with them. In 1884, W. F. Mallalieu, at the Methodist Episcopal general conference at which he was made a bishop, presented a memorial on justice to labor. It was referred to the "committee on the state of the church," in whose files it remained safely interred. That was the year in which the United States Bureau of Labor was established. At the general conference of 1888, the bishops reported that they saw "millions of laborers compactly united under leadership likely to become unscrupulous, chafing under real or fancied grievances." Apparently they were more apprehensive about possible breach of the peace by organized labor—possibly remembering the Molly Maguires, whose violent career in the Pennsylvania coalfields had been ended by Pinkerton's men a dozen years earlier—than about any industrial injustices that needed correction. At any rate, they had nothing to suggest for either, because "we sympathize with that antipathy which Americans feel toward commingling of church and state in official action." (They got over that!) The Deaconess Society furnished a link between the poor and the church and an agency for service, but the church was apparently most interested in it as a means by which the church could maintain its "hold" on labor and the immigrant. By 1896, the episcopal address began to show more awareness of the other phase of the situation and to speak more strongly about the mutual duties of labor and capital, though still rather neutrally. The general conference of 1908 adopted a social creed which became the mold and pattern for the one adopted a few months later by the Federal Council of Churches. This was the most specific and the most outspoken demand for justice for labor that had, up to this time, been issued by any general church body, and it became a landmark in the history of the development of a social conscience in the churches. A still more definite and comprehensive statement was issued in 1928. Meanwhile, it is scarcely necessary to say, the Methodist Board of Temperance, Prohibition and Public Morals, under the executive direction of Clarence True Wilson, had become a powerful ally of the Anti-Saloon League, not to say its rival for publicity for the work which it carried on in its magnificent headquarters in Washington.

The reports of the Board of Home Missions of the Presbyterian Church in the U. S. A. in 1886 and again in 1888 showed concern about the problems of cities and immigrants, but it turned out that nothing was in view except evangelization. Again, in 1890, in reporting to the general assembly, the Home Board discussed "city evangelization," and "our foreign population," and regretted that less had been done among the Germans by the Presbyterians than by other denominations. In 1893, it listed among the hindrances to missions in the city "the spirit of uneasiness that pervades the masses" and "the arbitrariness of the trades unions," as well as socialism and "the more hideous form of communism which aims to destroy that fundamental principle of ethics which teaches that a man has an undoubted right to all the property he can acquire by the legitimate use of his powers." Through the next few years the minutes of the general assembly and the reports of the Board of Home Missions continue to make frequent mention of the problem of the cities and their foreign populations, but always in terms of evangelization or Americanization. Perhaps the visit and address of President Roosevelt at the general assembly of 1902, when the centennial of the Home Board was celebrated, brought some suggestion of other duties. The next year Charles Stelzle was authorized to study the workingmen with a view to finding ways of bringing them into the church. Still the problem was that of "increasing the hold of the church" on the laboring class. Stelzle, at the Markham Memorial Church in St. Louis, began to give a different meaning to his assignment. He had been a machinist before he became a preacher, and had kept his membership in the union. By encouraging the exchange of friendly delegates between church and union meetings, he built up much good feeling between them, and the church began to be interested in finding what it could do for labor and not merely what labor could do for it. Meanwhile, the Woman's Board had been carrying on schools and kindergartens, as well as missions, among the aliens in Chicago and Wisconsin. Through Stelzle's efforts, the Home Board's department of the Church and Labor was established in 1905, and for the first time there was explicit recognition of the necessity of studying the industrial problem for the sake of labor.

The national council of Congregational churches in 1901 appointed a labor committee, which has been known since 1904 as the industrial committee.

The Disciples of Christ, somewhat slower to enter this field, established a Board of Temperance in 1907; a Commission on Social Service in 1911, on motion of J. H. Garrison at the Portland convention; and later combined these two in the Board of Temperance and Social Welfare, of which the most conspicuous leader has been Alva W. Taylor. The convention of 1913 urged the colleges to establish chairs and lectureships in social ethics.

The Roman Catholic Knights of Columbus did some work comparable to that of the Y. M. C. A., but the church did not definitely organize for work in this field until, in 1919, the National Catholic Welfare Council, succeeding the National Catholic War Council and directed by a committee of bishops, began to formulate a social program and to set up machinery for its promotion.

The Federal Council of Churches of Christ in America, growing out of a league of open and institutional churches, had its roots in the soil of social questions from the start, and since its organization in 1908 it has not ceased to take an active part in dealing with social and industrial conditions which are in need of discussion, investigation or remedial action.

It is worthy of note that, although it has been customary to say that the American Protestant churches are predominantly rural in their tradition and strength, they were much slower in becoming aware of the social and economic problems of agriculture than of the rights and needs of industrial workers. There was, to be sure, a considerable amount of interest in the plight of the country church and a keen sense of the pathetically weakened condition into which many formerly strong old country churches had fallen by reason of the changes in rural conditions. But it was not until the session of the Federal Council in December, 1932, that the Social Creed of the Churches was rewritten to include some expression of concern for the economic injustices under which the farmers were suffering and the menace to the social fabric which was implicit in the prostrate condition of this basic industry.

Chapter XI

IMPERIALISM AND MISSIONS

If Mr. Pulitzer with his *New York World* and Mr. Hearst with his *New York Journal* had not been engaged in a titanic struggle for the mastery in the field of sensational journalism in the years immediately before and after 1898, it is quite probable that there would have been no Spanish-American war, and that the entrance of the United States into the wide field of world-politics, if and when it came, would have taken place under quite different conditions and uncomplicated by the possession of insular territory in the far East. Probably also the course of Christian missions would have been different; and the church in America, which has always derived much of its mood from the reaction of its missionary effort upon it, would have had a different tone during the years between the little war and the Great War. It would be unprofitable to follow out such ifs, but it is within the legitimate jurisdiction of history to say that the war of 1898 was brought on largely by the newspapers. The attitude of the American people at the decisive moment was, in the main, a somewhat sentimental but entirely honest, altruistic and high-minded response to a fictitious situation that had been set up by an unprecedented abuse of the power of the press.

The outbreak of the Spanish-American war found the churches as ready as they had been in 1861 to assist in the transfiguration of a national conflict into a crusade for righteousness and humanity. Indeed, they were interested in it only because they were so sure that it was just that. And the attitude of the churches and the church people was no different in that respect from the attitude of the lodges, the clubs, the commercial organizations, and all the other groups that make up the total social structure. America was for war, because the great mass of its people—religious and irreligious, clergy and laity—had become firmly convinced that the Spanish régime in Cuba was nothing but a continual carnival of brutality, that Spain was impotent, insolent, treacherous, and cruel, and that it was the dictate of common humanity, not to speak of Christianity and national self-respect, to go into Cuba and clean up the mess. Just how this impression had been produced, it is important to note.

Some of it was a natural and creditable reaction toward the pitiable conditions which actually existed in Cuba. Spain had clung rather desperately to the last remnants of her American empire. For more than half a century insurrection had been endemic in Cuba. An illiberal colonial policy had stimulated rebellion; and rebellion in turn had brought upon the island still more illiberal measures. In that vicious circle, Cuba became more miserable; Spanish policy became harsher; the military measures undertaken by Spain to stamp out insurrection and the guerilla operations of the insurrectos in behalf of Cuba libre kept the islanders on the verge of starvation; and the United States necessarily felt a growing sympathy with the Cubans, and a growing resentment against Spain for maintaining such a nuisance practically on our door-step. It was more than a nuisance; it was an embarrassment and, in a way, an insult, as though some bully were beating a child under our windows. The appeal to the heart of the nation to perform a service to humanity met with a response which was 90 per cent. sincere and disinterested.

But the appeal itself was about 90 per cent. fraudulent and fictitious. The picture of outraged Cuban innocence (usually symbolized by a feminine form) manhandled by Spanish ferocity was one that was for the most part manufactured in the newspaper offices. The primary and intended consequence of the publication of the lurid atrocity-tales and the making of sensational news when there was none sufficiently sensational to report, was the rolling up of huge sales for the *World* and the *Journal*. Incidentally and, so to speak, as a by-product, this journalistic campaign also brought on a war. It brought on a war because it produced an unreasonable hatred of the Spaniards, and an emotional disturbance which made it quite impossible to understand the realities of the Cuban situation. America went to war with Spain in all good faith in the name of humanity, chiefly because newspapers had interests of their own, not strictly humanitarian, in building up a war psychology. It is reported that a great newspaper proprietor sent a famous artist to Cuba in advance of hostilities to make war pictures. "But there isn't any war," protested the artist. "Never mind," replied the newspaper magnate, "You furnish the pictures and I'll furnish the war." And, to a very considerable extent, he did. The incident may or may not be authentic history; even if it is not, it represents what actually happened.

Political considerations also played a part, but not a decisive one. There were influential voices summoning the nation in the same direction with motives far less sordid. Theodore Roosevelt, whose influence with church people was deservedly strong, had for a long time been of the opinion that "what this country needs is a war." While he was a ranchman in Dakota in 1886, he had been keen for a war with Mexico and had offered to enlist a cavalry battalion among the "harum-scarum riders" of his Medora ranch and others in the vicinity. And in the same year, in the enthusiasm of a Fourth of July speech, he had expressed the opinion that he would "see the day when not a foot of American soil will be held by any European power." His wife said that in 1892, when he was eagerly watching the development of friction with Chile, they used "to call Theodore the Chilean volunteer and tease him about his dream of leading a cavalry charge" (H. F. Pringle: *Theodore Roosevelt,* p. 167). When the Venezuela affair was at an acute stage, he wrote to his friend Henry Cabot Lodge expressing the hope that it would lead to a war with Great Britain which would be fought out in Canada and issue in the annexation of that dominion. Such statements as this, of course, were not given general publicity, but they were in the background ready to influence public policy when an opportunity for war offered—and Mr. Roosevelt was Assistant Secretary of the Navy.

There were other statesmen whose patriotism was of this belligerent and expansive type, but for the most part the politicians of either party preferred that the war should be sponsored by the other, if there was to be a war. During the closing months of Mr. Cleveland's administration, his critics of the opposite party had denounced in ringing terms the "brutal stupidity and cowardice" of a foreign policy that had made no move toward recognizing either the independence or the belligerency of the Cuban insurrectos, and the Republican platform on which McKinley was elected in 1896 had declared in favor of recognizing their independence. But to recognize Cuban independence and act accordingly would involve almost certain war with Spain. McKinley was far too peaceable a man to desire a war; least of all did he want to start off his own administration with a war. The Republican victory in the presidential election of 1896 had been won on the argument that the Democratic administration of the conservative Cleveland had produced the financial depression from which the industrial East and the agrarian West were alike suffering, and that another Democratic administration under the radical Bryan would produce a panic. The first concern of the McKinley administration, therefore, must be to restore prosperity. It would be much more satisfactory if the Cuban business could be brought to a head during the months between McKinley's election in November and Cleveland's retirement in March, so that the costs of war and its interruption of the return of prosperity might not be debited to the incoming administration. McKinley himself took this view of the matter; Senator Lodge and Theodore Roosevelt expressed the same idea to each other in their correspondence; and Whitelaw Reid wrote to the President-elect that, while Cuba must doubtless ultimately be ours, it would be wise to avoid any break with Spain for the present.

The four months between the election of McKinley and the retirement of Cleveland were filled with incidents which illustrate the part played by the press in bringing on the war and the methods by which public opinion was manufactured to that end. Within one week after the assembly of Congress, in December, 1896, General Maceo, the leader of the Cuban insurrectionist forces, had been killed in action; Senator Cameron had introduced a resolution for the recognition of Cuban independence; and a Mr. Huau (otherwise unknown to fame) had given to the newspapers the information, which he said he had received in a private letter from Cuba, that General Maceo had been lured by a flag of truce and treacherously shot. The complete unimportance of Mr. Huau and the anonymity of his informant did not restrain the press from treating this piece of news as though it were of proved truth and giving it the utmost publicity. "The perfidy of Spain must have been the topic in hundreds of Protestant pulpits that Sunday morning. 'It will be a disgrace to Christian civilization,' one pastor cried, 'if, with the morning light, the wires shall not flash messages from every part of our nation to our representatives at Washington demanding that this outrage shall be avenged at the point of the bayonet and the mouth of the cannon'" (W. Millis: *The Martial Spirit*, p. 64).

A surge of righteous indignation accordingly converged upon Congress, and especially upon the Senate in which the Cameron resolution was pending. But Cleveland—with that magnificent insouciance which statesmen, even of his independence, never achieve so perfectly as during the closing months of a second term of the presidency— told a group of blustering congressmen that Congress could do as it pleased about declaring war; he wouldn't mobilize the army or navy, for he could buy Cuba for a hundred million dollars and a war would cost a great deal more than that. So the Cameron resolution, even supported by the sensational but unconfirmed Huau revelations, was allowed to die on the Senate calendar when it became apparent that the House would not pass it and when Secretary Olney pointed out that such a resolution, even if passed by Congress, would be "inoperative as legislation, and important only as advice of great weight voluntarily tendered to the Executive regarding the way in which he shall execute his constitutional functions."

The religious press was not yet clamoring for war, but it was helping to set up the justification for one when it should come. One religious paper declared (December 10, 1896) that "the murder of non-combatants, the butchery of prisoners of war, and assaults upon women and girls constitute the major portion of General Weyler's military operations," and the following week summarized the Spanish policy in Cuba as a "fiendish carnival of murder, treachery and rapine."

One of Mr. Hearst's most colorful contributions toward adding circumstance and detail to this picture of Spanish savagery was in connection with the story of the personal indignities offered to three Cuban young ladies on the American steamer *Olivette* in the harbor of Havana. They were searched by Spanish authorities for insurrec-

tionary documents which they were suspected of carrying concealed
on their persons. By the time Richard Harding Davis's indignant
account of this incident had been translated into New York Journalese,
it became a perfect certainty that the brutal soldiery had dealt most
indelicately with these girls, and the picture which Frederic Remington drew to illustrate the story showed one of the young women
standing stripped before her tormentors. With what headlines the
Journal accompanied this story and picture, and with what editorial
trumpeting for every drop of chivalrous blood in the country to boil
with indignation and every manly arm to be bared to strike the blow
of righteous vengeance, may be easily imagined. However, the suspicion that was stirred in some cynical minds by the fact that the
story was exclusive with the *Journal* presently found confirmation
when Mr. Pulitzer's *World*, jealous of this coup, found and interviewed the girls themselves, who said that the only searching had
been done by a police matron in decent privacy. The story was spoiled,
but its effect on the public mind remained.

Another possibility of inflaming the public mind lay in the rousing
of sympathy for those "American citizens" who were in prison for
complicity in the insurrection. These citizens were, without exception,
Cubans who had been naturalized and then returned to continue their
efforts for Cuba libre. The case of one Julio Sanguily was chosen as
a representative of the seventy-four then in confinement, and the
Morgan resolution, introduced into the Senate on February 24, 1897,
demanded his "immediate and unconditioned release." The debate
upon this resolution included accusations of the ghastliest atrocities,
all in quite general terms except a revival of the already exploded
Olivette incident. Then Senator Hoar proved that Sanguily's naturali-
zation was fraudulent, and Sanguily admitted his guilt by accepting
a Spanish pardon which Secretary Olney had negotiated. So that case
sputtered like a wet firecracker and went out. Something more romantic was needed. It was discovered in the wrongs and the beauty
of Señorita Evangelina Cisneros.

The Cisneros incident was also a Hearst promotion. This young
lady had voluntarily followed her father when he was exiled to the
Isle of Pines for insurgency; then she herself had been arrested and
sent back to Havana; and now it was reported that she was about

to be sent to a penal colony in Africa—for no other offense than the defense of her virtue against a brutal and lustful Spanish officer. No real facts were ever sought; probably they could not have been found anyway. The mere suggestion of beauty in distress and virtue imperiled was enough. Here was a chance to mobilize the sympathies of womanhood. "Enlist the women," was the cry. Monster petitions were prepared, bearing the names of tens of thousands of women. A fore-gleam of the later joining of North and South in one fervor of patriotism is found in the fact that, while the widow of Jefferson Davis was appealing to the Queen of Spain in behalf of Miss Cisneros, Julia Ward Howe, author of the Battle Hymn of the Republic, was appealing to the Pope. The climax came when the New York *Journal*, having worked up a nation-wide excitement about the case of this imprisoned girl, planned her rescue from the prison in Havana, which was actually carried out on October 10 by a *Journal* reporter—"the greatest journalistic coup of this age!" Her reception in New York produced a popular demonstration which lacked nothing but ticker-tape and shredded telephone books—both later developments in the technique of expressing civic enthusiasm. I am pleased to note that my own contemporary comment on the case was somewhat guarded: "The public knows little of Miss Cisneros and the merits of her cause, but it looks upon her as a personification of the cause of Cuba libre. She is by far the most attractive personal representative of that cause who has yet appeared." But it was just as true that the cause of Cuba libre was a generalization of the cause of the beautiful Miss Cisneros.

So it had been brought about, before the destruction of the *Maine*, on February 15, 1898, that the country had already been taught not only to sympathize with the Cubans on account of the actual merits of their case, but to hate and despise Spain, and that the support of the church people had been enlisted by making it appear that the prospective war was a crusade in the interest of humanity. After the tragedy of the *Maine*, there was a brief period of calm, motived by the desire to be—and especially to appear to be—judicial. "Let us await the result of the investigation." But the actual mood was not wholly unlike that of the editor of the *Independent* who, thirty-three years earlier, had declared that Jeff Davis should be fairly and impartially tried, and hung. Any lack of positive evidence that Spain had, either officially or unofficially, blown up the battleship of a friendly power, was amply compensated by the general conviction that that was just the sort of thing Spain would do. That conviction was partly the result of the long continuance of really bad conditions in Cuba; but to a much greater extent it was the result of the fabrications and exaggerations of a sensational press which had appealed to the most generous impulses of the people by the most ignoble means and for the most ungenerous purposes.

When war was declared, two months after the destruction of the *Maine*, it was supported by "the practically unanimous consent of the people," as was testified by a score of religious papers. Its motive seemed to be one of pure idealism. "It is a war in the interest of humanity and of the rights of the oppressed. It is a war that looks to peace. . . . Its disinterestedness appeals to the moral sentiment of mankind, and future historians can but vindicate the justice and righteousness of our cause" (*Christian-Evangelist*, May 12, 1898). The self-denying ordinance by which, in the very act of entering upon the war, we declared that we would not take Cuba for our own, gave the last needed touch to our consciousness of perfect altruism. Nobody at the moment was thinking about Puerto Rico or the Philippines. Few Americans had ever heard of the Philippines. Among those who had might be mentioned Mr. Theodore Roosevelt, Assistant Secretary of the Navy, who had schemed for the appointment of Commodore Dewey to the command of the Asiatic squadron, and who sent him the order which started him to Manila Bay.

The war for the liberation of Cuba turned out to be also a war in the far East, and when Spanish rule or misrule in the Philippines had been overthrown, America was confronted with something which was either an opportunity, a duty, or a temptation, according as it might be viewed. Events moved rapidly, but not more rapidly than public opinion developed; and religious opinion kept pace, stride by stride, with patriotism in its most expansive mood. Within two weeks after the editorial justifying the war in Cuba, which has just been quoted from a good average exponent of mid-western religious sentiment, the same editor was considering what we ought to do with the Philippines and wondering whether the hour had not struck for Christian America and American Christianity to play a larger part upon the world stage.

"Are we justified, with all our wealth, our power, our educational and religious development, our civil and religious liberty, our free institutions, in maintaining an isolated position and standing aloof from the great tasks which the civilized nations of the earth must perform in behalf of the world's progress?" (*Christian-Evangelist*, May 26, 1898).

During the summer and autumn of that year, the pulpit and the religious press, still in a warm glow of patriotism and uplifted by the vision of new horizons, were busily translating the possible possession of an Asiatic archipelago into terms of a new kind of Christian service to backward peoples. When Congress met in December, it had as its most challenging problem the question of the extension of national sovereignty to cover the Philippines. The arguments for it were both economic and idealistic. Senator Beveridge, in his maiden speech in the Senate, demanded that we keep the islands. He had already made himself an expert on the subject by a quick trip to the Philippines immediately after his election. Exhibiting a nugget of gold, he cried: "I picked this up on the ground in one of these islands. There are thousands of others lying about." To which Senator Hoar replied, in one of the briefest speeches ever made in the Senate: "The Devil taketh him up into an extremely high mountain and showeth him all the kingdoms of the world and the glory of them and saith unto him, 'All these things will be thine if thou wilt fall down and worship me.'"

But Beveridge and the other expansionists could also quote Scripture to their purpose. "God has made us adepts in government," he said, "that we may administer government among savage and senile peoples, . . . and of all our race he has marked the American people as his chosen nation to finally lead in the regeneration of the world. This is the divine mission of America. The judgment of the Master is upon us: 'Ye have been faithful over a few things. I will make you ruler over many things.'"

How could Christian patriotism fail to rise to such a challenge? It rose with reasonable unanimity, except in circles where traditional opposition to increasing the power of the Federal government bred suspicion of this new doctrine that it was commissioned by God to uplift the world, and in certain other circles in which, quite apart from the question of Federal power and states rights, the idea of forcing civilization down the throats of alien peoples at the point of a bayonet seemed to smack more strongly of commercialism than of Christian patriotism. On the whole, however, the churches were quite ready to give a religious sanction to the project of taking up the white man's burden.

President McKinley encouraged this view of the duty of Christian America and sought, and to a great extent gained, the support of religious opinion on these grounds. Explaining his attitude toward expansion to a group of his Methodist brethren, he said: "I am not ashamed to tell you that I went down on my knees and prayed Almighty God for light and guidance more than one night. And one night late it came to me this way: there was nothing left for us to do but to take them all and educate the Filipinos and uplift and civilize and Christianize them and by God's grace do the very best we could by them as our fellow men for whom Christ also died." But he was also aware, as he phrased it on another occasion and to a different audience, of "the commercial opportunity to which American statesmanship cannot be indifferent."

The pulpit and the religious press in general had not only supported the war as an unselfish and humanitarian enterprise but received from expansionist policy a strong impetus to foreign missionary work. That such popular preachers as T. DeWitt Talmage had been eager for war before it came and zealous for its prosecution after it started, is less significant than that the great missionary boards and the ministry and laity generally took up the foreign missionary cause with new zeal derived from the infusion of a fresh patriotic impulse. At a great ecumenical missionary conference held in New York in 1900, Cleveland, McKinley, and Roosevelt appeared together on the platform—"a past president, the present president and a future president," as the author's father wrote to him at the time with prophetic foresight.

The Philippines offered a field where, for the first time, what was essentially foreign missionary work was to be conducted under the American flag. Furthermore, it was a field which the denominations were entering together. A great change in their attitudes toward one another had occurred since the opening of the West and it was universally agreed that they should enter this field not as competitors in a race, jostling each other for inside positions on the track, but as colleagues in a common Christian enterprise. In 1902, an evangelical union was formed by missions of the five principal denominations engaged in missionary work in the Philippines and the territory was divided among them to prevent duplication of effort and waste of resources. A union theological seminary was established in Manila by the same five denominations for the training of a native ministry. In spite of the imperialistic impulse in which it originated, mission work in the Philippines has not only expressed that degree of unity that already exists among the American churches but has given increasing recognition to the spirit of independence and the nationalistic aspirations of the native people.

The year of entrance into the Philippines was also the year of the Boxer rebellion in China. Political events following that crisis favored missionary expansion there also. And with the rise of new educational and cultural movements in the ancient empire came a new willingness to accept the combined educational and religious influences of the occident. Until the revolutions and the nationalistic awakening following the World War, China was a sphere of influence in which American Christianity operated with great success.

It would be outside the purpose of this discussion to treat in detail of the development of missionary activities in the various foreign fields, but the part which the promotion and spirit of missionary work has played in the life of the American churches is an essential aspect of the story of these churches. From the Spanish-American War until the World War the amount of money given annually for the support of foreign missions rose rapidly; the statistical reports of converts gained and schools and hospitals conducted corresponded with the increase in expenditures; and for the most part the dominant ideal was that of conferring upon alien and needy peoples the blessings of American Christianity. Even within this period, however, there was recognition in the case of Japan, the most advanced of the Oriental nations, of the necessity of giving a large place to native leadership. In 1907, for example, three Methodist missions united to form the Japanese Methodist Church by which the churches themselves were put under Japanese control, leaving the institutions of higher education under the direct control of the missionaries. A federation of churches in Japan, formed in 1911, included twenty-four bodies and four-fifths of all the native Christians. A federation of Christian churches in India was the result of conferences held in 1909.

The World War and its aftermath wrought another change in the conception of the missionary problem and consequently in the attitude of the churches at home. In general, the missionaries on the field have been quicker than their supporting constituencies at home to sense the need of adjustment to new needs and conditions. During the decade and a half after the Spanish-American War, American Christians undoubtedly thought of foreign missions in more imperialistic terms than they ever had before, or than they have since.

Chapter XII

DENOMINATIONAL EVENTS AND CONTRIBUTIONS

Most of the details of the history of the several denominations necessarily lie outside of the scope of this work. Interesting and important as these are, their recital must for the most part be left to the denominational historians who can recount the achievements of the several denominations as separate bodies, the reasons for their separateness, and the grounds of their greatness and glory. We must concern ourselves chiefly with the movements of the common Christian mind, the issues which drive planes of cleavage through all denominations transverse to those which divide them from each other, and those outstanding facts and personalities which rise high enough to be visible across denominational boundaries and to form features in the general landscape of the period. Still, it must be remembered that the greater part of the story of Christianity in our time is the story of what has been done through, or at least in, denominations, and it will be proper for us to recount briefly some of the main items in the record of the more important denominations. For all minutiae, however, the denominational histories must be consulted.

Methodists

Publication was the first activity of the Methodists after preaching. The Methodist Book Concern was organized in 1789 in New York, forty-two years before the founding of the first Methodist college that had vitality enough to survive until now. The division of the funds of the Book Concern was one of the most difficult problems raised by the division of the church. The Book Concern passed through a trying period, in the late 'seventies, when extensive frauds in high places cost it many thousand dollars, and the attempt to investigate and remedy the abuses met with an inexplicable amount of obstruction.

The admission of lay delegates to the general conference was granted in 1872. This had been a point of hot controversy for many years, and the Methodist Protestant Church had seceded partly on this issue in 1830. The growth of a responsible and educated body of laymen made the change imperative. It marked a recognition of the passing of the pioneer stage; as usual, the recognition lagged considerably after the event. Until 1932, the annual conferences, the area of whose jurisdiction is generally somewhat less than separate states, were still made up wholly of ministers. A newspaper poll conducted by the *Northwestern Christian Advocate* in 1931 showed a large majority, especially of laymen, in favor of the admission of laymen to the annual conferences, and a corresponding change in the church law was made by the general conference in the following year.

The admission of women to the general conference had a long and stormy history. Women were elected but they were not seated—not even when the honored Frances E. Willard was chosen in 1888. She was admitted, in marble, to Statuary Hall in the Capitol building at Washington, but not to the Methodist general conference. The conference itself had seemed to settle the question in favor of the women in 1872 when, in admitting laymen, it defined the term as including all members of the church who were not members of annual conferences. But the women were not seated until 1904.

The centenary of 1866, celebrating the one hundredth anniversary of the first appearance of Methodism in America, included a successful drive for nine million dollars for educational and other enterprises. Most of this amount was raised and spent locally, and the country was pretty well sprinkled with "centenary churches." The centenary of 1919, marking the centennial of John Stewart's mission to the Wyandotte Indians, was made the occasion for an attempt to raise a hundred million dollars by the northern church and thirty-five million by the southern for the enlargement and support of the missionary programs, based on a comprehensive survey of the fields and of Methodist "world service."

The centralization of authority in the Methodist church has always given occasion for a certain amount of criticism. Of the criticisms from the outside, the most famous was a book called *The Great Iron Wheel*, by R. J. Graves, a Baptist attack on Methodist bureaucracy, the first edition of which was published in 1853 and the thirtieth in 1860. "Parson" Brownlow wrote a reply to it. More important were the criticisms of the administrative system from within. There has been a steady stream of them. The area system of episcopal jurisdiction was adopted in 1912. The Methodist episcopate is not a separate and higher order of ministry, but an administrative office. There is a strong current of opinion in favor of limiting the tenure of it to a term of years.

Methodist Episcopal young people's organizations began with the Church Lyceum (1872), designed to stimulate the intellectual interests of both young and old. It was an adoption by the church of the then popular secular lyceum system. The Young People's Methodist Alliance (1883) was organized at the Des Plaines camp-meeting, near Chicago, by Doctor and Mrs. Lowry, who preached "entire sanctification, perfected love, a fuller baptism of the Holy Spirit, and a more complete consecration." The Alliance combined a reading course (like Chautauqua), the temperance society technique of the pledge, an evangelistic emphasis, and the pietistic fervor which later became the special characteristic of the Holiness groups. Its pledge read as follows: "I enjoy or will seek the blessing of heart purity as taught in the Scriptures. I promise to abstain from the use of tobacco and of all intoxicants as beverages, to refrain from card-playing and dancing, and from attending the theatre, the opera, the circus and all other places of questionable amusements. I agree to have stated seasons of private prayer, to pray for my pastor and for the members of the Young People's Methodist Alliance, to study the Bible each day, and to give daily thought to the winning of souls by personal conversation, letter writing, tract distribution, prayer, and other means." The Alliance soon had 500 local societies and two full-time representatives. The Oxford League (1884) was fathered by Bishop Vincent. Designed to encourage "study, piety, and service," it did not include the distinctive "Holiness" features of the Alliance. It grew slowly for a time, then rapidly in 1888. The Young People's Christian League (Boston, 1887) aimed to coördinate existing local societies. It prepared a reading course and published prayer-meeting topics. The Methodist Young People's Union (Detroit, 1887) was also designed to consolidate all existing Methodist young people's movements and to provide them with an improved system. It was not too modest: "We believe that the theory of our movement is unassailable, and the statement of that theory in our constitution is nearly perfect." All of these were merged in the Epworth League in 1889. The leaders of Christian Endeavor protested against taking the distinctive features of that movement as the basis for a denominational organization without the Christian Endeavor name. The Epworth committee replied that these "distinctive features" of Christian Endeavor were all "familiar reminiscences of Methodism." The Epworth Leagues have continued to be the important organizations of the Methodist churches, north and south.

As Methodism became more urbanized and less revivalistic, there separated from it various groups which laid great stress on the idea of "complete sanctification" and which prized the liberty of unbridled expressions of emotion and conviction as the Spirit gave them utterance. Not less than twenty-five Pentecostal and Holiness organizations have been formed since 1880. Their members are, for the most part, rural, poor, ignorant, and emotional. The cultural advance of Methodism has been facilitated by the sloughing off of this element among which a fiery religion is compensatory for the consciousness of financial, social, and intellectual inferiority.

After futile suggestions looking toward the reunion of the northern and southern branches of Methodism in the years immediately after the Civil War, both sides settled to the cultivation of their own fields. Union projects were dropped, but friction also diminished. At present the division between them is little more than administrative separateness on geographical lines.

An eminent representative of the Methodist Episcopal Church, South, lists the following items as landmarks in the progress of that church since the Civil War: "Lay representation in the general conference given; laity rights given to women; Negro members organized into the Colored Methodist Episcopal Church; woman's missionary society organized; board of church extension organized; Sunday school, Epworth League and educational boards set up, now consolidated under Board of Christian Education; branch houses of publishing house established at Richmond, Dallas, and San Francisco; Southern Methodist University at Dallas and Emory University at Atlanta; time limit removed from pastors; the goal set, but not quite realized, of the Centenary missionary movement of $35,000,000, and endowment of $10,000,000 for superannuated preachers; the building of thirteen hospitals; the setting up of autonomous conferences on foreign fields; the Judicial council, by which bishops are relieved of the responsibility of deciding on points of law" (Dr. W. P. King).

Baptists

By the time of the Civil War, the Baptists had pretty well outgrown the reputation which they had enjoyed in colonial and early Federal days of being ignorant fanatics, Ishmaelites among the respectable denominations. They had adopted methods of worship and of propaganda not widely at variance with those of other evangelical bodies, and they had both founded and patronized educational institutions. Twenty-five permanent Baptist colleges had been established before 1860—while the Presbyterians had forty-nine, the Methodists thirty-four, and the Congregationalists twenty-one (D. G. Tewksbury: *The Founding of American Colleges and Universities before the Civil War*, New York, 1932). Beginning with some prejudice against an educated ministry, the Baptists, like the Methodists and Disciples, had been somewhat backward in founding colleges, but by this time they had all got over this feeling. They knew how to make a little money go a long way in education, not only in the early period, but later. The Baptist historian, Vedder, says that in 1900 the 105 colleges and universities, ninety academies and seven theological seminaries under Baptist control had total assets of "the great sum of $44,000,000," which represented an increase from only $7,000,000 in 1870.

In the case of the Baptists, as with the Methodists, the division over slavery produced a separation which has been perpetuated on other grounds after the disappearance of its cause. Among them also, while efforts at reunion have been unsuccessful, bitterness has disappeared. The southern Baptist churches, always less hospitable to outside influences and modernistic tendencies, have been the most fertile field for the growth of fundamentalism. Southern Baptists (not including Negroes) outnumber northern Baptists almost three to one.

And the Negro Baptists almost equal in numbers the white Baptists in the South. (Northern Methodists, on the other hand, are almost twice as numerous as southern white Methodists and the latter have almost double the total membership of the three large Negro Methodist churches.) The recent heavy immigration of Negroes to the northern states has naturally affected the Baptists more than any other denomination.

The Baptist Congress, growing out of the "social unions" which began to be organized in 1864, was originally intended as a forum for discussion of the problems of religion by laymen, but it presently became the chief assembly of the northern Baptists for the consideration of everything except the actual business of the missionary societies, and the voice of the ministry predominated. When there was active discussion of the project of union between the Baptists and Disciples, a joint congress of the two bodies was held in 1908 and a joint committee recommended that such congresses be held thereafter biennially. The proposal was ratified by the Disciples but not by the Baptists, and not long thereafter the Baptist congresses ceased to meet. The organization of the Northern Baptist Convention seemed to make them unnecessary.

The union of the northern Baptists and the Free-will Baptists, which became effective in 1909, signalized the passing of the theological interest which had been the ground for their separation. The regular Baptists were no longer so strongly Calvinistic as to make it seem worth while to maintain a separate organization to bear testimony to the freedom of the will.

Educational progress among Baptists had already made great advance when the establishment of the University of Chicago in 1892 brought about a notable increase in their prestige in this field and furnished a striking illustration of an institution of denominational origin, conceived rather as the denomination's contribution to culture and scholarship than as an instrument for the propagation of its own distinctive tenets. This, however, was not accomplished without producing much difference of opinion within the fold. For the liberalism of the new university not only served as a rallying point for the more modernistic element of the denomination, but furnished a point against which the more conservative group crystallized its opposition.

In spite of the existence of a large fundamentalist element among the northern as well as the southern Baptists, the former have been much permeated by liberal tendencies toward open communion and open membership.

Besides conducting foreign missions in various parts of Asia and Africa, the Baptists, like the Methodists, have given considerable attention to the spread of their views in various European countries, especially in France, Germany, and Italy. In all of these cases, the effort has been to encourage autonomous movements. This has been notably the case in connection with the extensive Baptist movements in Russia and Scandinavia.

Presbyterians

The union of the New School and Old School Southern Presbyterians in 1864 and the New School and Old School Northern Presbyterians in 1869 and the continued inability of the northern and southern groups to unite with each other show how social, political and geographical considerations may outweigh theological. When the two northern bodies, after cautious preparation merged in a united general assembly (Philadelphia, 1870), they gave their allegiance to the Presbyterian Board of Foreign Missions and to the consolidated boards of Home Missions and of publication, and withdrew from the ABCFM in which the New School had until that time continued to coöperate with the Congregationalists. For accuracy in nomenclature it should be remembered that the two Presbyterian churches are not "northern" and "southern," but the Presbyterian Church in the United States of America and the Presbyterian Church in the United States. Nevertheless, the thirty-six colleges and seminaries of the latter are all south of the line of the Missouri Compromise; and of the sixty-five institutions of the former, all but sixteen are north of it and fourteen of these sixteen are in the border states.

While Presbyterian history after the Civil War was marked by one deepened cleft of division, the total tendency has been toward unity within the denomination. Efforts to unite the northern and southern churches have occurred from time to time, generally on the initiative of the northern assembly, but without success. Part of the Covenanters and part of the Seceders (the Associate Presbytery) had united long before in the Reformed Presbyterian Church, which in turn had divided into New Side and Old Side, both of which believed that the constitution of the United States was fatally defective because it did not explicitly recognize a "covenant with God" as the basis of civil government, but the latter insisting that members should bear witness to this belief by refusing to vote until this defect was remedied. The Reformed Presbyterian Synod at Pittsburgh, in 1883, unanimously adopted resolutions advising all officers and members of the church to avoid the use of tobacco, opposing prohibition, and "joining the Episcopal general convention and the Methodist general conference in asking the government to keep faith with the Indians." Other strains of Scotch Covenanters and Scotch and Irish Seceders combined to form the United Presbyterian Church, among the characteristics of which was the condemnation of instrumental music (until 1881), and still are the exclusive use of the psalms instead of hymns and opposition to all secret societies. It is a group with very conservative theology, great zeal, and no small proportions (178,000 in 1929). The union of the Cumberland Presbyterian Church with the Presbyterian Church in the U. S. occurred in 1906, leaving behind, however, a body of considerable size (now over 60,000) which refused to concur in the union. In 1876, an "Alliance of the Reformed Churches throughout the World holding the Presbyterian System" was organized. It contemplated coöperation and sympathy rather than union among the sixty divisions of the Reformed family which constituted it.

The Presbyterian Church in the U. S. A.—that is, the northern church—includes about 72 per cent. of the total membership of the nine Presbyterian bodies in the United States. With reference to its internal organization, mention should be made of the formation of a Board for Aid of Colleges, in 1883; the raising of the first large pension fund for retired ministers in 1888; and in 1922 a general overhaul of the machinery of the church and the organization, out of the various boards and agencies that had sprung up, of four boards: the Board of National Missions, the Board of Foreign Missions, the Board of Christian Education, and the Board of Pensions. Along with this came the formation of the Permanent Judicial Commission, which handles all judicial cases, and the Executive Council, which manages all urgent business, subject in both cases to the approval of the General Assembly.

The course of doctrinal controversy within Presbyterianism has been sufficiently suggested in discussing the heresy trials that have already been mentioned—the cases of Swing, Briggs, Henry Preserved Smith, and McGiffert. Of these, the case of Professor Briggs was the most important in its influence upon the church. It marked the first great impact of Biblical criticism upon the church as a whole, and led to a reconsideration of the relation of the theological seminaries to the general assembly and to the withdrawal of Union Seminary from Presbyterian control.

While the trial of heretics was proceeding in terms which gave little indication that Presbyterianism had any hospitality for modern thought, there was a strong movement for a revision of the Westminster Confession. The first step was a proposal for the revision of the list of proof-texts accompanying the shorter catechism. It had been discovered that, however true its doctrines might be, some of the supporting textual evidence lacked cogency. In 1889, responding to overtures of fifteen presbyteries, the assembly sent down to all the presbyteries a question as to whether they desired a revision of the Confession and, if so, in what respects. It is interesting to observe that diversities of opinion did not follow the former line of cleavage between Old School and New School. In the assembly of 1890 it was reported that 134 presbyteries favored some sort of doctrinal restatement, while only sixty-eight were opposed to any change. Most of those wishing revision desired to be relieved of the obligation to believe that infants dying in infancy were lost, and almost as many wished a more explicit statement of the love of God for all men. It was somewhere in the course of this discussion that the suggestion was offered that a footnote might be added to the effect that the doctrine of reprobation was not to be understood as excluding the love of God. Whereupon old Dr. Howard Crosby arose in the assembly and, with uplifted hands, cried: "Brethren, has it come to this, that the Presbyterian Church proposes to relegate the love of God to a footnote?" The revision was made, but failed of adoption by the presbyteries, and the matter was dropped until 1902, when textual revisions were adopted covering, among other matters, the salvation of those dying in infancy, two chapters were added on the Holy Spirit and on the Love of God, and a Brief Statement of the Reformed Faith was approved to serve as a supplement to the Westminster Confession, not as a substitute for it, by presenting the desired modifications as an interpretation of the historic standards. The extreme fundamentalist movement has found its chief support among the Presbyterians and Baptists.

In 1905, a Book of Common Worship was adopted, for optional use, indicating a trend toward more liturgical forms, especially in the city churches.

It would be superfluous to say that the Presbyterian churches of all groups have carried on educational and missionary work with unflagging energy. In recent years very strong statements on social matters have been put forth; and the existence of Labor Temple in New York, as well as the support of social settlements, testifies to the interest of Presbyterians in this field of work.

Unitarians

The first delegate conference of the American Unitarian Association met in December, 1864. In the spirit of good will and rejoicing appropriate to the closing months of the war, it seemed that all the differences between the more mystical and the more liberal elements had been settled by compromise on a rather orthodox position. When an attempt was made to have a definite creed adopted by a national conference in April, 1865, it was found that no such reconciliation had occurred. The proposed creed contained these words: "We believe in one Lord Jesus Christ; the Son of God and His specially appointed messenger and representative to our race; gifted with supernatural power, approved of God by miracles and signs and wonders which God did by him; and thus by divine authority commanding the devout and reverential faith of all who claim the Christian name." This was not adopted, though it was reported that it expressed the views of a majority of the delegates. The conference did adopt a constitution in the preamble of which the delegates were called "disciples of the Lord Jesus Christ." The more radical element was willing to define the purpose of Christianity as a general diffusion of love, righteousness, and truth, and wished to make Unitarianism broad enough to include all who were sympathetic with the spirit of Jesus.

The theological affirmation of the conservative and evangelical Unitarians leaves one wondering what their separation from the orthodox Congregational churches half a century earlier was all about.

Those to whom both the supernaturalism and the Christian exclusiveness implied in the constitution were odious started a movement the next year to have it amended in the direction of a freer association of all religious persons who were willing to unite, without reference to belief in the uniqueness of Jesus. Out of this protest grew the Free Religious Association, organized May 30, 1867, with a membership chiefly but not entirely drawn from the Unitarian group. Emerson was the first signer of its roll of members. This Association was vague and desultory in its activities, and vaguer still in keeping its records, but it served to coördinate the tendencies in the direction of a more inclusive fellowship. The more radical views gained a large following in the West, where the Western Unitarian Association showed itself hospitable to them and the periodical *Unity*, published in Chicago, became their organ. The Unitarian Church was almost split by this divergence of opinion. The result of the long effort to write a Unitarian creed was the adoption of a resolution by the National Conference of 1870 to this effect: "Reaffirming our allegiance to the gospel of Christ . . . we invite to our fellowship all who wish to be his followers." The Parliament of Religions, held in Chicago in 1893 and to a considerable extent promoted by Jenkin Lloyd Jones, meant more to the Unitarians than to the evangelical Protestants who participated in it without any intention of putting Christianity on the same plane with the ethnic religions which were represented in it. The following year the Unitarian Association altered its constitution to meet the more liberal views. The Free Religious Association, its work accomplished and its position substantially adopted by the general body, faded out and died as casually as it had lived.

Since 1894, or even a little earlier, the chief emphasis has been upon ethical culture and upon those universal elements which Christianity holds in common with other great religions. The principal divergence within the body has been between the theists and the "humanists," the latter rejecting even the most modernized and cautiously stated idea of God. Having no great zeal for propaganda, and being content to make an almost purely intellectual appeal with no recourse to the popular arts by which masses of men are swayed, the Unitarians have made no great growth numerically. Their standing complaint against the liberals in other denominations is that they "ought to be Unitarians." Unitarianism in the United States was originally a protest against the rigors of strict Calvinism, as Universalism also was. But other ways of escape from Calvinism have become so numerous that neither of these pioneering denominations of liberals has been to any great extent a beneficiary of the general movement toward liberal thought.

Congregationalists

Congregationalism probably stands less in need of a separate history than any other American denomination. It has had fewer distinctive characteristics, and less denominational consciousness, and has been more open to influences from without and more productive of influences that went out than any other of the principal religious groups.

Before the Civil War the New England churches had already undertaken a vigorous work in the West, both educational and evangelistic. Chicago became the western capital of Congregationalism by the establishment of Chicago Theological Seminary in 1854 (opened to students in 1858) and the beginning of publication of the *Advance* in 1867. After the first national convention, at Albany in 1852, and a convention at Boston, 1865, which adopted the "Burial Hill declaration" of faith, the denomination made its general structure more organic by establishing in 1871 a series of triennial councils. But congregational independence was so thoroughly a part of the system that when the "creed of 1883" was issued, by a commission appointed by the previous council, it was expressly provided that it carried no authority other than the persuasiveness of its statements and the influence of the names signed to it. The Boston correspondent of the *Christian Union* wrote: "Looking back two years, to the time when the attack on Newman Smythe began, the new creed registers an extraordinary advance in Congregational popular opinion. The works of Horace Bushnell, *Old Faith in New Lights, The Freedom of the Faith*, etc., have scattered seed-thoughts broadcast which an iron-clad orthodoxy could no more resist than an iceberg could turn back the path of the summer sun. This movement, and its culmination in the undogmatic and catholic creed, marks an epoch in the denomination." Yet it was a conservative creed, as explicit in its trinitarianism as the Nicene, and with even a *filioque* clause. But it was an undogmatic creed because it was not dogmatically imposed. It was a statement of what twenty-five well-informed men believed to be the actual beliefs of most Congregationalists at the time. However, it left them free to change, and so they have, until Congregationalism probably contains at present a larger percentage of liberal thinkers than any other evangelical denomination. The character of Congregationalism, in this and other respects, has been chiefly determined by its emphasis upon education, and its steadfast maintenance of the independence of the congregation within the larger body and of the individual within the congregation.

Lutherans

The history of Lutheranism in America has been determined largely by two facts: first, that it has been the faith of immigrant groups either recent enough in their arrival or resistant enough to Americanization to preserve a lively sense of their racial origins; second, that it has been doctrinally conservative, not with an emotional or revivalistic emphasis but with a substantial basis of theological scholarship.

Germany and the Scandinavian countries have been the principal sources of Lutheran immigration. The church has lost heavily by the failure of its immigrants to keep the faith. In 1897, it was estimated that one-third of the Norwegians and Swedes in the United States were still church-members, but only one-twelfth of the Danes. It is not possible to state the percentage of Lutherans who are not of these racial and linguistic groups and very definitely aware of the fact, but it would be very small. While entirely loyal and patriotic, even in the trying times when their adopted country was at war with the mother-country of many of them, the Lutherans have therefore always labored under a sense of a certain detachment from the main body of the population. This has been emphasized by a feeling of the necessity of guarding against certain liberalizing tendencies which were at one time called "Americanism." For a generation before the Civil War, some of the strong men of the church—notably Schmucker and Kurtz —had attempted to secure such modification of the Lutheran doctrines as would remove the obstacles to closer fellowship with the other denominations. Schmucker's enthusiasm for this was so great that he may be counted as perhaps the most prominent advocate of Christian unity in his generation. But before the war that question had been definitely settled in favor of the maintenance of the strict standards of doctrinal purity of historic Lutheranism. A second source of doctrinal discord, and one that really produced division as the other did not, was the fact that some of the German immigrants had belonged to that Evangelical church which had been produced by the union of Lutherans and Reformed in Prussia in 1817, while others were from the strict Lutherans who had resisted that union and had therefore become victims of the severe repressive laws by which the Prussian government, especially from 1830 to 1846, had tried to compel their acquiescence.

Both of these facts—diversity of racial and linguistic origins and different degrees of adherence to "pure" Lutheranism of the strongly anti-Calvinistic type—have contributed to produce the many divisions of American Lutheranism. In addition, it should be noted that the various waves of migration brought their separate organizations with them, and that Lutheranism in Europe never had any standardized form of general organization independent of the state, so that unity in the new country was something that had to be created rather than merely preserved. Very considerable progress has been made toward an effective unification of Lutheran forces, particularly in the organization (1918) of the United Lutheran Church in America by the consolidation of the General Synod, the General Council, and the United Synod in the South; and by the formation of the Evangelical Lutheran Synodical Conference of North America by the joining of four synods. The maintenance of a system of parochial schools is a feature of the Lutheran program which is unique in American Protestantism, and it may be one reason why, in spite of the difficulties that have been mentioned, the Lutherans have continued to be one of the most rapidly growing religious bodies in the United States.

Episcopalians

Throughout the whole course of its recent history, the Protestant Episcopal Church has been in varying degrees disturbed by the pull of its desire for fellowship, on the one hand, with the other Protestant

churches and, on the other, with the other Episcopal churches. There
has always been within it a party that found its closest spiritual kin-
ship with Congregationalists, Presbyterians and the like, and another
party which considered the "Protestant" in its name a misnomer and
yearned for fellowship with Rome—or, if that were not possible, at
least with the Oriental Catholics. The extraordinary thing is not that
such diversities of view should exist but that, in spite of them, the
peace and progress of the church have been so little hindered.

In the first years after the Civil War, the conflict between high
church and low church was keen, as it was also at the same time in
England and had been for a generation. Different degrees of ritualism
produced friction and mutual criticism. The Oxford movement was
so recent and vivid a memory that incense and any elaboration of
vestments were viewed by some as sure signs of a Romanizing
tendency. Nevertheless, the high church practice on the whole was
gaining ground and the defections were few. Still more trouble arose
from differences as to the degree of fraternizing that might be permitted with churches having no episcopally ordained ministry. The
case of Doctor Tyng and his controversy with Bishop Horatio Potter
became classic. The rector was reprimanded by the bishop for having
preached in a Methodist church, and the incident aroused so much
acrimony that a split between the high and low church parties was
feared. A low churchman of the diocese of New York contributed the
following doggerel expressive of the opinion that the bishop was
straining at the gnat of fellowship with Protestants while swallowing
the camel of Romanism:

> I saw a bishop lying flat,
>   Choking in gasps of agony,
> Trying to swallow down a gnat
>   That in his gullet chanced to fly.
> The insect had, while on the wing,
> Seemed buzzing out Tyng Tyng Tyng Tyng.
>
> Again I looked. With mouth agap
> The bishop takes a stertorous nap,
> When lo! a camel staggers by
> Loaded with priestly panoply;
> Bales of vestments on his hump,
>   While here a crucifix appears,

A box of candles galled his rump,
  And smoking censers scorched his ears.

Before, behind, a savory crowd
  Of greasy monks, with alb and cope,
Intoned and chanted, crossed and bowed
  Like Father Agapius or the Pope.
The bishop slept; he took no note;
  The caravan marched down his throat.

*   *   *   *

Was't Rome I saw, or was it not her?
Or did I dream, dear Bishop Potter?

But the bishop did not swallow the camel, nor the camel the bishop. Elsewhere the rôles were reversed, and in Chicago, for example, at the Church of the Ascension, in 1883, the very high church rector had a sharp conflict with the low church Bishop McLaren. The spirit of caricature was not found on one side only. After the general convention of 1883, at Boston, the high church Dr. J. H. Hopkins reported that "the dying mule of Protestant fanaticism gave its last kick at Boston in its long war against ritualism."

The prestige of Phillips Brooks, who, though he stood aside from party wrangling, was clearly evangelical and liberal in his sympathies, was one of the forces which produced a temporary swing of the pendulum in the other direction. Within recent years the difference has received a new formulation. Now it is Anglo-Catholicism, rather than ritualism. The new term shows a deeper understanding of the real issue. The stress on the Catholic idea of the church and the practice of ancient Catholic ceremonies are apparently on the increase, and meanwhile two things have happened which have given a freer course to this tendency. One is that there has been such an adjustment of Episcopal Catholicism to the processes of modern scholarship that it requires no indiscriminate resistance to critical attitudes; the other, that it has been found, both by experience and by reason, that one may hold with the utmost strictness to the idea of a catholic church without being either logically or practically required to believe that the acceptance of the primacy of the Bishop of Rome is the criterion of catholicity.

The Protestant Episcopal Church has always had prestige and prop-

erty out of proportion to its members. At present it is growing in
numbers more rapidly than Protestantism as a whole, and much more
rapidly than the Roman Catholic Church in this country. Its administrative effectiveness was greatly increased by the organization of a
National Council in 1919, composed of twenty-four bishops, priests
and laymen and headed by the Presiding Bishop, who is thus practically an archbishop without the title. It points with pride to the fact
that nine Presidents of the United States have been Episcopalians.

The Disciples of Christ

Separating from the Baptists about 1830 on the issue of "restoring
primitive Christianity" in certain particulars which they considered
essential to the reunion of the church on the apostolic basis, the
Disciples of Christ grew rapidly in the Mississippi valley. By 1849,
they had an annual national convention, which was a mass meeting
without representation of the churches or authority over them, and a
missionary society, which, however, did little or nothing until many
years later. Their first effective organization was by states. Colleges
and papers came into existence, always without official control by the
churches, but promoting their interests none the less. The Disciples
escaped division in the Civil War, but during the years just before and
after it they were much disturbed by internal conflicts over the question as to what features of primitive Christianity ought to be restored.
Was it proper to use organs in public worship and to have missionary
societies, since the apostolic church had neither? The strict construc-
tionists on this point ultimately withdrew from all the organized work
of the main body, established their own colleges, read their own
papers, supported their own missionaries and evangelists without the
intervention of "unscriptural" societies. Since it was such common
enterprises, and not any general organization over the churches, which
had furnished the bond of union, the setting up of a distinct set of
enterprises constituted division. The census of 1906 recognized the
division by listing the anti-organ and anti-society group as "Churches
of Christ" and the others as "Disciples of Christ." Together they had,
in 1932, nearly two million members, three-fourths of whom belong to
the latter group, sometimes called (by comparison) the "progressives."

The main body of Disciples have ceased to bear any peculiar marks of their plea for the restoration of primitive Christianity. They practice immersion, refuse to set up creeds, observe the Lord's Supper weekly, and maintain the independence of the local congregation, because they believe these to have been the practices of the apostolic church and to be the only possible basis now upon which the church can unite—and union is their great objective. But because congregational independence and individual liberty of opinion are so firmly embedded in their habits of thought, they have developed tolerance for a wide range of opinions. Within their ranks and in full fellowship and good standing may be found some of the most liberal and some of the most conservative religious thinkers in America. A few liberal churches practice "open membership"—that is, the reception of unimmersed members—and a large percentage of the preachers and active laity have no objection to it except the fear that it would create another division.

The national convention was reorganized on a delegate basis in 1912, but the arrangement did not work and the convention again became a mass meeting. In 1919, all the missionary and benevolent societies were consolidated to form the United Christian Missionary Society. Discontent with the management of this society—with the alleged liberalism of some of its missionaries, and with what was considered the autocracy of so much consolidation in one "official" agency—led to the transfer of much support from it to a group of "independent agencies," under the stimulus of a very conservative religious paper. The Disciples have always been suspicious of anything approximating ecclesiastical control, but amenable to editorial influence. Considering that they are, on the average, rather less inclined to modernistic views of religion than some of the denominations with a richer cultural background, the fact that the most influential undenominational journal of liberal religious opinion, *The Christian Century*, developed out of a Disciples paper, is an evidence of the liberty of individual thought within the denominations. Liberal Disciples would also say that it illustrates the modern meaning of Alexander Campbell's avowed purpose to advance the unity of Christians by "making the doors of the church as wide as the gates of heaven."

Jewish Congregations

Among the German Jews who had come to the United States during the great migration before the Civil War were many of liberal sentiments. Out of this group grew the Reform movement, led by Rabbi Isaac M. Wise, who became the first president of the Hebrew Union College in Cincinnati. There was no national organization of synagogues until 1873, when the Union of American Hebrew Congregations was formed. The vast immigration from Russia and Poland during the last two decades of the nineteenth century and the first few years of the twentieth brought a great influx of orthodox Jews. In 1877, there were less than a quarter of a million Jews in the United States. Fifty years later their number was estimated at four million. This estimate has to do with race, not with religion; but enough of them are adherents of the Jewish faith to support something more than 3,000 congregations which are organized in three federations—Reform, Conservative and Orthodox.

Chapter XIII

ROMAN CATHOLICISM IN AMERICA

The growth of the Roman Catholic Church in numbers, wealth and prestige has been one of the most notable factors in the religious and social history of America since the Civil War. In 1865, the Catholic population of the United States was approximately three million, which was 9.65 per cent. of the total population. By 1900, it amounted to twelve million, or 15.78 per cent. of the whole; in 1920, approximately twenty million, or 18.76 per cent.; in 1930, about twenty-three million, according to the most generous figures, or practically the same per cent. The Protestant churches meanwhile had increased their total membership from about five million in 1860 to thirty-two million in 1930.

While the numerical increase of Roman Catholicism has been almost entirely due to immigration and while immigrants are usually poor at the time of their arrival and for at least a few years thereafter, the property holdings of the church have increased at an even more rapid rate than its numbers and more rapidly also than those of the Protestant churches.

The relation of Catholic growth to immigration has been the subject of several studies which have arrived at widely differing conclusions. One theory has been that the church has radically failed to hold the allegiance of the immigrants and their posterity. The Abbé Villeneuve in 1890 estimated that the number of Catholics in the United States would have been twenty million more than it was if Catholic immigrants and their descendents had kept the faith. In 1891, Mr. Cahensly, in a memorial to the Pope, estimated the loss at sixteen million. Twenty years later he revised his estimate and put the loss at ten million. Gerald Shaughnessy in *Has the Immigrant Kept the Faith?* (New York, 1925) argues rather convincingly that the losses have been no greater than "that defection of Catholics which ordinarily takes place among any population." The conversion of non-Catholics has not, to any considerable extent, affected the figures. Of the 883,000 converts during the century ending with 1920 (Shaughnessy's estimate) probably less than 300,000 are now living. The remainder of the twenty million Catholics now in the United States are made up of Catholic immigrants and their descendents, plus the descendents of the 30,000 Catholics who were in the country in 1790, plus the Catholic inhabitants of the territory that has been annexed. Mixed marriages have been a factor the net result of which would be difficult to determine. While the church's requirement that all children of such marriages shall be brought up in the Roman Catholic faith ought to make mixed marriages a means of more rapid increase, Catholic authorities universally recognize that this is not so.

The net result of any careful study of the available data must be the conclusion that, while the Roman Catholic Church has made rapid gains, the statistical curve affords no ground whatever for either the hope or the fear that it will take the country. The most thorough recent study of this question will be found in *Will America Become Catholic?* by John F. Moore (New York, 1931). He says: "In numbers, in cohesion, in educational activity and in many avenues of philanthropy and benevolence, it has become the outstanding single Christian denomination. But, while stating this clearly, I must add that, according to my reading of the evidence, the Roman church has not yet achieved increases which, regarded progressively, would 'make America Catholic' within any foreseeable period of the future" (p. 60).

It is true, indeed, that the most important deflection of American life from the Puritan pattern which had prevailed in New England and to some extent elsewhere was due to the increasing flood of immigration and the consequent growth of the Roman Catholic Church. Many Protestants and many persons of no religion whatever have viewed the growth of Catholicism since 1865 with alarm, though the organized political expression of this antagonism has never again reached the magnitude or the intensity that it had in the 'forties and 'fifties. But, on the other hand, there were others, especially those who were interested in a plentiful supply of cheap and docile labor, who not only welcomed and promoted immigration but considered the Roman Catholic Church a valuable instrument of social control.

Immigration created problems for Catholicism while vastly augmenting its numbers and strength. The society of St. Raphael, in 1891, appealed to Pope Leo XIII to provide for the various immigrant groups priests and bishops of their own nationality, as well as to approve a program of separate parochial schools for each nationality whose curriculum should "always include instruction in the national language." This would not only have encouraged the perpetuation of unassimilated alien groups but would have amounted to the establishment of a series of relatively independent national churches. The Pope rejected these suggestions as "neither opportune nor necessary" (Mode: *Source Book,* p. 481). But even after the failure of this Cahensly movement to secure the organization of the foreign language churches into separate administrative units, the maintenance of separate racial and linguistic congregations continued to be a definite policy of the church.

It is not safe to generalize too hastily about the effect of immigration upon either the immigrants themselves or the total religious condition of the country to which they come. The main questions are, of course, whether the immigrants keep the faith with undiminished devotion, whether children keep it, and whether, if so, their religion tends to unify them with the country of their new allegiance or to maintain their old nationalistic and racial qualities and loyalties. Shaughnessy's claim that the church has suffered no very serious loss of its immigrant members can be accepted only if one accepts also his criterion of membership by which no one is accounted to have left the church if he maintains a general attitude of friendliness, accepts its sacraments at the high moments of life and death, and attends its services a few times in a lifetime. The immigrant may take one or another of four attitudes: he may hold his old religion unchanged; or hold it with modifications; or adopt another; or have none. Shaughnessy suggests five possible tests of a Catholic: attend mass regularly and contribute (too strict); attend mass frequently and take the sacrament at least once a year (too strict); attend neither regularly nor frequently but take the sacrament once a year and bring up his children in the faith (too strict); neglect all requirements except baptism, religious marriage and the calling of a priest in the hour of death (Shaughnessy's own criterion); practically abandon the church but summon a priest at death (too loose).

Moving to a new country affects the immigrant's relation to the church far more than it does the number of those who maintain some sort of connection with it. A study of a large number of individual cases, chosen at random, shows two opposite tendencies. Some, finding themselves in a new and strange environment, cling to their church more strongly than before because it furnishes the only bond with their old life. For these, the parish is even more important in their lives than it was back home, because it alone represents familiar community and national interests in an alien environment. This is quite commonly the case among Polish immigrants. With others, the assimilation of the spirit of the new country as they understand it and the pressure of new interests either reduces their connection with the old church to a merely nominal allegiance or destroys it entirely. It is not alone in the Catholic Church that these influences are felt. Perhaps it would be fair to say that a change of environment strengthens whatever tendency was already strongest in the individual's relation to his church. If he was lax in his devotion, he becomes more lax; if ardent, more ardent. The same thing holds true with reference to migration within a country.

The Catholic Church has, for example, lost heavily among the Italians. The census of 1916 shows 3,300,000 persons of Italian birth or parentage in the United States, but only 1,936,000 adherents, in even the loosest sense, of churches in which the Italian language is used even part of the time. The number who attend churches which use only English would certainly be more than balanced by the number whose membership in Italian churches is purely nominal. The loss in this racial group must be nearly or quite 50 per cent.

The question as to whether the Roman Catholic Church has undergone modification in its American environment is one that can be answered in two ways according as one has in mind, on the one hand, the basic doctrines and principles of the church itself as maintained by the hierarchy which constitutes the *ecclesia docens* and set forth in those books which bear the *imprimatur* and *nihil obstat* of ecclesiastical authority; or, on the other hand, the actual attitudes and mental processes of the lay members and many of the clergy. Roman Catholicism as a system of faith and as an organized institution for the control of whatever the church considers as pertaining to religious belief and moral conduct has not been Americanized. The minds of millions of Catholics undoubtedly have been. Tendencies toward liberalization were manifest in the work of Father Hecker, in the program of modernism and in the attitudes of such high ecclesiastics as Cardinal Gibbons and Archbishop Ireland.

Father Hecker, founder of the Paulist order and editor of the *Catholic World*, became a convert to Catholicism after being in turn a Lutheran, a Methodist and a worker with a radical working-men's party and the society of transcendental socialists at Brook Farm. He united a deep and ascetic piety with ardent social enthusiasm, and in 1868 he was expressing the hope that the majority of the people of America would be Roman Catholics by 1900. But his avowed purpose was not only to "Catholicize America" but also to "Americanize Catholicism"—not by any diminution of papal authority but by taking the emphasis from obedience and the passive virtues and the esthetic aspects of religion and putting it upon reason and self-reliance and the independent action of the individual. In the biography of Father Hecker, published after his death in 1888, his distinctive ideas attained wider publicity than they had in his life. Archbishop Ireland, in the preface to that biography, called him the ideal American priest and reinforced his appeal for a modern type of churchmanship. "Each century calls for its type of Christian perfection. At one time it was martyrdom; at another, the humility of the cloister. Today we need the Christian gentleman and the Christian citizen. . . . His [Hecker's] was the profound conviction that in the present age, at any rate, the order of the day should be individual action—every man doing his fair duty and waiting for no one else to prompt him." This and other liberal sentiments in regard to the Americanization of Catholicism were condemned by Pope Leo XIII in his letter of January 22, 1899, to Cardinal Gibbons "Concerning new opinions."

Father Hecker's temperate propaganda for the conversion of Prot-estants was so moderate in its tone, so skilfully couched in the vocabu-

lary of contemporary thought, and so sympathetic toward the temper
and the aspirations of the American people that a writer in the
Independent who had attended one of the missions of this "seven-
footer with a long divided beard" described his method as "Jesuitical."
But there is no ground for doubting his sincerity. After his death,
and when a visible difference—not to say an open controversy—had
arisen between the conservative party of no compromise and those
Catholics who were more hospitable to modern ideas and more in
sympathy with the American mind, there came to be a group of
distinguished prelates who were generally recognized as representing
this more liberal attitude: Cardinal Gibbons, Archbishop Ireland, Archbishop Keane, rector of the Catholic University at Washington, Mgr.
O'Connell, former rector of the American College at Rome, Mgr.
O'Gorman, bishop of Sioux Falls, S. D., and Archbishop Kain of
St. Louis. These men fraternized with non-Catholics more than any
members of the Roman Catholic hierarchy ever had before, or ever
have since. Cardinal Gibbons opened with prayer the Parliament of
Religions at Chicago in 1893. Archbishop Keane read papers before
Protestant assemblies, and expressed ideas very like Hecker's at the
International Scientific Congress of Catholics at Brussels in 1894. Mgr.
O'Connell advanced similar views at the Catholic Scientific Congress
at Freiburg in 1897. Cardinal Gibbons and Archbishop Ireland gained
an unprecedented degree of popularity and prestige among non-
Catholics. Few, indeed, were the Protestants who did not yield the
tribute of their admiration to these towering personalities and feel
that they could make common cause in behalf of a better America
with a Catholicism dominated by their spirit. But in the course of the
war on "Americanism," it became evident that this spirit was not to
be allowed to become dominant. The Vatican gave to Abbé Maignan's
criticism of Hecker the *imprimatur* which the Archbishop of Paris
had refused. The Jesuit, Delattre, ended his critique of *An American
Catholicism* with the sentiment, "Christianity is docility." Pope Leo
XIII, with a clear reference to Cardinal Gibbons, forbade Catholics to
take part in mixed congresses. The era of fraternizing was, for the
time at least, at an end.

The movement known as Catholic modernism began specifically
with the adoption by certain French theologians of methods of Biblical

study which had originated principally among non-Catholic German scholars. The war upon it became serious with the encyclical *Providentissimus Deus*, in 1893, and came to its climax in the encyclical *Pascendi* of Pius X, in 1907. After that, it is fair to say that modernism was dead. Along with its assumption of the right of scholarship to arrive at its own conclusions in regard to Biblical questions, modernism in general had encouraged a somewhat free attitude toward the authority of the church. It was not a question of denying any of the dogmas of the church—for that was something which no modernist of standing ever did—but of lacking docility toward its discipline. "They disdain all authority and brook no restraint," said Pius X. "Relying upon a false conscience, they attempt to ascribe to a love of truth that which is in reality the result of pride and obstinacy. . . . With consummate audacity they criticize the church." "Some of you," he says, quoting Gregory IX, "puffed up like bladders with the spirit of vanity, strive by profane novelties to cross the boundaries fixed by the Fathers." The way to exterminate this "growing band of rebels" is, in the words of the encyclical *Pieni l'animo*, of 1906, to "demand strictly from priests and clerics that *obedience* which, while absolutely obligatory upon all the faithful, constitutes for priests a principal part of their duty," and to exclude absolutely "those who show inclinations toward disobedience to discipline, and its parent, intellectual pride." Everything is to be condemned which "points toward new orientation of Christian life, new directions for the Church, new aspirations of the modern soul, a new social vocation for the clergy, a new Christian civilization, and other like things."

While this death-sentence of modernism in all its forms and with all its implications was perhaps directly called forth by tendencies in France and Italy, it can scarcely have been without direct reference also to conditions in the United States. At any rate, it was addressed to the whole church, and it was received without protest or opposition. Thereafter, modernism in any form among the Roman Catholic clergy in the United States did not exist. Mr. Michael Williams, the eminent editor of the Catholic *Commonweal*, writing in 1928, says: "The Catholic Church in the United States knows that the Modern Mind is simply the sum of all the heresies against which the Catholic Church has struggled elsewhere, more or less successfully, since its beginning." This being true, whatever differences there may be, if any, between Roman Catholicism in the United States now and Roman Catholicism in other places and at other times, are not due to changes in the church but to changes in the attitude of its lay members toward it and toward the civil, secular and non-Catholic society which constitutes their environment. Upon that point it is easy for any one to gather his own impressions and form his own opinions, but difficult for any one to collect adequate data to serve as the basis for a generalization deserving to be classed as knowledge.

Much of the history of the Roman Catholic Church in America can be seen by surveying the proceedings of the three Plenary Councils of Baltimore. (See Peter Guilday: *A History of the Councils of Baltimore*, New York, 1932.) The first of these, which was the first national Catholic council in the United States, was held in 1852. At that time it was expected that the council would sound its note either for slavery or for abolition, says Guilday. "There was no more unity in Catholic ranks on the slave question than in those of the prominent Christian churches at that time." But no word was spoken on the subject. When it was seen that silence was to be the policy (quoting Guilday): "Catholics realized more acutely than ever the real meaning of the church's place in American life, and non-Catholics appreciated the fact that here was a body of American spiritual leaders who meant to bring to the disturbed condition of the times the one asset the country needed: peace and calm. . . . By their silence our prelates divorced this burning political question from Church affairs and gave to the deliberations of the council that unity of Catholic outlook which was basic to the legislation that was passed." As a measure of self-protection, this was doubtless wise, but it may be questioned whether those non-Catholics who viewed the slavery issue as a moral as well as a political question were so appreciative of the church's detachment from it.

The Second Plenary Council of Baltimore, meeting in 1866 when the war was over and slavery was no more, issued a pastoral letter which said: "We could have wished that, in accordance with the action of the Catholic Church in past ages in regard to the serfs of Europe, a more gradual system of emancipation could have been adopted." But the Catholic Church in America had carefully guarded

its unity by refraining from any word or action favoring emancipation by any system, gradual or other, until the struggle was over.

Bishop Spaulding, of Baltimore, ranking member of the American
hierarchy, was greatly stirred by the splendor of the vestments in the
procession at the opening of this council, and felt that the throng of
witnesses must be impressed by the visible strength and glory of the
church which here manifested a unity that had survived the war with
increased prestige. "The ship of state," he wrote, "had been wrenched
from its moorings. . . . The sects had been torn asunder and lay in
disorder and confusion. . . . All were ready to applaud any power
that had been able to live through that frightful struggle unhurt and
unharmed; and when the Catholic Church walked forth before the
eyes of the nation, clothed in the panoply of undiminished strength
and of unbroken unity, thousands who but a while ago would have
witnessed the manifestation of her power with jealous concern, now
hailed it with delight as a harbinger of good omen" (*Life of Bishop
Spaulding*, p. 305). On this ground, popular and universal acclaim
ought perhaps to have been given also to the Masonic order—which
the Council condemned, along with the Odd Fellows, the Sons of
Temperance and other secret societies—for it also had gone through
the war undivided.

At the Council of 1866, "mixed marriages were more strongly
condemned and marriage before non-Catholic ministers was strongly
condemned." The words, in part, were: "Matrimonia Catholicorum
cum haereticis semper detestata est ecclesia." The decrees of this council, consisting chiefly of a recodification of the doctrines and laws of
the church, filled 526 quarto pages. It was noted with satisfaction that
the Catholic population (3,842,000, according to Shea), the number of
priests and the number of churches had all just about doubled in the
fourteen years between the first and the second Councils of Baltimore.

By the time of the Third Baltimore Council, eighteen years later,
the Catholic population had again about doubled, though the figures
are in dispute among Catholic authorities. There had been little growth
in the South, but much in the eastern cities by immigration, and much
in the rapidly growing West and Northwest chiefly through immigration but partly also through the zeal of the orders devoted especially
to missions, among which Father Hecker's Paulists were the most

conspicuous. This Council of 1884 decided to found the Catholic University, at Washington, which was opened in 1889, and ordered priests to refrain from all political discussion in the pulpit or in public.

The school question has perhaps been the occasion for as much mutual opposition and ill will between Catholics and non-Catholics as any other item in the church's program. Again it must be remembered that the purely secular American public school system is the result of the modification of an earlier plan of education in which religion played an important part. As the prevailing religion of all of the states was Protestant—Roman Catholics forming only 1 per cent. of the total population at the beginning of the Federal period—the schools were naturally Protestant. Several provincial councils of Baltimore were held before the first of the plenary councils. The first provincial council, in 1829, made a general declaration in favor of schools under Catholic auspices. The next two, in 1833 and 1837, were silent on the subject. The council of 1840 protested against sectarian (i.e., Protestant) teaching in public schools, but said nothing about parochial schools. This was the year in which Gov. William H. Seward of New York recommended foreign-language Catholic schools supported by taxation for the children of immigrants, and it was in the next year that Bishop Hughes organized a Catholic party which nominated its own candidates for the legislature on the platform of "public money for the support of Catholic schools." However, the next three provincial councils, those of 1843, 1846, and 1849, were again silent on the subject, though this was the time of the hottest debate on the public school question and the time when the Presbyterians were starting their parochial school system. The First Plenary Council of Baltimore, 1852, made a general statement encouraging Catholic education but proposed nothing definite. The Second was more emphatic about it. Before the Third, the Congregation of the Propaganda in Rome had issued an Instruction, in 1875, forbidding the attendance of Catholic children at schools which jeopardized their faith. The Third Plenary Council of Baltimore, 1884, was thoroughly aroused on the subject and it is from this time that the development of parochial schools on a large scale begins. Almost one-fourth of its decrees were devoted to education. The clergy were commanded to establish schools, and the laity to patronize them. "We not only exhort

Catholic parents with paternal affection, but we *command* them with all the authority in our power, to procure a truly Christian education for their dear offspring; to defend them from the dangers of secular education during the whole term of their infancy and childhood; and finally to send them to Catholic and especially parochial schools" (Guilday, p. 238). It was ordered that a school be built beside every parish church within two years.

The campaign to secure public funds for the support of the Catholic schools had gone on rather steadily during the 'seventies and it continued intermittently thereafter. A petition to that effect was presented to the Buffalo city council in 1875 and rejected by it. Bishop Purcell, of Cincinnati, in 1876, issued an address "to the people of the United States" demanding for Catholics exemption from taxation for the support of non-Catholic schools. Plans which amounted to the recognition of Catholic schools as a part of the public school system and their support by public funds have from time to time been locally operative. Such were the Poughkeepsie, New York, plan which was in effect from 1873 until 1891, and the Faribault, Minnesota, plan, fostered by Archbishop Ireland, which was in operation in that place for two years beginning with 1891 and a few years longer in other towns in Minnesota which had large Catholic majorities. These compromises all proved unsatisfactory. Protestant sentiment continued to disapprove the support of sectarian schools by public money, while Catholic sentiment found that the arrangement conceded too much to the public school system. The latter feeling was exhibited and intensified by the "Bouquillon controversy," which arose in 1891 after the publication of a pamphlet in which Father Bouquillon, a professor in the Catholic University, argued that the state has a right to educate its citizens, to set minimum academic requirements for all schools, and to inspect all schools as to hygiene and public morals. These apparently harmless propositions, according to a Catholic authority, "precipitated an educational controversy among Catholics which was without parallel in American Catholic history. . . . Bouquillon's views were greeted with a storm of criticism which clearly showed that they were out of harmony with the views held by most American Catholics" (Burns: *Growth and Development of the Catholic School System*).

The shift of opinion, however, has been in the direction of Bouquillon's more liberal view. The American Federation of Catholic Societies, meeting at Buffalo in 1906, declared that the secular teaching in Catholic schools, but not the religious instruction, should be paid for out of public school funds, and that parochial schools should be subject to state inspection with reference to secular subjects. A recent comprehensive statement of Catholic opinion says that Catholics favor a public school system which will include denominational schools for diverse denominations (McClorey: *The Church and the Republic*, New York, 1927).

On the other side, there have been occasional secular attacks on the whole system of parochial schools even when voluntarily supported. The Oregon law aimed to put them out of business, together with private schools of every sort, by requiring all children to attend the public schools. This law was declared unconstitutional by the supreme court, and most Protestants approved the decision.

The story of the Catholic contribution to the struggle for the rights of labor and the betterment of the condition of the poor would begin with Father Hecker and come down to Father Cox of our own day. Not unrelated to it would be the record of the services of Catholic sisters as nurses in the Civil War—together with members of at least one Episcopal sisterhood and many Protestant women who belonged to no order—and the continuing and extensive work of Catholic charities. It would include chapters from the life of Cardinal Gibbons, and it would have to be expanded into a wide stream of narrative to cover the work of the National Catholic Welfare Council, organized in 1919, which is now the most potent Catholic organization for the promotion of social work as well as the interests of the church.

If only one episode can be selected, it may properly be that of Cardinal Gibbons and his defense of the Knights of Labor. He tells of it in his *Retrospect of Fifty Years*, published in 1916, when he was the last survivor of the Vatican Council. "Those who live in these days," he says, "cannot conceive the state of society in the 'seventies and 'eighties. The money of the country was not only concentrated into the hands of a very few people, but by means of this money this very small oligarchy was put in the position of getting complete control of our free institutions." Several organizations in the interest of labor arose during Cleveland's first administration, and they were generally attacked—not without some ground—as destructive and revolutionary. "And indeed, the oppression of the wealthy was driving the poor into excesses of which the anarchist riots in Chicago were but one example." Many ecclesiastics were alarmed by the organization of labor. The Canadian bishops obtained from the Holy See a condemnation of the Knights of Labor for Canada. But Cardinal Gibbons was more "alarmed at the prospect of the church being presented as the friend of the powerful rich and the enemy of the helpless poor." He consulted with President Cleveland, and had Mr. Powderly, president of the Knights of Labor, appear before a meeting of the twelve archbishops to explain the "secrecy" of the order. He explained it satisfactorily, and the archbishops voted, ten to two, not to condemn the order and to try to keep the Pope from condemning it. When Archbishop Gibbons went to Rome, in 1887, to receive the red hat, he presented to the Cardinal Prefect of the Congregation of Propaganda a statement on behalf of the Knights of Labor, whose president, he said, "declared that he is a devoted Roman Catholic; that he practices his religion faithfully and receives the sacraments regularly; that he belongs to no Masonic society or other association condemned by the church; that he knows nothing in the organization of the Knights of Labor contrary to the laws of the church; that, with filial submission, he begs the pastors of the church to examine their constitution and laws and to point out anything they may find objectionable, promising to see to its correction" (p. 193).

It was a good brief for the Knights of Labor, and its warning against the danger to the church if it "seeks to crush by an ecclesiastical condemnation an organization which represents 500,000 votes and which commands so much respect" may have had weight in determining the attitude of the Vatican when, four years later, in 1891, Pope Leo XIII issued his great "labor encyclical," *Rerum Novarum.* If the president of the Knights of Labor had not been a Roman Catholic, the result might have been different.

It was not without justice that a bronze statue of Cardinal Gibbons was unveiled in Washington, D. C., on August 14, 1932, on the semicentennial of the Knights of Columbus. The date was also almost exactly one-third of a century after the Pope's rebuke of Cardinal conspicuous. This Council of 1884 decided to found the Catholic University, at Washington, which was opened in 1889, and ordered priests to refrain from all political discussion in the pulpit or in public.

The school question has perhaps been the occasion for as much mutual opposition and ill will between Catholics and non-Catholics as any other item in the church's program. Again it must be remembered that the purely secular American public school system is the result of the modification of an earlier plan of education in which religion played an important part. As the prevailing religion of all of the states was Protestant—Roman Catholics forming only 1 per cent. of the total population at the beginning of the Federal period—the schools were naturally Protestant. Several provincial councils of Baltimore were held before the first of the plenary councils. The first provincial council, in 1829, made a general declaration in favor of schools under Catholic auspices. The next two, in 1833 and 1837, were silent on the subject. The council of 1840 protested against sectarian (*i.e.*, Protestant) teaching in public schools, but said nothing about parochial schools. This was the year in which Gov. William H. Seward of New York recommended foreign-language Catholic schools supported by taxation for the children of immigrants, and it was in the next year that Bishop Hughes organized a Catholic party which nominated its own candidates for the legislature on the platform of "public money for the support of Catholic schools." However, the next three provincial councils, those of 1843, 1846, and 1849, were again silent on the subject, though this was the time of the hottest debate on the public school question and the time when the Presbyterians were starting their parochial school system. The First Plenary Council of Baltimore, 1852, made a general statement encouraging Catholic education but proposed nothing definite. The Second was more emphatic about it. Before the Third, the Congregation of the Propaganda in Rome had issued an Instruction, in 1875, forbidding the attendance of Catholic children at schools which jeopardized their faith. The Third Plenary Council of Baltimore, 1884, was thoroughly aroused on the subject and it is from this time that the development of parochial schools on a large scale begins. Almost one-fourth of its decrees were devoted to education. The clergy were commanded to establish schools, and the laity to patronize them. "We not only exhort

Catholic parents with paternal affection, but we *command* them with
all the authority in our power, to procure a truly Christian education
for their dear offspring; to defend them from the dangers of secular
education during the whole term of their infancy and childhood; and
finally to send them to Catholic and especially parochial schools"
(Guilday, p. 238). It was ordered that a school be built beside every
parish church within two years.

The campaign to secure public funds for the support of the Catholic
schools had gone on rather steadily during the 'seventies and it continued intermittently thereafter. A petition to that effect was presented
to the Buffalo city council in 1875 and rejected by it. Bishop Purcell,
of Cincinnati, in 1876, issued an address "to the people of the United
States" demanding for Catholics exemption from taxation for the
support of non-Catholic schools. Plans which amounted to the recognition of Catholic schools as a part of the public school system and
their support by public funds have from time to time been locally
operative. Such were the Poughkeepsie, New York, plan which was in
effect from 1873 until 1891, and the Faribault, Minnesota, plan, fostered by Archbishop Ireland, which was in operation in that place for
two years beginning with 1891 and a few years longer in other towns
in Minnesota which had large Catholic majorities. These compromises
all proved unsatisfactory. Protestant sentiment continued to disapprove
the support of sectarian schools by public money, while Catholic sentiment found that the arrangement conceded too much to the public
school system. The latter feeling was exhibited and intensified by the
"Bouquillon controversy," which arose in 1891 after the publication
of a pamphlet in which Father Bouquillon, a professor in the Catholic
University, argued that the state has a right to educate its citizens,
to set minimum academic requirements for all schools, and to inspect
all schools as to hygiene and public morals. These apparently harmless propositions, according to a Catholic authority, "precipitated an
educational controversy among Catholics which was without parallel
in American Catholic history. . . . Bouquillon's views were greeted
with a storm of criticism which clearly showed that they were out of
harmony with the views held by most American Catholics" (Burns:
Growth and Development of the Catholic School System).

The shift of opinion, however, has been in the direction of Bou-

illon's more liberal view. The American Federation of Catholic
cieties, meeting at Buffalo in 1906, declared that the secular teaching
 Catholic schools, but not the religious instruction, should be paid
· out of public school funds, and that parochial schools should be
bject to state inspection with reference to secular subjects. A recent
mprehensive statement of Catholic opinion says that Catholics favor
ublic school system which will include denominational schools for
verse denominations (McClorey: *The Church and the Republic,*
:w York, 1927).

On the other side, there have been occasional secular attacks on the
1ole system of parochial schools even when voluntarily supported.
1e Oregon law aimed to put them out of business, together with
ivate schools of every sort, by requiring all children to attend the
iblic schools. This law was declared unconstitutional by the supreme
urt, and most Protestants approved the decision.

The story of the Catholic contribution to the struggle for the rights
 labor and the betterment of the condition of the poor would begin
th Father Hecker and come down to Father Cox of our own day.
ot unrelated to it would be the record of the services of Catholic
ters as nurses in the Civil War—together with members of at least
e Episcopal sisterhood and many Protestant women who belonged
 no order—and the continuing and extensive work of Catholic
arities. It would include chapters from the life of Cardinal Gibbons,
d it would have to be expanded into a wide stream of narrative
cover the work of the National Catholic Welfare Council, organized
 1919, which is now the most potent Catholic organization for the
motion of social work as well as the interests of the church.

If only one episode can be selected, it may properly be that of
rdinal Gibbons and his defense of the Knights of Labor. He tells
it in his *Retrospect of Fifty Years,* published in 1916, when he was
: last survivor of the Vatican Council. "Those who live in these
/s," he says, "cannot conceive the state of society in the 'seventies
1 'eighties. The money of the country was not only concentrated
o the hands of a very few people, but by means of this money this
y small oligarchy was put in the position of getting complete con-
l of our free institutions." Several organizations in the interest of
or arose during Cleveland's first administration, and they were

generally attacked—not without some ground—as destructive and revolutionary. "And indeed, the oppression of the wealthy was driving the poor into excesses of which the anarchist riots in Chicago were but one example." Many ecclesiastics were alarmed by the organization of labor. The Canadian bishops obtained from the Holy See a condemnation of the Knights of Labor for Canada. But Cardinal Gibbons was more "alarmed at the prospect of the church being presented as the friend of the powerful rich and the enemy of the helpless poor." He consulted with President Cleveland, and had Mr. Powderly, president of the Knights of Labor, appear before a meeting of the twelve archbishops to explain the "secrecy" of the order. He explained it satisfactorily, and the archbishops voted, ten to two, not to condemn the order and to try to keep the Pope from condemning it. When Archbishop Gibbons went to Rome, in 1887, to receive the red hat, he presented to the Cardinal Prefect of the Congregation of Propaganda a statement on behalf of the Knights of Labor, whose president, he said, "declared that he is a devoted Roman Catholic; that he practices his religion faithfully and receives the sacraments regularly; that he belongs to no Masonic society or other association condemned by the church; that he knows nothing in the organization of the Knights of Labor contrary to the laws of the church; that, with filial submission, he begs the pastors of the church to examine their constitution and laws and to point out anything they may find objectionable, promising to see to its correction" (p. 193).

It was a good brief for the Knights of Labor, and its warning against the danger to the church if it "seeks to crush by an ecclesiastical condemnation an organization which represents 500,000 votes and which commands so much respect" may have had weight in determining the attitude of the Vatican when, four years later, in 1891, Pope Leo XIII issued his great "labor encyclical," *Rerum Novarum.* If the president of the Knights of Labor had not been a Roman Catholic, the result might have been different.

It was not without justice that a bronze statue of Cardinal Gibbons was unveiled in Washington, D. C., on August 14, 1932, on the semicentennial of the Knights of Columbus. The date was also almost exactly one-third of a century after the Pope's rebuke of Cardinal

Gibbons for attending mixed congresses and the papal letter condemning "Americanism."

The religious orders are an immensely important factor in the ecclesiastical organization. Without them the whole program of educational and charitable work would be impossible. They furnish the private soldiers in the army of the church, the mass of laborers who do its educational and benevolent work. Serving without pay, subject to the rigid control of their superiors, bound by irrevocable vows which make it impossible to withdraw without the utmost difficulty, and almost totally cut off from normal domestic relations and from all social ties apart from their orders and their work, they constitute a wonderfully disciplined and devoted and inexpensive force for carrying on the enterprises of the church. Sixty-nine orders for men and 180 orders for women are represented in the United States. Of the men's orders, some are devoted largely to nursing, others to teaching, still others to conducting missions and retreats. There are 3,537 Jesuits in the United States, 1,585 of whom are priests, 1,612 "scholastics" and 434 lay brothers. The membership of the women's orders numbers in the neighborhood of 75,000. When one considers that there are more than 1,000 Catholic hospitals, orphanages and homes for the aged, chiefly "manned" by women of the religious orders, and over 700 academies for girls, staffed entirely by them, and parochial schools in 7,000 parishes with more than 2,000,000 pupils, nearly all taught by "religious," the number does not seem disproportionate to the work. Of completely cloistered nuns, there are very few. In general, the monastic life of both men and women is as far removed from pious indolence as one could well imagine.

The National Catholic Welfare Council, 1919, grew out of a congress of twenty-seven Catholic organizations, held in Washington in 1917, which had led first to the National Catholic War Council. In 1921, the Archbishop of San Francisco, reporting for the Welfare Council, said: "In eight months we have coördinated and united the Catholic power of this country. We feel ourselves powerful because our union has become visible. All our Catholic organizations report an increase of energy and do not doubt that, thanks to the N. C. W. C., we can bring Catholic coöperation to its apogee." It has departments, each presided over by a bishop, on education, legislation, social action, lay organizations, and the press, and an executive department which "keeps itself in direct contact with the government, to which it makes known the Catholic point of view on legislation such as the prohibition bill, the tariff, and the classification of religious objects" (Bressières: *L'Union Catholique*, Paris, 1924, p. 194). The National Council of Catholic Men "has several million members. It has already led several campaigns, notably against the encroachment of the state in the field of education" (Bressières, p. 195).

The Knights of Columbus, organized in 1882, have taken on new vigor since the war, not only in their original activity of supporting Catholic education and in providing for Catholic young men such facilities as the Y. M. C. A. has made familiar and popular, but in directly combating the influence of the Y. M. C. A. in certain European countries, notably in Italy.

The growth of the numbers and influence of the Roman Catholic Church has occasioned in many non-Catholic minds an alarm which has found expression in various organizations and which has often been capitalized for political or commercial purposes. Fairly to evaluate these movements would require a study not merely of the facts regarding their activities but also of the Roman Catholic practices and attitudes against which they protested. It is impossible in this book to enter that highly controversial field, but a brief summary of the anti-Catholic movements may be given.

The Civil War brought to an end the Know Nothing Party which had been, in the days of its greatest strength, much more a refuge for those who wished to believe that slavery was a minor issue than a crystallization of anti-Catholic sentiment. After the war, *Fifty Years in the Church of Rome,* by Father C. P. Chiniquy, an ex-priest, carried on the tradition of lurid anti-Catholic literature which had been established by "Maria Monk," whose book, published in 1835, had been followed by the colorful revelations, neither very creditable nor very credible, of the numerous company of ex-nuns, ex-monks and "escaped" this and that which enlivened the course of the "native American" movements in the 'forties and 'fifties.

The "A. P. A." was the first of the modern anti-Roman organizations. Founded as the American Patriotic Association, at Clinton, Iowa, in 1887, by 1893 it had 70,000 members in twenty states. The arrival of Mgr. Satolli in Washington in the latter year as the first apostolic delegate to the church in the United States (but popularly supposed to be a diplomatic representative from the Vatican to the American government) furnished a talking-point for its promoters. The political method of the A. P. A. was to try to control the primaries, and its ritual of initiation required an oath not to vote for a Catholic under any circumstances and not to employ a Catholic if a Protestant was available. In 1894, it had seven weekly papers. It opposed the nomination of McKinley in 1896 on the ground of some rumor that, though a Methodist, he was under Catholic influence. But Mark Hanna brought it into line by persuading some leading members that this rumor was without foundation and employing them (on generous terms) to travel through the Mississippi valley states, visiting the lodges and converting their brethren. It was not nationally important after 1900, though it retained enough vitality to take a part in the campaign of 1912.

There was a conspicuous burst of Roman Catholic energy in 1908 and the years immediately thereafter. The diocese of Baltimore celebrated its centennial. The United States was taken from the jurisdiction of the Congregation of the Propaganda and was no longer treated as missionary territory. The first American Catholic missionary congress was held in Chicago in November, 1908. The jubilee of Cardinal Gibbons was celebrated with acclaim. Two new American cardinals were appointed. A eucharistic congress was held in Montreal. The Knights of Columbus took on new life in 1914. All of these events increased Catholic morale. Talk of "making America Catholic" became more frequent and more confident. With the large increase in the number of Catholics, the daily press, naturally hesitant about offending either subscribers or advertisers belonging to a group so large and so cohesive, became much more deferential in its treatment of the Roman Catholic Church.

The "Guardians of Liberty," organized in 1911, were headed by General Nelson A. Miles. Their principal periodical, *The Menace*, published at Aurora, Missouri, was reported to have 1,400,000 subscribers in 1914. An effort was made to have its mailing privilege cancelled, but a trial in a Federal court on the charge of sending obscene matter through the mails ended in an acquittal. At the same time there was almost an epidemic of anti-Catholic periodicals. A commission appointed by the Knights of Columbus to investigate propaganda hostile to the church found sixty-one such papers. By 1917, all except two or three of these had disappeared.

If the war wiped out this swarm of ephemeral scare-sheets, the years immediately after it brought the most successful of all the anti-Catholic movements, the Ku Klux Klan. Organized in 1915, it had no great growth until after the Armistice. It found a fertile field in the general alarmist temper of the time, of which the anti-red hysteria of 1920 was one symptom. Simmons, the organizer, and Clarke, the professional promoter, who got eight dollars out of every ten-dollar initiation fee, were out in 1922, succeeded in the place of supreme power by Hiram W. Evans as Imperial Wizard—a Disciple, a Mason and a dentist, "the most average man in America," by his own estimate. The membership was estimated at 4,500,000 in 1924. It still included Jews, Negroes and Catholics as the objects of its antipathy, but its methods became somewhat less violent and crude. As a matter of fact, the Protestant churches suffered a great deal more from its domineering and divisive tactics than the Roman Catholic Church did from its direct attacks. There was some prospect that the Klan would be the chief political issue in the campaign of 1924. It narrowly escaped denunciation by name in the Republican convention, and it was the hot spot in the Democratic convention where a resolution specifically repudiating it failed by only three votes and probably affected the result of the McAdoo-Smith rivalry for the nomination.

The part played by anti-Catholic sentiment in the presidential campaign of 1928 cannot be adequately discussed within the space here available. The following facts are clear: that there was a certain amount of violent opposition to the Catholic candidate quite in the worst tradition of the A. P. A. and the Ku Klux Klan; that the Roman Catholic Church, while loudly proclaiming that religion should not be allowed to enter into the election and while restraining its pulpit from partisan utterances, marshaled its press and all the less conspicuous agencies at its command in support of the Catholic candidate; that many Protestants and persons of no religion accepted the term "bigot" as a true characterization of all who took a candidate's religious affiliation into account, and, not desiring to fall under the curse as bigots, were the more inclined to support the Catholic candidate in order to prove their liberality; that many, who did not feel that any candidate should be voted for or against solely on account of his religion, nevertheless considered that the electorate has a right to take into account a candidate's whole range of organizational connections as forming part of the picture of his personality and probable course of action. It is impossible to give an accurate estimate of the relative proportions of these forces and the actual weight which the religious issue had in determining the result of the election. My own judgment is that it worked to the disadvantage of the Catholic candidate but did not turn the scale against him.

Chapter XIV

PROTESTANT UNITY AND THE FEDERAL COUNCIL

The three great movements which have characterized the American church in the last half century have been, first, a widening and deepening interest in social problems in the light of which divisive doctrines have lost much of their importance; second, a liberalized view of religion in which they have lost much of their certainty; and third, a tendency toward coöperation and unity among the sundered families of faith. The first of these tendencies has furnished the motive power for the third and the second has removed many of the obstacles to it.

Economic considerations have also had their weight in driving the churches together, for it has been observed in many fields that they must either combine or collapse. But in general they have been drawn rather than driven into these more coöperative attitudes and the impulse to unification has gained more from the desire of the churches to increase the efficiency of their work than from fear of losing their own lives.

The multiplicity of denominations, each carrying on its work independently through a period of rapid territorial expansion and numerical growth and a period of new and complicated problems presented by an urban and industrialized society, produced a situation such that, when the whole field and the religious forces at work in it were broadly surveyed, there appeared to be a vast amount of zeal and energy expended with no general plan whatever. Viewed from the standpoint of the separate denominations, the work was, to be sure, purposive and in many cases orderly. The improved organization of denominational machinery for missions, benevolences and education had achieved that. No one could say that the Methodists or the

Episcopalians, for example, were without system, and even those denominations with the least ecclesiastical authority, like the Baptists and Disciples, or those with the least denominational coherence, like the Congregationalists, had created powerful organizations for the promotion and support of the enterprises which they undertook. But when a particular geographical area, whether urban or rural, was observed, the confusion of disunited Protestantism became apparent. The detailed county maps and the diagrams showing the distribution of population and churches in cities, prepared by the Interchurch Survey made this painfully evident. Similarly, the consideration of specific problems, such as those of industry and international relations, revealed the fact that the churches spoke with no united voice and that their energies were applied to the solution of these problems almost at random.

Almost from the beginning of the entire period which we have under consideration there has been some degree of awareness of these conditions on the part of the most sensitive minds. And during the last thirty years some of the most earnest thought and endeavor of the churches themselves, as well as of their more advanced leaders, has been devoted to attempts to remedy this situation.

An analysis of the whole general movement toward unity may be given under the following headings, some of which have already been discussed:

1. Denominations having union their specific and avowed objective. The Disciples of Christ have announced this as their goal from the beginning of their existence, and the Episcopalians have not ceased to stress the essential unity of the church. The efficiency of both as agencies for the promotion of unity has been limited by the fact that both insisted upon union on specific programs which they already held.

2. Voluntary coöperative organizations of individuals with or without specific approval by denominational assemblies but, in either case, involving no commitment of the denominations as such. Among these were the American Bible Society, International Sunday School Association, Young Men's Christian Association, Young Women's Christian Association, Woman's Christian Temperance Union, Evan-

gelical Alliance, Young People's Society of Christian Endeavor, and the Religious Education Association. These have promoted acquaintance, established habits of coöperation, developed a spirit of unity by exercising it, produced practical results which justified them and trained a new generation less denominationally minded.

3. Coöperative organizations of denominational boards. Such are the Home Missionary Council, the Council of Women for Home Missions, the Foreign Missions Conference of North America, the Committee on Cooperation in Latin America, the Council of Church Boards of Education, the International Missionary Council.

4. The reunion of certain divided denominations. Here are to be mentioned the consolidation of various Lutheran bodies, the reunion of the Old School and New School Presbyterians and of the Presbyterians and Cumberland Presbyterians and of certain smaller Presbyterian groups, the union of the Baptists and Free-will Baptists. The continued efforts at reunion between northern and southern Methodists and between northern and southern Presbyterians, and to some extent between northern and southern Baptists, have produced no definite result but illustrate the same tendency.

5. Unions of separate denominations. In this field the efforts have been many but the actual achievements few. The formation of the United Church of Canada by Congregationalists, Methodists and Presbyterians is worthy of note though it falls outside of the geographical limits of our discussion. The union of the Congregationalists and the Christian Church in 1930 was perhaps the first case of the union of two important denominations not belonging to the same stock. Other overtures are pending such as those between the Congregationalists and Universalists and between Methodists and Presbyterians. The latter is especially noteworthy, not only because of the size of the two groups and the complete separateness of their traditions but because they represent a theological cleavage which was, or was supposed to be, absolute. The Presbyterians are Calvinists (or should we say *were* Calvinists?) and the Methodists are Arminians. But Professor Moffatt has wisely observed that "Presbyterianism is older than Calvinism." The Presbyterian General Assembly in 1932 expressed a willingness to accept an administrative episcopate if that would smooth the path to union with other bodies. The "Free Church

in America," the organization of which was effected in December, 1932, by a joint commission of Unitarians and Universalists, lacks only the final vote of approval by the national conventions to sanction it as a common agency for much of the work of these two liberal denominations.

6. Coöperation and union in foreign missions. In this field, union has advanced farther than in any other. It includes educational work in union colleges and theological seminaries, medical work and hospitals, Bible societies and book repositories, and federated or united national churches. The United Evangelical Church of the Philippines was formed in 1929 by the union of Congregationalists, Presbyterians and United Brethren.

7. Movements for general organic unity, finding expression in an extensive series of overtures and conferences which cannot be mentioned in detail, with the Stockholm and Lausanne conferences as the high points up to date, and the annual conference of the Christian Unity League as an important agency for the promotion of the whole program.

8. The community church movement, approaching the problem from the side of the local situation and its needs and proposing the union of the Christians in a neighborhood rather than the union of churches as such.

9. The Federal Council of Churches, the distinguishing characteristic of which is that it represents an official coöperation of the denominations themselves authorized by their assemblies or councils or conferences of highest jurisdiction. The members of its directing committee are chosen by the ruling bodies of the several denominations to serve as delegates and representatives of the denominations. This is not quite true in the case of those strictly congregational bodies whose national assemblies are themselves not delegate bodies and therefore cannot officially act for the entire group. But even in such cases the conventions doubtless express the consensus of opinion of their denominations in giving adherence to the Federal Council and in appointing representatives to sit in it. So we have, in the Federal Council, the nearest approach to a parliament of Protestantism that it is possible to have considering the diversity of forms of organization in the different constituent denominations; but it is a parliament

which neither exercises nor claims the right to exercise any authority over the member bodies. It acts as their agent, not as their ruler.

The organization of the Federal Council of Churches of Christ in America came as the culmination of a series of events which occurred in the fourteen years from 1894 to 1908. These were its immediate antecedents. Its more remote causes include, on the one hand, all those influences which made for the increase of the spirit of unity among the churches and those activities in which that spirit found expression; and on the other, everything that fostered, or expressed, or pertained to, the increasing emphasis upon that aspect of religion which concerned what people do and how they live from Monday to Saturday.

This series of direct antecedents began with the organization of the Open and Institutional Church League in 1894. An open church was one in which the seats were free. The abandonment of the old system of renting pews represented the passing of the idea that the church was a proprietary institution, like a club, existing to minister edification and spiritual comfort to those who had been admitted to its membership and who paid for its support. Some denominations had never had rented pews; with others, especially the older ones and those in the older communities, renting pews had been the usual practice. Rev. Charles L. Thompson, of the Madison Avenue Presbyterian Church, New York, who became one of the founders of the League, was an ardent free-pew man. At the same time there had been wide discussion and some adoption of the institutional church idea. An institutional church was one which did other things besides conduct church services and a Sunday school. It was generally an old church in a location which had been abandoned by the original constituency of the church and occupied by a poorer and often by a foreign population. It had fewer members within easy reach, but more needy people, and these needy people generally needed other things worse than they needed to be preached to. It was the time when "college settlements" and "social settlements" were being founded. With these examples before their eyes, socially minded religious leaders saw that a church so situated was confronted not by a predicament, as had usually been supposed, but by an opportunity. The institutional church, with its classes and clubs, its friendly visitors and relief agencies and sometimes its employment bureau, was the result. Such a church had not only a minister but a staff, and its plant worked seven days in the week. The term "open church" came to have a larger meaning than merely that its pews were open to all comers. The Open and Institutional Church League was a league of that kind of churches. The churches which coöperated in it were Presbyterian, Methodist, Baptist and Congregational, but the denominations as such had no relation to it.

In the following year, 1895, a Federation of Churches and Christian Workers of New York City was formed. Originally projected at a meeting of the alumni club of Union Theological Seminary, its purpose was that of "applying the gospel to every human need, and of so readjusting and directing its agencies that every family in the destitute parts of our city shall be reached." Local federations on similar lines were formed in several other cities.

These two organizations functioned usefully for some years. In 1900 they jointly called a meeting which took action leading to the formation of a National Federation of Churches and Christian Workers. It was composed chiefly of local churches and city federations, though there were also representatives of the New York State Federation, the Interdenominational Commission of Maine, the Connecticut Bible Society, and the Pennsylvania Evangelical Alliance. The meeting at which this organization was perfected, at Philadelphia, 1901, was counted a great landmark in the history of unitive Protestantism. And so it was. But the organization was soon found to be heterogeneous and unwieldy. It was like a national convention of precinct workers. At a still more notable meeting, at Washington in 1902, the general secretary, Dr. E. B. Sanford, proposed that steps be taken toward the formation of a Federation with the backing of the denominations themselves and composed of members to be officially designated by them. Steps were immediately taken toward the calling of a conference of official representatives of whole denominations to consider the feasibility of such a federation.

After much preliminary work and a three-year campaign of education, the Interchurch Conference on Federation was held in Carnegie Hall, New York, in November, 1905. It outlined a plan, drafted a constitution, and appointed an executive committee to secure ratification by denominations and the appointment of representatives.

The first meeting of the Federal Council of Churches of Christ in America was held at Philadelphia on December 2, 1908. The principles on which federation rests, as stated by Dr. Samuel McCrea Cavert, are:

1. Responsibility for coöperative work rests on the denominations.
2. Diversity must not mean divisiveness.
3. Churches are now ready for coöperation in many great tasks.
4. The path to larger unity lies through the field of action.
5. Freedom to hold varying views as to the ultimate form in which the spirit of Christian unity will find expression.

The strength of the Federal Council's appeal alike to conservative and to liberal churches, to those which made organic unity an avowed objective and to those which were suspicious of union efforts, lay in the fact that it devoted its efforts to practical problems and avoided theological statements, and that its coöperative program involved neither commitment nor prejudice to any further step in the direction of unity. Twenty-eight denominations became members of it, not counting the Protestant Episcopal, which felt itself unable to become fully a member but coöperated almost as completely as though it were.

The work of the Federal Council covered an immense and growing variety of common interests, as well as the promotion of local and state federations. It gave attention to such traditional and expected enterprises as evangelism, religious education, foreign missions, the encouragement and direction of the Negro churches, and the relief of suffering Protestant churches abroad. Its war-time activities included the designation of chaplains, religious and social ministries in the camps and over-seas, the collection of funds for relief, and war work of every description. Before the war it was engaged in enterprises of international good will and the promotion of the ideals of peace; after the war, in economic and industrial questions and international relations. At the first quadrennial meeting, in 1908, resolutions were adopted, following the patterns of those adopted by the Methodist general conference a few months earlier, which became a social creed of the churches. These Fourteen Points—antedating President Wilson's famous Fourteen by ten years—indicate the progress which the church had made since the days when Christian business men were exhorted simply to "make money according to the laws of business and spend it according to the laws of God." And since many of these points implied legislation for their enforcement, they also register progress from the point where the spokesmen of religion were saying that government has nothing to do with the relations between capital and labor except to guarantee freedom of contract. The representatives of twenty-eight denominations took their stand:

For equal rights and complete justice for all men in all stations of life;

For the right of all men to the opportunity for self-maintenance, the right ever to be wisely and strongly safeguarded against encroachments of every kind;

For the right of workers to some protection against the hardships often resulting from the swift crisis of industrial change;

For the principle of conciliation and arbitration in industrial dissensions;

For the protection of the worker from dangerous machinery, occupational disease, injury and mortality;

For the abolition of child labor;

For such regulations of the conditions of toil of women as shall safeguard the physical and moral health of the community;

For the suppression of the "sweating" system;

For the gradual and reasonable reduction of the hours of labor to the lowest practicable point, and for that degree of leisure for all which is a condition of the highest human life;

For a release from employment one day in seven;

For a living wage as a minimum in every industry and for the highest wage that each industry can afford;

For the most charitable industry that can ultimately be devised;

For suitable provision for the old age of the workers and for those incapacitated by injury;

For the abatement of poverty.

The Federal Council did not stop with the enunciation of general principles. By the investigation of the steel industry—carried on by the

Interchurch World Movement but with the moral support of the Federal Council—it drew to itself much ill will from those who resented the interference of the churches with their profits, but it revealed the facts regarding the prevalence of the twelve-hour day, and went so far toward proving it not only an evil but one not economically or technically necessary in that industry that the United States Steel Corporation soon came to a general adoption of the eight-hour system which it had before declared impossible. Its attitude on international questions since the war, its resolutions in favor of radical reduction of armaments, its opposition to militarism in all its forms, and its tolerance toward liberal, social and economic doctrines have brought upon it the criticism and condemnation of militaristic nationalists and the devotees of a *laissez-faire* system of competitive capitalism in industry.

In the promotion of united efforts, the Federal Council has been careful not to get ahead of its constituency—the churches which are members of it. It has therefore sometimes incurred criticism for timidity in not adventuring more boldly into fields of action which are now occupied by the churches separately but which invite consolidated action—such as home and foreign missions. But it is an organization *of* the churches, not *over* them, and it is of the essence of it that it can take out of the hands of the denominations nothing which they do not willingly commit to it.

Some of the efforts toward unity on the part of a few denominations may serve as samples to indicate the general trend.

The Congregationalists, alone of the large denominations, approved the plan of union proposed by the American council on organic union, 1923; passed strong general union resolutions, 1923; negotiated with the Protestant Episcopal Church, 1923; favored union with the Presbyterians, 1925; negotiated for union with the Universalists, 1927; expressed willingness to give up their distinctive name for "Churches of Christ," 1927; united with the Christian Church, 1931.

The Methodist Episcopal Church adopted ringing resolutions declaring that it will work and worship with any church that works with Christ and will "keep step with any church that marches toward the goal of his desire," 1920; approved plan of union with the Methodist Episcopal Church South by vote of the general conference, 1924, and by referendum, 1925; proposed union with the Presbyterian Church in the U. S. A., "organic union without reservation or condition," 1928; made new plans for union with Methodist Episcopal Church South, and Methodist Protestant Church, 1932, on which action will be taken by the M. E. South in 1934.

The Methodist Episcopal Church South by vote of its general conference accepted the plan of union with the Methodist Episcopal Church, 1924, but the project was defeated by the annual conferences; appointed a commission on interdenominational relations, 1930.

The Northern Baptist Convention united with the Free Will Baptists, 1909; feels difficulty in approaching the subject of organic union because it does not have organic union among its own congregations; approved conference with the Disciples of Christ on "unity of program," 1928, but adopted a minority report rejecting the favorable joint report of this conference, 1930.

The Presbyterian Church in the U. S. A. established a standing committee on church coöperation and union, 1903; united with the Cumberland Presbyterians; proposed union of all evangelical churches, 1918, when the general assembly declared "our profound conviction that the time has come for organic union of the evangelical churches of America"; in pursuance of this resolution, formulated a plan of union which was approved by the general assembly of 1920 but defeated by the presbyteries; united with the Welsh Calvinistic Methodist Church, 1920; adopted a proposed plan of union with the Presbyterian Church in the U. S., the United Presbyterian Church and the Reformed Church in the U. S., 1920, which has been discussed rather continuously ever since; conferred upon union with the Congregationalists, 1924 and 1925; conferred with the Methodist Episcopal Church since its overture in 1928; offered to accept an administrative form of episcopacy to make union with the Methodists possible, 1922.

The Disciples of Christ have always stressed union as one of their original purposes; made overtures to the Baptists in 1907 and at other times; created a commission on Christian union, 1910; proposed "unity of program" with Baptists, 1928, and approved the joint committee's report, 1929.

The Lutherans have achieved unification of several of their formerly separate synods, especially by the notable unions of 1932, but they have in general insisted that union with other denominations is impossible without a degree of doctrinal agreement which does not exist.

Chapter XV

THE CHURCH AND BIG BUSINESS

In following the fortunes of the Federal Council we have got somewhat ahead of the story of the development of other aspects of American cultural and religious life which are less pleasant to contemplate. We have been considering the remedies which the common Christian mind began to apply, under the stimulus of its more courageous and advanced leaders, before we have quite sufficiently noted the disease and the extent to which the church itself was infected with it.

"The Man with the Hoe," a poem written by a then unknown California schoolteacher, Edwin Markham, took the country by storm immediately upon its publication in 1899, because the country was ready for it. Economic conditions had developed to such a point that the essential truth of the picture was recognized, and the social conscience had developed a sufficient degree of sensitiveness to be able to respond to it. A generation before, it would have aroused no interest. A generation later it would have been only one among many expressions of human sympathy and of appeal for the righting of ancient wrongs grown newly poignant. But this was the period of populism, of a fresh outburst of agrarian discontent, and of a new awareness of the injustices of the social order. Bryan's revivalistic appeals for the rights of the common man still rang in the ears of the West, rebellious against the "money power," and were to ring again, and they had troubled and alarmed the complacent East. Prosperous urban pastors might denounce him, but everybody knew there was something the matter. Doctor Parkhurst of New York, Dr. Robert S. MacArthur, of Calvary Baptist Church, New York, and Doctor Talmage, then of Washington, all denounced Bryan from their pulpits

THE CHURCH AND BIG BUSINESS

in 1896; and Rev. Cortland Myers, of the Baptist Temple, Boston, said that his Chicago platform was "made in hell." The diagnosis might be wrong, the Nebraska doctor might be a quack, and his prescription might be rank poison, but the wisest knew and the plainest felt that society was suffering from a grave malady in spite of its opulence—perhaps because of it. With all the laurels of a recently won war—the aroma of which was slightly tainted by the odor of the "embalmed beef" scandal—and with all the thrill of entering upon a new and glorious mission for the uplift of our already restless and reluctant wards in our recently acquired Pacific archipelago, it was an open secret that all was not well in the nation's vitals.

The church, or at least a part of it, was ready for the quickening word. It had already been prepared for it by the beginning of its activity in the slums, and by the movement for the "open and institutional church." The science of sociology had been born, and "Christian sociology" was being studied by a few and talked of by many. The dangers of concentrated corporate wealth were gaining recognition, and not only in radical quarters. Long before, in 1873, the chief justice of the Wisconsin supreme court, Judge E. G. Ryan, had declared publicly to a university audience: "The question will arise in your day, though perhaps not fully in mine, Which shall rule, wealth or men? Which shall lead: money or intellect? Who shall fill public stations: educated and patriotic freemen, or the feudal serfs of corporate capital?" Before 1900, the question whose rise Judge Ryan foresaw had arisen. President Schurman of Cornell University, only a little later, in 1906, said: "We are coming to measure man—man with a heart and mind and soul—in terms of mere acquisition and possession, and waning Christianity and waxing mammonism are the twin specters of our age. The love of money and the reckless pursuit of it are undermining the national character."

Henry Cabot Lodge, though allied by birth and fortune with the moneyed element and closely associated with political conservatism, called attention "to the darkest sign of all, the one in which money and the acquisition of money by taking it from some one else through the process of law seems in the last analysis rampant in every portion of the community and at the bottom if not at the top of almost every proposed reform, every political issue and every personal ambition." He was equally alarmed at "the gigantic modern plutocracy and its lawless ways" and the frantic and undisciplined endeavors of the proletariat to avoid work and to rob the rich of their accumulations.

Lodge's young friend, Theodore Roosevelt, began his political career with an attack upon a form of corruption in New York that was political in method but avaricious and predatory in substance. In 1897, he wrote to Lodge: "The really ugly feature of the Republican canvass is that it does represent what the Populists say, that is, corrupt wealth. . . . Both Platt and Tracy represent the powerful unscrupulous politicians who charge heavily for doing the work—sometimes good and sometimes bad—of the bankers, railroad men, insurance men, and the like."

These men—Ryan, Schurman, Lodge, Roosevelt—were not reckless radicals or irresponsible extremists. They were not even professional reformers. Two of them were very shrewd politicians, who spoke their frankest words secretly to each other, in private letters which have come to the eyes of the public only after their death. But all of them saw that prosperity was, in part, a national disease.

"The Man with a Hoe" was the most eloquent and effective single protest against the dehumanization of man by the processes of an acquisitive society.

In reviving its concern for these matters, religion was not entering a new field but re-entering one which it had occupied long ago and lost a while. The medieval church, taking the world for its parish and all life for its field of control, did not hesitate to make codes for the conduct of secular affairs. It mitigated some of the horrors of war by the truce of God and forbade the taking of interest as usury. To be sure, men took interest and fought seven days in the week when the exigencies of the campaign required it, but they had to do these things with a bad conscience, aware that the church condemned them.

The Puritan church also attempted to control conduct in detail. But the gradual failure of the program by reason of the odium attaching to its compulsive and restrictive measures and its change from a dominant majority to a querulous minority drove it back into the circumscribed area of doctrine, worship and ordinances.

As new problems arose following the industrial revolution—and in

America following the concentration of industrial power in the hands of a few—the church had to learn all over again to recognize the moral implications of secular programs. In the agrarian upheaval which found expression in the silver campaigns of 1896 and 1900 and in the program of reform in the interests of human rights set forth by the populists even before those dates, the church was in the main silent. Only slowly and as the abuses of industrial control in the interests of wealth cried to heaven for abatement, did the Christian conscience begin to concern itself with industrial problems.

The problems as well as the constituency of the churches were traditionally rural. The church had for many years been developing a technique for ministering to the needs of homogeneous rural or village communities through the services of clergy universally respected as having superior culture and a higher social status than their parishioners as well as holding in trust the revealed truth of religion. The situation was radically changed when the church's constituency was no longer either rural or homogeneous, when the diffusion of education brought increasing numbers of the laity up to the level of equal intelligence (and often above it, in their own estimate at least) and when the voices of science and philosophy, which were now heard on the street as well as in academic halls, were challenging much that had been proclaimed as divine revelation.

But meanwhile the church was itself a part of that industrial society the defects of whose processes, so far as they concerned the human factors involved in them, furnished its most serious problems. The churches were themselves corporations, with problems of budgets and building funds and endowments. The church had already discovered its laity as an element of its spiritual power. Moody had helped in that, and such organizations as the Baptist social union; and the admission of laymen to the Methodist general conference was one of the many ways in which that discovery had been registered. But with the growth of big business and great fortunes, and the simultaneous expansion of the church's institutions to a point requiring much more adequate financing, the church became more sensitively aware of the layman's money as a very present help in time of trouble. Rich men in increasing numbers found their places on the boards of colleges and missionary societies. The "consecration of wealth" became a favorite topic of edifying discourse. It was, indeed, a very proper and necessary topic, though too often it was assumed that the portion of a man's wealth which he devoted to a religious use lent a vicarious sanctity to the part which he kept for himself, regardless of the methods by which both parts might have been acquired. In the earlier days, the *religious mind, patriotic and progressive, saw in the work of the empire-builders who led in the construction of the western railroads*— no matter at whose expense—agents for the opening up and development of the country and the consequent extension of the kingdom of God, and was as little inclined as any other section of public opinion to be fastidiously critical in regard to methods. It wanted righteousness, of course, but it also wanted results of a visible and tangible sort. So now, the Lord's work had to be done and it cost money. Money could be got only from the people who had it. Efficiency was the watchword.

Similarly, the churches were little inclined to criticize Mr. Roosevelt's method of acquiring the Canal Zone. We wanted the canal, didn't we? Well then, the man who could get the strip and dig the ditch was the man for us. Besides, Roosevelt had already talked so loudly of righteousness and the square deal, and had given so many proofs of good faith in doing so where only Americans were concerned, that the churches were scarcely inclined to criticize one doubtful deed of so good a man. The canal zone was a gift-horse whose dentition need not be subjected to a too meticulous inspection.

But there were areas of sensitiveness. Great scandal was occasioned by the revelation that some of the richest churches in New York, Trinity Church in particular, drew a large part of their income from the rental of shamefully crowded and unsanitary tenements (Charles Edward Russell, in *Everybody's Magazine*, 1908). Following the sensational magazine articles by Lincoln Steffens in which "The Shame of the Cities" was exposed, and the dishonesty and inefficiency of municipal governments was disclosed with names, dates and places, "muck-raking" (Roosevelt's derogatory term) came into high favor. Business ethics improved with the discovery of how unethical big business had hitherto been. Ida Tarbell's *History of the Standard Oil Company*, 1904, told some things that had been forgotten and many more that had never been generally known. Mr. Rockefeller, who had built a fortune without precedent by practices now condemned, gave money more generously and more wisely than any other possessor of wealth on any comparable scale had ever done. No very rich man—except misers—had ever spent so little on himself. He never had a yacht, a racing stable, a Fifth Avenue house, a Newport mansion, a home in London or Paris, a villa on the Riviera, or an art gallery. He never gambled, never drank, never gave a costly ball or any other kind. His perfect confidence that his financial methods had been in accordance with the will of God and his success a signal mark of divine favor was as absolute as Mr. Bryan's belief that his program represented the will of God—even though the tangible confirmation was lacking in the latter case. "God gave me my money," said Mr. Rockefeller. (See John T. Flynn: *God's Gold*.) About such a case the church was frankly, and quite properly, puzzled. Some qualms about the acceptance of "tainted money" were the extent of its disturbance. Some of those who opposed the acceptance of tainted money by the churches were social liberals, like Washington Gladden, who saw religion making itself an acquiescent partner in anti-social processes by sharing the profits; others were theological conservatives who were alarmed by the prospect that religious liberalism would be heavily subsidized. The essential fact was that Mr. Rockefeller's long life had spanned a changing order.

In 1902, at the time of a serious coal strike, Mr. George F. Baer, president of the Reading Railroad, said: "The rights and interests of the laboring man will be protected and cared for not by labor agitators but by the Christian man to whom God in His infinite wisdom has given the control of the property interests of this country." No more bald and concise statement of the feudal point of view as applied to modern capitalism and industry could have been framed. It is a landmark of social progress that an important financier could not only think that but could dare to say it only thirty years ago. It is also a sign of social progress prior to that date that religious opinion in general promptly found voice to repudiate this claim that God had chosen and commissioned a favored few to control the property interests of the country and to deal out to the laboring men such benefits as the wisdom of the "Christian" overlords might deem suitable for them. "Divine-right Baer" was held up to equal scorn in the religious press and in the labor press.

Great insurance companies were found to have skeletons in their vaults. More generally than ever before, public opinion in favor of plain honesty in government and business became articulate, and to some extent effective. Of all of this, Theodore Roosevelt was the personal symbol, and his anti-trust crusade an important expression. The *laissez-faire* policy was fast losing its respectability.

The period following the Spanish-American War found the church confronting a multiplicity of problems which, if not new, were at least presented in more complex forms. The shift of population from country to city continued with accelerated speed. The social problems which had for a generation been a matter of concern to a few leaders of Christian thought and action had begun to make some appreciable impact upon the mind of the church as a whole. The moral and cultural problems, especially as affecting youth, were met by new experiments in religious education in place of, or in addition to, the old Sunday school program of mere Bible study. The rapid growth of the state universities, following and accompanying the even more rapid multiplication and development of high schools, complicated the situation of the denominational colleges with respect to both their finances and their administration. The church colleges had, on the one hand, to keep faith with the churches in order to secure support; and on the other, they had—or thought they had—to secularize their programs in order to get students in competition with the state universities. As a matter of fact, the colleges did very well during these years between the two wars. High school and college attendance was increasing enormously. The country was prosperous and, after so many slashing attacks upon unethical methods of acquiring wealth and so much Rooseveltian trust-busting and corporation-baiting, a good many rich men were the more anxious to prove that wealth was not unmindful of its social responsibilities. Giving to colleges stepped up to a higher level. It was well for the colleges that it did, for the standardizing agencies were requiring more endowment and more Ph.D.'s on faculties. The Carnegie pension system for teachers, applicable only to colleges not under denominational control, led many colleges which had always supposed that they were denominational to discover that they were not.

Various social changes conspired to lend respectability to what had formerly been considered Sabbath-breaking. The easy attitude toward Sunday observance was no longer a matter of beer gardens and the practice of a "continental Sunday" by recent immigrants from the continent—against which the defenses of the evangelical conscience were reasonably proof—but of Sunday papers larger, louder and funnier than heretofore, of Sunday baseball and golf, and of the new instruments of mobility which made the country accessible to city-dwellers—the bicycle, then and especially the automobile. More important than any of these, perhaps, were the movies.

The church as a whole showed more resourcefulness and achieved more success in meeting the financial responsibilities of this new age than in other respects. Not only were the endowments of its colleges vastly increased during the first fifteen years of the new century, but there was corresponding development in the charitable and social institutions and in the budgets both of local churches and of home and foreign missions. The churches were institutionally prosperous. They were vaguely troubled by a strange new consciousness of human rights imperiled by the working of the industrial and financial machinery to which they owed their own support, and they were not indifferent to the human waste of the process, but they still had unshaken faith in the system.

Chapter XVI

THE CHURCHES AND THE WORLD WAR

In discussing the Churches and the World War, I am more interested in noting the attitudes of the churches toward war, and toward *this* war, than in describing in detail their activities in meeting the war-time situation.

The awakening of the churches to the fact of their duty in connection with actual social situations, and the development both of the machinery for response and the habit of response to social needs had gone far enough by 1917 so that, if there was to be a war at all, it could be taken for granted that the churches would take an even larger part in it than they did in the Civil War. For whatever else a war is and does, it certainly presents a complex of abnormal and exigent social situations. All institutions and all persons feel the demands which these situations make upon them with an intensity proportional to their sense of social responsibility. This was obviously true of the great majority who supported the war. It was equally true of those who, acting as recalcitrant individuals or as members of small protesting groups, felt that they were serving a larger social good by resisting the decision of the government and of the churches.

It is a familiar saying that the church has always been for war when there is war and for peace when there is peace. Or it can be stated without the touch of cynicism which seems to lurk in that aphorism by saying that the church has always, or generally, cherished the love of peace as an ideal; but it has always, or generally, been patriotically amenable to the suggestion that any particular war in which the country is engaged at the moment is a legitimate exception. It would be out of place in this connection to discuss the ethics of war and the question as to whether the church ought always to condemn it; but it is only saying what every one knows—certainly what every one who ever lived through a war knows—to say that every war generates its own justification in the mind of the nation that engages in it, and that the natural forces which produce this rationalization operate just as strongly upon religious minds as upon any others. Whether or not, in a particular case, these forces are strong enough to overcome the presumption against a process so destructive of the moods and values that religion habitually exalts, depends upon the quality of the religion and the patterns of thought and behavior of the people who hold it. As a matter of fact, during the past seventeen centuries the Christian mind has generally been able to adjust itself with little difficulty or delay to the approval of any war in which the community might be engaged.

It was not always so. During the first two centuries of the Christian era the church did not allow its members to serve in the army, and in the third century only a few of them did so. When the Roman state extended its protection to the church, the church reciprocated by giving its sanction to the state and withdrew its objection to a function seemingly so essential to the state's very existence. Patriotism became a Christian virtue and war the normal expression of it. Within another century the loyalty of *non*-Christians had fallen under such grave suspicion that, by the year 416, only Christians were permitted to serve in the army. After that it was a long while before any question was raised as to the legitimacy of war as an institution in a Christian social order. The church itself took on so many of the qualities of a state that it would have seemed an act of sheer suicide for it to have repudiated violence. The Protestant reformation introduced no change in this view, for Protestantism also relied upon the protection of the secular arm and the patronage of governments which were themselves upheld by their armies. It was a Christianity thus schooled in coöperation with the state and in the approval of whatever seemed essential to the welfare of the political society that was transplanted to America.

In the days immediately preceding the Revolutionary War, the New England clergy were active in the patriotic cause, "establishing from Holy Writ the legal right of resistance to unconstitutional action and often in burning phrases urging their people to resist even to bloodshed" (A. M. Baldwin: *The New England Clergy and the American Revolution*, p. 123). They took an active part in recruiting volunteers for the colonial army, and served not only as chaplains but often as officers. The war with England in 1812 and the war with Mexico found the church similarly ready to lend the sanction of religion to their country's cause and to the military methods by which it was supported.

Into the Civil War the churches, both North and South, entered with unprecedented fervor. On the northern side, "the Bible and especially the writings of St. Paul were cited to show that God was the source of civil authority and that he required obedience to civil authority from all the people." Secession was therefore heresy as well as treason; the rebellion was "the most hellish since Satan seceded from the government of Heaven"; and the baptism of blood acquired almost the sanctity of a sacrament (C. B. Swaney: *Episcopal Methodism and Slavery*, p. 300). On the southern side, in the words of Rev. Dr. Smythe of Charleston, "the war now 'carried on by the North is a war against slavery and is therefore treasonable rebellion against the Constitution of the United States and against the word, providence, and government of God" (Kirby Page: *Jesus or Christianity*, p. 215). For both, the cause was a holy cause and the war a holy war.

In 1876, the *Independent* described war as the best school of the manly virtues, and found in an occasional war an indispensable stimulus of patriotism. Two years later it envisaged peace—but only an enforced peace at that—so faintly and so remotely that it conceived of a possible alliance of the United States and the British Empire "at a distance of not more than three centuries," which would guarantee perpetual peace by being too strong to be attacked.

Yet there was a certain amount of peace sentiment, oftener than not springing from humanitarian rather than religious motives. "Here is the challenging paradox—that the chief opponents of war in the last 200 years have been men having no visible alliance with the creeds or institutions of the Christian religion" (W. H. P. Faunce: *Religion and War*, p. 78). The first peace society in the United States was organized in 1815. Many others, chiefly local, were formed both in the United States and in Europe. The first international congress of peace societies was held in London in 1843, chiefly at the instigation of a Quaker, Joseph Sturge. The peace societies often bitterly criticized the church for its failure to support them, not that they did not derive a good deal of their strength from religious people, but that most of these were of sects that were deemed queer and extreme, like the Quakers, while the respectable churches and the responsible leaders held aloof. International peace congresses, representing peace societies, not governments, were held not infrequently through the latter half of the nineteenth century. A Seventeenth Universal Peace Congress met in London in 1908, with representatives of 280 peace societies from twenty-three countries. By this time the religious motive in the movement was dominant. But the peace societies themselves have generally not stood out against war when it came. They had not seriously studied the relation of the state to the church, the individual and the individual conscience.

In 1896, the New York Peace Society was established and Mr. Carnegie gave ten million dollars to finance the peace movement. A national peace conference met in New York in 1907, and annually thereafter. The national association of Cosmopolitan Clubs, led by Louis P. Lochner, was formed for the same purpose. The Federal Council of Churches, at its first meeting in 1908, had appointed a standing committee on peace and arbitration, which later became the Commission on International Justice and Good Will. In 1911, Edward Ginn, the publisher, endowed the World Peace Foundation. In 1912, the American Peace Society, then celebrating its centennial, established headquarters at Washington and took on new life. The American School Peace League was formed. The Church Peace League was organized, including clergymen of all denominations. The Church Peace Union, endowed by Mr. Carnegie and later called the World Alliance for International Friendship through the Churches, was formed in 1914. It survived the war that it could not prevent, and had councils in twenty-six countries in 1922. It was holding an International Church Peace Conference in Constance, Switzerland, August 2–5, 1914, when the war broke out, and the delegates had considerable difficulty in getting home.

The church and churchmen were prominent in the peace movement in the early years of this century, but had no monopoly of it. Many of its most prominent leaders were more eminent for other things than for their activity in organized religion, and some were not churchmen at all. The list included Lyman Abbott of the *Outlook*; Hamilton Holt of the *Independent*; Charles W. Eliot, Nicholas Murray Butler, A. Lawrence Lowell and David Starr Jordan, university presidents; Andrew Carnegie and James J. Hill, financiers; Carrie Chapman Catt, feminist; Jane Addams, social worker; James A. Choate, lawyer and diplomat; William Howard Taft, ex-President. The condemnation of war found approval in all quarters, and the pulpit which was soon to resound with the call to arm was now singing the sweet songs of peace.

In 1914, American idealism was, nominally, triumphant in government also. Woodrow Wilson, the Christian scholar in politics, with strong pacifist leanings, was President; and William Jennings Bryan, a typical conservative evangelical in politics with an even greater antipathy to militarism and imperialism than to modernistic doctrines in religion, was Secretary of State.

In spite of the official neutrality of America during the first phase of the European war, there was a general reaction of horror at the invasion of Belgium, and this was intensified by the exaggerated tales of atrocities. The Germans were no longer just "Germans." They became "Huns." The term is said to have owed its use in this connection to the report that the Kaiser instructed the German soldiers sent to China in 1900, at the time of the Boxer rebellion, to conduct themselves "like Huns," so that for a generation to come no Chinese could look upon a German without terror. But Hunnishness, even under that name, has an even longer lineage. When the French army invaded and devastated the Palatinate on transparently sophistical excuses in 1688, during the reign of Louis XIV, contemporary German writers characterized the French soldiers as "Huns" (Ogg: *Europe in the Seventeenth Century*, p. 314).

While the religious mind was more committed to the ideals of peace, it was perhaps also more responsive to the propaganda of the allies which depicted Germany as a beast over-riding all considerations of decency and humanity and it was quick to accept the suggestion that the frankly anti-Christian philosophy of Nietzsche and the radical doctrines of German theologians had furnished the theory on which the German policies were based.

German propaganda was most effective in reaching American citizens of German extraction, who were mostly Lutheran and Catholic, the Irish, with their traditional hatred of England, who were mostly Catholic, and the Jews, who had good ground of antipathy to Russia. The sentiment of Anglo-Saxon Protestantism was largely pro-ally. Many university men who had academic association with German scholarship were sympathetic with Germany but not many of these were evangelical Protestants. And there was a contingent of super-patriots who found it easy to demonstrate their loyalty by reviving ancient anti-British prejudices.

A curious manifestation of pacifist idealism was given by Mr. Ford's peace ship which sailed in December, 1915, with the quixotic notion of ending the conflict by the unofficial mediation of a group of American citizens. The moving spirits of this enterprise, however, were not closely connected with the churches.

The religious press for the most part maintained an attitude of comparative neutrality and approved of the administration's efforts to keep America out of the war. Even the sinking of the *Lusitania* produced no such sudden flare of zeal for a crusade as had the sinking of the *Maine*. Theodore Roosevelt, however, as contributing editor of the *Outlook*, early began to demand American participation in the war. In general, eastern sentiment was more favorable to intervention than western, though after the die was cast in April, 1917, the West was quick to answer the criticisms upon its pacifism by superior zeal for enlistment.

While the issue of American intervention hung in the balance, preparedness organizations on the one hand and peace organizations on the other were busy with propaganda: on the one side, the Navy League, the National Security League, the American Defense Society and the American Rights Committee; on the other, the American League to Limit Armaments, the American Union Against Militarism, the Women's Peace Party, and the League to Enforce Peace. The program of the last mentioned contained many features afterwards incorporated in the League of Nations. While churchmen were more numerous and more prominent on the peace side than on the preparedness side, it can scarcely be said that the main impetus of the non-intervention movement was specifically religious.

Certainly it was not a religious motive which determined the attitude of the Socialist party which was violently opposed to participation in the war. To some extent the Socialist attitude was colored by the presence of a large proportion of Germans in their ranks. From the first it was fairly evident that if there were intervention it would be on the side of the Allies. Later America's entrance into the war produced division in the Socialist Party, one group feeling it necessary to give loyal support to the government and the other staunchly maintaining its pacifist attitude. Conspicuous in the latter group was Eugene Debs, who not only went to prison for his pacifist opinions but stayed there three years after the war was over and conducted his campaign as Socialist candidate for the presidency in 1920 from his cell in the Federal penitentiary—and received twice as many votes as any Socialist candidate before or since.

By the beginning of 1917 the social conscience of the church had advanced to the point where all liberal-minded people in it detested war in general, but where that detestation was ready to be swallowed up in a sense of the urgency of this particular situation. The strongest argument for this war was that it was to be a "war to end war." In fact, it was already conceived as that before we entered it. Lyman Abbott wrote: "The armies of the Allies are in the strictest sense of the term officers of peace. They are fighting for peace. They might as well bear upon their banners the inscription, 'Blessed are the peacemakers, for they shall be called the children of God.'"

Doctor Fosdick did not believe that any war could end war, and he denounced war as un-Christian. But he believed that the only time to prevent a war is before it happens; that after a war has started, "for example, after the assault on Belgium had been started," there is nothing to do but see it through, Christian or not. Similarly, G. B. Smith (*Principles of Christian Living,* p. 194) held that "the all-important moral problem is to prevent the declaration of war."

The lofty idealism of President Wilson and his patient adherence to a peace policy for nearly two years after the sinking of the *Lusitania* had much to do with carrying the churches with him into the war when the final decision was made. But if they had been more inclined than some other organizations to heed the President's injunction to maintain neutrality in thought as well as deed in the early stages of the conflict, when war was declared and George Creel's propaganda bureau began its effective work, the church did not simply become patriotic—it had always been that—but it became in the highest degree bellicose.

"Never before in history had such a campaign of education been organized; never before had American citizens realized how thoroughly, how irresistibly a modern government could impose its ideas upon a whole nation and under a barrage of publicity stifle dissent with declarations, assertions, official versions and reiteration." It scarcely needed the espionage act of June, 1917, to whip the churches into line. Most of them were already in line, clergy and laity. Relatively few remembered that they had ever had a conscience against war. War in the abstract was still a hideous thing, but this particular war was different. It was in the first place a war against that inhumanity which had been shown (by the lurid and largely false evidence presented by Rev. Newell Dwight Hillis, among many others) to be the congenital characteristic of Germans; and it was a war to end war. A few ministers and college professors resisted—a good many in the aggregate but a very small percentage. "Clergymen were unfrocked and sent to prison for over-emphasizing the sermon on the mount" (Beard, *The Rise of American Civilization*, II, 643).

Columbia University, whose president had been a leading advocate of peace, took the lead among educational institutions in ridding itself of professors whose patriotism was rated at less than 100 per cent. A. Barton Hepburn, member of its board of trustees, wrote: "It is very difficult to discharge professors once employed. They make common cause and howl about academic freedom. We have had trouble along this line in Columbia, where they taught sedition and disloyalty and that enabled us to get rid of eight or ten at a time."

The extent of the church's surrender to the mood of war can be best indicated by reference to specific statements and acts:

Even before war was declared, Episcopal ministers at their conferences passed resolutions that America should enter the war. In this respect they outdid the other churches for the others did not support war until diplomatic relations were broken.

"The Massachusetts Clerical Association, an Episcopal body, voted for war early in March. Episcopal clergymen were also prominent in the great April crusade when a distinguished delegation of parsons hastened to Washington to combat the un-Christian influence of the pacifists who were then making their last stand" (Granville Hicks, in the *American Mercury*, February, 1927).

Practically every denomination that held a convention in 1917 passed a resolution favoring the war.

The American Unitarian association resolved "not to grant financial aid to any church which employs a minister who is not a willing, earnest, outspoken supporter of the United States in the vigorous and resolute prosecution of the war."

The idealistic motive for war was set forth persuasively in a little volume entitled *Religion and War*, by Yale Divinity School professors. Dean Charles R. Brown wrote: "We entered the war because we were not willing to stand by and allow other nations to be crippled and broken in the resistance they were offering to lawlessness and crime, and in the defense they were making for the principles of justice and freedom which are the glory of our national history."

Professor Frank C. Porter: "Jesus teaches unlimited non-resistance where only personal and selfish interests are at stake; but resistance unto blood for the sake of the Kingdom of God and his righteousness."

Professor D. C. Macintosh, who later was made internationally famous by his failure to obtain citizenship because of his refusal to take an oath to obey any future law, regardless of conscience, wrote: "If these gallant soldiers are not sons of God, there are no sons of God among us. . . . His likeness can be seen in their faces, marred with the grime and the blood of battle for a just and holy cause" (*God in a World of War*, p. 57).

Rev. N. D. Hillis, arch-propagandist, though of Quaker descent, wrote: "The symbol of Prussia is a soldier with a firebrand in one hand, a bombshell in the other, breathing fire from his nostrils as he tramples down with his feet of mail Belgian women and children." He toured the country with an illustrated lecture on German atrocities, and wrote sermons to be sent to all ministers for Liberty Loan drives.

He became a perfect prophet of hatred. He doubted whether the "Hun" would ever turn from the wickedness of his ways "until his own land is laid waste, until he sees the horrors of war with his own eyes, and hears the groans of his own people with his own ears, sees his own land laid desolate, finds his own heart crushed with anguish." "Society has organized itself against the rattlesnake and the yellow fever. The boards of health are planning to wipe out typhoid, cholera, and the black plague. Not otherwise, lovers of their fellowmen have finally become hopeless with reference to the German people. They have no more relation to the civilization of 1918 than an orang-outang, a gorilla, a Judas, a hyena, a thumbscrew, or a scalping-knife in the hands of a savage. These brutes must be cast out of society." He looked favorably upon the suggestion of sterilizing German men and segregating German women, so that the strain might be extinguished.

Doctor Cadman, Dr. Charles E. Jefferson, Rabbi Wise, Walter Rauschenbusch (himself a German), Washington Gladden—all near pacifists before the war—were convinced and converted by the atrocity stories. Charles Parkhurst, editing *Zion's Herald*, forgot his pacifism and leaped into the fray. Henry van Dyke said: "I'd hang every one, whether or not he is a candidate for mayor (this with reference to Morris Hillquit, the Socialist), who lifts his voice against America entering the war." Faunce, Fosdick, Douglas Mackenzie, and Shailer Mathews wrote books exposing the errors of pacifism. Lyman Abbott approved the dismissal of Cattell and Dana from Columbia, and argued for the expulsion of LaFollette from the Senate and for the arrest of all pacifists. Hillis considered it little less than treason to listen to Fritz Kreisler play the violin. Billy Sunday—but why quote him?—prayed characteristically: "Thou knowest, O Lord, that no nation so infamous, vile, greedy, sensuous, blood-thirsty, ever disgraced the pages of history. Make bare thy mighty arm, O Lord, and smite the hungry, wolfish Hun, whose fangs drip with blood, and we will forever raise our voice to thy praise." (Applause.) This was in a prayer in the House of Representatives in January, 1918. Horace Bridges put Ethical Culture on the right side by writing an article for the *Atlantic Monthly* on "The Duty of Hatred." Father Ryan wrote in the *Catholic World* on "The Limits of Free Speech."

The churches' participation in the World War was rationalized by the belief that great spiritual benefit would accrue to the men in the trenches. "The fighting man is nourishing his soul on the gospel. The man in the trenches is committing his life to God" (*Northwestern Christian Advocate*, April 25, 1917).

In a sermon to the soldiers in camp, Rev. F. B. Harris declared: "The soldiers who go over the top go not simply with His command; they go with Him" (*Ibid.*, March 7, 1918).

Replying to a criticism upon the church for its failure to support the war adequately (an article entitled "Peter Sat by the Fire Warming Himself," in the *Atlantic Monthly*), Rev. O. S. Duffield said: "It will never be forgotten that at the altars of the church the ministry persuaded thousands upon thousands of our boys to dedicate themselves to the great cause as the holiest crusade of the Christian centuries" (*Ibid.*, March 7, 1918).

And again, showing denominational as well as Christian pride in supporting the war: "The Christian church is in the war. And Methodism must do its share in the war. In Bishop McDowell's fine phrase, 'We do not intend that any church shall have more stars in its service flag than we have.' [And none did.] Of course, the Methodist Church will, as it has ever done, stand by the government to the last trench" (*Ibid.*, March 15, 1918).

The leading organs of evangelical opinion had little sympathy with war resisters and conscientious objectors. "There are but two possible attitudes for Americans to assume. They are either for or against the government. They are either patriots or traitors" (*Christian Advocate*, February 13, 1918).

The Methodist press had preached peace and commended arbitration in the years before the war and approved Bryan's arbitration treaties in 1913. It was rather slow to catch the war fever in 1914 and 1915 and was hesitant about accepting stories of atrocities. There were optimistic hopes about the reviving effect of war on religion. "The English soldier boys are going to war to learn of Christ in his true essence, and coming back home to stir the church" (*Northwestern Christian Advocate*, March 8, 1916).

By the time America entered, the war was thoroughly idealized and by the time it ended it could be boasted that "Methodism's world program" was "first in war, first in peace" (*N. Y. Christian Advocate*, November 21, 1918).

The espionage act of June 15, 1917, was intended to curb the activities of those persons in the United States who adhered to the cause of the enemy. It was used, however, to punish and restrain all sorts of radicals who were opposed either to all war or to this particular war, those who were suspected of being German sympathizers, and those who considered the war as capitalistic. The I. W. W. promoted strikes, especially in the mining and lumber industries in the West. Obstructing the war was with them a less important consideration than attacking capitalism. But "criminal syndicalism" became a convenient form of indictment. Those who opposed war on social grounds, like Roger Baldwin, director of the American Civil Liberties union, based their attitude on opposition to the principle of conscription. Along with these may be listed the radical socialists who viewed the conflict as a struggle not of nations but of classes, and opposed it as a capitalistic war.

Religious opposition to the war included: (1) Bodies having a long and honorable tradition of pacifism such as the Quakers and Mennonites. These were, in general, willing to do non-combatant service and their scruples were generally respected. (2) A number of minor sects, usually quite unknown to the draft boards which had to do with them, whose other-worldly tenets included objection to wearing buttons, shaving, saluting, or wearing uniforms, as well as non-resistance. (3) Persons whose religious connection was with denominations not committed to non-resistance but who were personally and on principle opposed to war. These suffered more harsh treatment at the hands of the government than either of the other two classes. Purely individual scruples against war unaccompanied by symptoms of fantastic nonconformity about other social practices seemed to many draft boards to be only a pretense motivated by cowardice, and many possessors of such scruples went to Leavenworth and Atlanta, and stayed there long after the war was over.

The trustees of the Church Peace Union, including Protestants, Catholics and Jews, which had been holding its first international peace conference at Constance when the war broke out, voted to devote their services and the income of their two million dollar Carnegie fund to promoting "the moral aims of the war"—whatever they were. Three or four of the trustees, including Dr. Peter Ainslie, dissented on the ground that the war had no moral aims. Bishop Paul Jones (Episcopal), a leader in the Fellowship of Reconciliation, the most extreme group of Protestant pacifists, was forced to resign his diocese, Utah, on account of his opposition to the war. He was still without a diocese in 1932, but he came within a few votes of being restored to active service by the General Convention at Denver in 1931.

The wartime activities of the churches were many and varied. As soon as war was declared, the Y. M. C. A. and the Knights of Columbus mobilized as welfare agencies. The Federal Council of Churches organized a general Wartime Committee. The Roman Catholics formed the National Catholic War Council. Through these and other agencies the churches served the soldiers in the camps and in the field, in both secular and spiritual ways. The distribution of cigarettes was counted to them for righteousness, and the doughnuts of the Salvation Army were twice blessed by blessing them that took and them that gave. Religious services were held and entertainment was furnished. The churches sold Liberty Bonds, organized their women to knit sweaters and trench helmets, and released their ministers to serve in the Y or as chaplains. They hung service flags behind their pulpits, and glorified the service and the sacrifice which the stars of those flags symbolized. In a thousand ways they built morale in the interest of the nation's cause and, as they earnestly believed, in the interest of the better world which was to emerge from the whirlwind of the war. They made it a holy war.

That the churches were still devoted to the ideal of peace is indicated by the promptness with which they rallied to the support of the President's policy with reference to the League of Nations. Their overwhelming sentiment in favor of joining the League was not the expression of a deliberate and informed judgment upon the merits of the proposal, whatever may have been its merits; it was rather a vote by acclamation in favor of the conviction which had sustained their faith through the struggle—that this *must* be proved to be a war to end war.

The subsequent development of the mind of the church on the subject of war must be considered later. For the present it will suffice

to illustrate by the example of two sets of denominational pronouncements the general curve which the change has followed.

The Northern Baptist Convention, 1915, passed resolutions favoring
arbitration and decrying "the evils of militarism, the delusions of
armaments as a protection against war." In 1917: "Whereas our
country is at war in defense of humanity, liberty and democracy . . .
we do solemnly pledge to the President and government of the United
States our whole-hearted allegiance and support (and) dedicate ourselves to our just and righteous cause." In 1922: "War as a method of
settling international dispute is 'barbarous, wasteful, and manifestly
contrary to every Christian ideal and teaching." In 1924: "Whereas
the Christian conscience of the world is coming to recognize that war
is neither inevitable nor necessary; that it is contrary to the teachings
and spirit of Jesus Christ; that it is the most colossal and ruinous social
sin that afflicts humanity today. . . . Resolved that war is a wrong
method for settling international disputes, and because it is wrong,
the church must not only condemn war, but must take an active part
in discovering and promoting the things that make for peace."

The sentiment of the Congregationalists can be discovered by a
study of the files of their most representative periodical, the *Congregationalist*. In 1892, this paper contained only one article on war, and
that one urged a round-the-world cruise of the American fleet to show
the world our power. In 1913, there were thirteen articles on war and
peace, all against militarism and an increased army and navy. In 1915,
there were twenty-six articles, predominantly anti-German, incidentally
anti-war. In 1917, war becomes a constant theme, at first with the
hope that we may keep out, then with insistence that if we go in it
must be without hate or greed. When we were once in, it was as
patriotic as any, but not rabid. Defending the religious press in general
against the unfounded charge of coolness in the war, it said: "The
religious press has been clear and emphatic in its constant justification,
. . . in its endeavor to mobilize all the resources of the Christian
Church behind the fighting men, in its exposure of German trickery
and cupidity, in its denunciation of German atrocities, in its insistence
that we stay in the war to the last dollar and the last man" (August
25, 1918). Since 1924, the Congregational national council has passed
resolutions denouncing war as un-Christian.

Chapter XVII

POST-WAR PROSPERITY AND PERPLEXITY

When the fighting was over, there was a brief period rather of exaltation than of exultation before the days of disillusion came. The conflict had been costly beyond all precedent or expectation, but, after all, it *had* ended war. Our great war President had convinced every idealist that the high objectives had been gained. A new world order was to be ushered in. The "one guilty nation" had been chastised and had been compelled to sign a confession that its punishment was just. Anyway, its power was broken. The defeat of Germany meant the defeat of militarism. Now there was to be a League of Nations, a league of perpetual peace. The treaty of Versailles drew a new map of Europe and made a righteous allotment of territory to the several governments. The war had been ghastly, but there would never need to be another. The church was proud that it had lent its sanction and its assistance in a crusade so glorious.

An account of the activities of organized religion and its status in America in the years since the war could be written by filling out with details the following propositions:

1. The churches shared in the idealistic interpretation of the peace as they had in that of the war. Even after the war had lost its glamor and suspicion rose that the Treaty of Versailles might not be a perfect and permanent adjustment, the religious mind tended to cling to the concept of a league of nations and to insist, with a tenacity which increased with the passing years, that war must be considered as an antiquated, outlawed and un-Christian institution.

2. The churches enjoyed the benefits of the two periods of economic prosperity—the one immediately after the war and the one which

began after the slump of 1921 and worked up to its climax and crash in 1929—and suffered, as business did, from some institutional over-expansion in the flush years. They shared also in the embarrassments and retrenchments of the lesser and the greater depression.

3. They played a large part in putting prohibition into the Constitution and in creating sentiment relative to the issues which arose in connection with it thereafter.

4. They shared in the general perturbation of the public mind over the various forms of post-war radicalism which seemed for a time to menace American institutions and the familiar social and religious order, and harbored reactionary and intolerant movements on a colossal scale.

5. But simultaneously there was also a great quickening of the social conscience within the churches and the appearance of a vast body of new liberal sentiment on international, inter-racial and industrial questions.

6. The number of church members increased somewhat less rapidly, and even decreased slightly in proportion to the population. Expenditures for religious purposes, especially for church buildings, increased rapidly during the years of prosperity, 1922–1929, even more rapidly than the general index of prosperity.

7. The community church movement extended its reach. The total number of churches showed some decrease, owing to the union of formerly competing congregations and the falling off of enthusiasm for expansion into new fields merely for denominational aggrandizement.

8. There was evident concern about the church's apparent loss of prestige and authority in the face of the increasing competition of secular interests and the popularization of critical attitudes. But that the public was still interested in religion, perhaps more genuinely interested in it than ever, was shown by the appearance of more discussions of religious questions in general periodicals and a greater tendency on the part of both church and non-church people to consider religion as something to be frankly and critically discussed.

9. There was a radical change in the foreign missionary situation, resulting partly from loss of the church's traditional certainty that it

had a definite message of salvation which must be given to the non-Christian world at all costs, partly from fuller recognition of the educational and social aspects of the missionary problem as distinguished from the evangelistic, and partly from the growing nationalistic spirit of the native churches (along with the countries to which they belonged) and the recognition of their right to develop an "indigenous Christianity."

The devotion of the churches generally to the idea of international peace has been expressed in the strong support that many religious leaders have given to the idea of joining the League of Nations; the still stronger and more effective support of the outlawry of war; the passing of absolute anti-war resolutions by many religious bodies and the signing of an unconditional renunciation of war by thousands of ministers; encouragement of all proposals for reduction of armament; and interest in the removal of the causes of war as indicated by the manifesto of thirty-five religious organizations in the United States to this effect: "We hold that since economic factors are primary causes of international suspicion and hostility that frequently lead to war, the churches should engage in the most serious study of such vital problems as foreign investments, war debts, raw materials, tariffs, armed intervention for the protection of property, and the whole question of the economic and political control of foreign peoples." By an interest, on the one hand, in social justice at home and, on the other, in international peace and good will, a vast range of economic and political questions have been brought within the circle of the church's attention.

It has already been remarked that President McKinley, a Methodist, ascribed to divine guidance his decision to take possession of the Philippines. President Harding, a Baptist, should also have credit for no less a sense of the need of religion. Soon after his election, and while he was making up his cabinet, he said: "It will help if we have a revival of religion. . . . I do not think any government can be just if it does not have somehow a contact with omnipotent God. . . . I have always been a great reader of the Bible. I have never read it as closely as in the last weeks when my mind has been bent upon the work that I must shortly take up. . . . I don't mind saying that I gladly go to God Almighty for guidance and strength in the responsibilities that are coming upon me."

The period of greatly enlarged gifts for both educational and religious purposes began near the beginning of the century. Note such movements as the Methodist centenary, the Disciples Men and Millions movement, the World Service movement. After the war began a period of inflation in church building and promotional programs. The patriotic belief still persisted that out of the war would issue a new spirituality which would transform the world. The church triumphantly trumpeted that "the world will never be the same" after such a costly lesson in sacrifice for the common welfare. Well, it never was—but it was not the spirit of sacrifice which had transformed it. Accustomed by contemplation of war expenditures to thinking of figures preceded by dollar signs and trailing illimitable vistas of ciphers, the churches conceived ambitious projects for financing the Kingdom of God which would have seemed absurd even ten years earlier. Liberty Loan drives had developed a technique of money raising as well as boldness in setting objectives. To build a million-dollar church seemed a matter of no great difficulty. And besides, the country was for a time terribly prosperous with the mushroom prosperity that follows a war (especially a war somewhere else) and terribly happy that the war was over.

In 1918, the general average of preachers' salaries was given as $937. Even this meager sum, which meant that the average Protestant church member paid about $4 a year for the support of his minister, may have been higher than the facts warranted. For if the 125 million dollars which is said to have been the total of the salaries is divided by 170,000, the number of ministers, the average works out at about $735. Many of the 170,000, however, were not in active or full-time service. The reports indicate quite definitely, however, that more than one-half of the ministers received less than $700, and that less than 1 per cent. received as much as $3,000. The reported averages ranged from $1,223 in the larger cities to $573 in villages and towns under twenty-five thousand; and by states from $2,200 in the District of Columbia and $1,800 in California down to $564 in Arkansas and $562 in Kentucky.

The period of prosperity following the slump of 1921 saw a long-overdue increase in the meager salaries of the ministry.

The Inter-church World Movement in its ambitious prospectus

revealed the mood of the church at the time and its disastrous failure revealed the weaknesses of that mood.

The Inter-church World Movement was born of the desire to coördinate activities of all churches, to render the most complete service to the whole country. Wartime drives for the sale of Liberty bonds and for funds for the support of war work had given courage to face figures of astronomical proportions. The whole-hearted support which the churches had given to the great common enterprises during the war suggested the belief that the public generally, regardless of church membership, would support this great concerted movement of the churches.

The Inter-church Movement proposed: (1) A comprehensive survey of the needs of the field and the organizations and resources of the churches. (2) A comprehensive plan for meeting the needs. (It was in effect a five-year plan.) (3) The formulation of a consolidated budget for the work of all the churches and their institutions. (4) A tremendous unified campaign to raise the money required for the budget. Very considerable progress was made toward the completion of the first three items. The surveys in particular were carried out with great skill, in some regions with great detail and incidentally at great expense. The plans were stated for the most part in terms of principles. More detailed programs would have come later. The budget was for the most part a compilation of the askings of the various coöperating denominational organizations. The campaign for funds fell flat.

The prohibition movement was in one aspect a part of this social movement of the churches. The W. C. T. U. and the Prohibition Party had found practically all of their support in the evangelical Protestant churches and the Anti-saloon League was to a considerable extent what it claimed to be: "the churches organized to fight the saloon." Nevertheless, after a temperance campaign waged sporadically for fifty years, only five states—Maine, New Hampshire, Vermont, Kansas and North Dakota—had state prohibition in 1898. After 1903, there were but three, for New Hampshire and Vermont in that year went back to the local option system.

Two factors outside of the immediate field of church influence tended to make the liquor business unpopular. The first was its unholy alliance with politics (Gordon: *When the Brewers Had the Strangle Hold*); the other was the awakening consciousness of large employers of labor in regard to the effects of alcohol on efficiency and safety in industry. But the churches, especially Methodist and Baptist, began to take a more active part in the campaign for prohibition. Bonfort's Wine and Spirits circular, October 25, 1914, said "We must realize that the entire Methodist Church is a solid, active, aggressive, and obedient unity in this war on our trade." The charge of clericalism and political ambition for the church, which has been frequently reiterated, had its origin at least as early as that year when the secretary of the liquor dealer's association said: "It is the Methodist Church which is obsessed with the ambition to gain control of the government." The president of the brewers' association in the same year listed the Methodist and Baptist Churches, the W. C. T. U., the Epworth League and the Anti-Saloon League as the chief enemies of the trade (*Brewers' Association Year Book for 1914*).

Other churches were somewhat less unanimous. The Anti-saloon League got little support from Episcopalians and Lutherans and none at all after its earliest days from Catholics. In the hope of creating an institution which would preserve whatever values the saloon had as a poor men's club without its manifest drawbacks, Bishop Potter in 1904 assisted in the opening of what was called the Subway Tavern in New York, not to encourage drinking, but to encourage moderation in drinking for those who were going to drink anyway and to give them a decent place in which to do it. The institution never flourished. The Anti-saloon League fought it as a surrender to the enemy. The liquor dealers fought it because of its implied criticism of the normal conduct of their business. And the prospective patrons did not flock to it in any considerable numbers because they did not want to do their drinking under conditions dictated by reformers.

The years from 1903 to 1916 were years of intensive propaganda and skillful political activity on the part of the Anti-saloon League and especially its active head, Wayne B. Wheeler. Attention was turned from preaching temperance to the organization of all the enemies of the saloon for political action. The story of the Anti-saloon League under the title *Pressure Politics*, by P. H. Odegard (New York, 1928), is not ill-named. Added to the influence already mentioned were the sense of the danger from drunkenness among Negroes in the South and the fact that the southern states were dominated more than any others by the influence of the two churches which were most active in the prohibition cause. The following states adopted state-wide prohibition: Georgia and Alabama, 1907; Mississippi and North Carolina, 1908; West Virginia, 1912; Virginia, 1914; Arkansas and South Carolina, 1915. Eight southern states were dry by 1915. This wave of political prohibition passed from the South to the West. Arizona, Colorado, Oregon, and Washington, 1914, Idaho and Utah, 1916.

Simultaneously, the local option movement had made great advance in the states which did not have state prohibition.

Nevertheless, while a large percentage of the area and population of the United States was subject to local prohibition, the Anti-saloon League year book for 1915 reported that the total consumption of wines and liquors in the United States in 1914 was greater than that in any preceding year.

The effect of these restrictive measures had been to make the rural districts and towns dry and to leave the larger cities wet. It is, of course, in the larger cities that those foreign populations are largely centered which are outside of the influence of the evangelical churches and whose traditions are more definitely tied up with the unrestricted use of alcoholic beverages. It was in the cities, also, that the liquor interests had their closest alliance with politics.

In 1913, the Webb-Kenyon bill, passed by Congress over the veto of President Taft, prohibited the shipping of liquor into dry territory, thus doing away with the "original package" decision which had made it possible to ship direct to consumers in dry states. This was the first important victory of the dry forces in Congress. The fact that they could secure the passage of the bill over a presidential veto showed that, for that purpose at least, they had two-thirds of Congress behind them, and encouraged them to make the final assault upon the enemy's stronghold. In December of that same year, 1913, a resolution providing for the submission of a Federal prohibition amendment was submitted in both houses of Congress. Unfavorable committees killed these bills but similar ones were introduced the following year.

By 1914, fourteen states had adopted state prohibition and with the addition of smaller districts which were dry by local option 47 per cent. of the population and 70 per cent. of the area of the United States was dry. Between this date and the adoption of the prohibition amendment the following states were added to the list that had state prohibition: In 1915, Arkansas, Idaho, Iowa, South Carolina, and Alabama. In 1916, Michigan, Montana, Nebraska, South Dakota. In 1917, Indiana, New Hampshire, New Mexico, and Utah. In 1918, Wyoming, Florida, Ohio, Nevada, and Texas. The adoption of prohibition in practically all of these states, with perhaps some slight exception in the case of the 1918 group, was entirely independent of the influence of the war. The war had its effect, however, in bringing about the restriction upon the use of grain for the production of alcohol (Act of 1917) and in the passage of the measure for wartime prohibition. The latter, however, never went into effect, for before the date set for its going into effect (July 1, 1919) two things had happened: The war was over, and the prohibition amendment had been submitted and ratified.

The wartime psychology, with its emphasis upon the conservation of food and the necessity of maintaining labor at its highest efficiency, undoubtedly had a part in moving Congress to submit the eighteenth amendment. It is, however, a gross perversion of fact to argue that prohibition was slipped over "while the boys were overseas." The Congress which passed the bill and practically all of the legislatures which ratified it were elected before the declaration of war. When national prohibition became effective 68 per cent. of the population and 94 per cent. of the area of the United States was already locally dry. The amendment became part of the Constitution in January, 1919, and the Volstead act went into effect January, 1920.

The Anti-saloon League continued its activity in efforts to secure state enforcement laws, appropriations to make these laws effective and the election of officials friendly to prohibition. In the pursuit of these ends it largely abandoned the enterprise of temperance education and relied upon law enforcement. Second only to the Anti-saloon League was the Methodist Board of Temperance, Prohibition and Public Morals, effectively headed by Dr. Clarence True Wilson. These two organizations, assisted in various degrees by other committees representing the churches, constituted a "pressure group" for political action. Whatever criticism is aimed at them for their attempts to "browbeat" congressmen and legislators must be viewed in the light of the fact that their work was possible only because of the existence of a vast body of prohibition sentiment among the people. Their policy of collating and publishing the records of candidates with reference to their attitudes to prohibition and of challenging the anti-prohibition organizations to do the same was an appeal to public opinion and it was effective as a campaign technique only to the extent to which the public opinion was on their side.

In the brief period of prosperity which intervened between the Armistice and the depression of 1921 there was an extraordinary number of strikes. Practically all of the fundamental industries were affected in greater or less degree. It is estimated that about four million workers were on strike at the same time in 1919. The cause was the failure of wages to rise in proportion to the new high level of prices, the general unrest following the war and the effort to unionize industries not already unionized. The case of the strikers was prejudiced by the association of reds and radicals with their cause. The Inter-church World Movement and the Federal Council of Churches conducted an investigation of the steel industry which led to the conclusion that the eight-hour day was practical, contrary to the belief of the managers of the United States Steel Corporation. The ultimate partial success of the strikers in this case was in no small degree due to the stand taken by representatives of the churches. And to this stand in the interest of labor was also due in no small measure the failure of the Inter-church Movement and the subsequent denunciation of the Federal Council by super-patriots as a dangerous organization.

The Harding régime was marred by some disgraceful incidents: the robbery of the Veterans Bureau by Col. Forbes; the Fall case; frauds by the Custodian of alien property; the election of Senators Newberry of Michigan, Smith of Illinois, Vare of Pennsylvania. Bootleggers and gangsters flourished. It came to be generally believed that the country was being swept by a crime wave. Statistics did not show any increase in the total volume of crime for the period, but certainly crime was bolder, more picturesque and more lucrative than previously. Municipal governments in certain cities, notably Chicago, reached new lows.

The confusion in Europe following the war, and especially the rise of bolshevism, led to panicky protest against all forms of liberalism and dissent. A partial explanation of this was the fact that there were outcroppings of communist sentiment and a certain amount of organized campaigning against the existing social order. It was the heyday of the I. W. W. A little later when self-appointed guardians of the republic began to make their black-list, it included every prominent intellectual of international mind with a conscience sensitive to social justice. The popular panic had fairly subsided, but in 1919 and for a few years thereafter the fear of red revolution was not confined to a small band of professional super-patriots. The House of Representatives refused to admit a duly elected socialist representative from Wisconsin and the New York legislature took similar action with reference to socialist members-elect. The outrage at Centralia, Washington, the deed of unidentified radicals, was followed by the lynching of a member of the I. W. W. Local and state authorities in the western states virtually suspended the bill of rights so far as the I. W. W. was concerned. Union labor fell under suspicion. There were many strikes in 1919. By the end of that year it was estimated that not less than two million workers in the United States were on strike. Some of these, under the conservative leadership of Samuel Gompers, could scarcely be accused by any one of wanting anything more radical than more pay, less work, or the recognition of their unions. Others, however, were demanding the nationalization of the mines, or the continuation of governmental operation of the railroads with labor given a voice in the management, or such agrarian readjustments as that proposed by Townley's Non-Partisan League among the farmers of the northwestern wheat-growing states. There was uncontestably a trend toward the left even in the orthodox labor organizations. And besides, there was a fringe of radicals more vociferous than numerous, mostly of foreign birth and all under the influence of foreign ideas, who looked upon the Russian experiment as the hope of the world and carried on communist or anarchist propaganda (very different things but sounding much alike to conservative ears) presumably with the support of money from Moscow.

It was estimated that in 1919 the membership of the Socialist Party numbered 39,000, the Communist Labor Party ten to thirty thousand, and the Communist Party thirty to sixty thousand (Gordon S. Watkins in *Atlantic Monthly*). This gave the radical parties, including the rather mild Socialists, a total strength at the maximum estimate of about one-tenth of 1 per cent. of the population or perhaps three-tenths of 1 per cent. of the voters. The fear of them was out of proportion to their numbers and that on two grounds: first, that even this number of advocates of violence might do untold damage; and second, that they might form a nucleus from which such ideas might spread among the laboring class, especially among those of foreign birth. There were enough bombing episodes to support this feeling. And on the other hand, there were unlawful and disorderly acts in defense of law and order. It was at this time that the strike of the Boston police force occurred, growing out of the unionization of the force and its affiliation with the A. F. of L. And out of that episode emerged a new hero and Calvin Coolidge was started on his road to greatness.

The steel strike began, not without the coöperation of certain radical organizers with a leaning to communism, and with the active promotion of the communist William Z. Foster. Before this got well under way came the great coal strike.

In opposition to these industrial perils and especially to the bolshevist menace that seemed implicit in them, the United States Attorney General, A. Mitchell Palmer—whose nerves were perhaps a little jumpy because his house had been bombed a few months before—made the wartime food and fuel control law the ground for securing an injunction against picketing and followed this up with a systematic campaign for the arrest and deportation of communist leaders to Russia. The heaviest blow fell on January 1, 1920, when simultaneous raids were made on communist headquarters in practically every state in the country that had a communist headquarters and hundreds of persons were arrested with or without evidence and scores of these were subsequently deported. The newspaper propaganda in support of this campaign fell little short of advocating the organization of a nation-wide vigilance committee to meet the red peril. To be sure, the *New York World* and a few other courageous papers declared and proved that there was no red peril, but sober argument had little weight to halt the progress of such hysteria. It had to run its course.

Before it did so, it had gone so much farther that it began to make itself ridiculous. William J. Burns estimated the number of communists at over 400,000. The National Security League raised it to 600,000. According to the president of the Allied patriotic societies the red radicals in America were holding ten thousand meetings every week and had established 350 newspapers in the last six months. Every sort of organization and every sort of paper which refused to join the red hunt or which had any sort of liberal social outlook was denounced as dangerous. The *New Republic*, the *Nation*, the *Survey* and the *Christian Century* were "revolutionary." Jane Addams, John Dewey, James Harvey Robinson, Norman Thomas and Rabbi Wise were charged with subversive radicalism. A little later, the whole Federal Council of Churches was similarly labeled.

In the Sacco-Vanzetti case, which dragged its weary length from the date of the original crime in April, 1920, until the execution of the two accused men in August, 1927, the sympathies of the more liberal churchmen and even of multitudes which had not previously been counted especially liberal were with the defendants. That the two men were technically anarchists was not denied. That either of them was in favor of the overthrow of the government by force was never proved. To many it seemed that they were being convicted of the specific crime upon no adequate evidence and were being denied a fair trial because of their political opinions.

It was natural that in the midst of this indiscriminate campaign against reds, radicals, and liberals of every tint and degree, there should be a resurgence of racial and religious intolerance directed at Negroes, Jews and Catholics. Of this the Ku Klux Klan was the chief though not the only vehicle. The Klan, organized in 1915, amounted to nothing until 1920, when a campaign of super-salesmanship and national hysteria brought it up to tremendous numbers and power. By 1924, its peak year, the membership was estimated by Stanley Frost at nearly four and a half million.

That there were anarchist activities of desperate character was undoubtedly true. Perhaps the most dramatic demonstration of this was the dynamiting in Wall Street on September 16, 1920. The prolonged investigation of this outrage failed to discover anything very definite but probably the first guess was right, that it was the work of anarchists. But even this conclusion, disturbing as it was, could scarcely support the theory that the country was honeycombed with organized bolshevism. By the following year the pendulum of public opinion began to swing in the opposite direction. While the Klan continued to grow, especially in the southern and mid-western states, the anti-red hysteria had about spent its force. It remained thereafter for certain patriotic societies to do what they could to keep up the suspicion against those who were devoted to promotion of peace and opposition to militarism. Perhaps America was diverted from this major folly by a multitude of minor ones. Radio broadcasting came in—not a folly perhaps, but at least a diversion and a vehicle for much harmless foolishness. Mah Jongg swept the country like a pestilence. Coué came along with the general wave of applied psychology with his assurance that everything would be right if we could say it was. A series of sporting events, pugilistic and other, demanded attention. Beauty contests became the rage and Miss Middletown ascended the ladder of fame until she sat upon its dizzy topmost rung as Miss Universe. The freer manners and morals of the post-war decade brought thrills to some and alarm to others but mental occupation to all. Among the personalities and topics that occupied the popular mind were King Tut, Einstein, cross-word puzzles, Floyd Collins, the kidnaping of Aimee McPherson, the Hall-Mills case, Leopold and Loeb, the Outline of History—and outlines of everything else—and Lindbergh's flight from New York to Paris.

Post-war prosperity had a set-back in the depression of 1921 which was doubtless one reason for the failure of the Interchurch Movement's hundred-million-dollar campaign. Yet in that same year the world's series broke all baseball records for attendance and gate-receipts, and the Dempsey-Carpentier prize fight set a record—for all time, it is to be hoped—when 75,000 persons paid $1,500,000 to see four rounds.

After the depression of 1921, there was a great wave of prosperity. Making allowance for the diminished purchasing power of the dollar, the real earned income per capita increased 28.7 per cent. from 1914 to 1926. It is estimated that in the flush days of the 1920's if the total assets and income of the country had been evenly distributed, each family of five would have had a capital of $15,000 and an income of $3,000 a year. But naturally there was no such even distribution, and the old cry that the rich were growing richer and the poor poorer continued to be heard. It is doubtful whether it was true at that time. The Federal Trade Commission in a study of national wealth and income reported that there appeared to be somewhat less concentration of wealth in 1923 than in 1912, and a study of income tax returns by the National Bureau of Economic Research led to the conclusion that the increase of the wealth of the wealthy had not reduced the incomes of those in the lower brackets—though of course it was still open to anyone to say that a more equitable distribution of this increment of wealth would have produced higher incomes for those in humble circumstances. Child-labor had decreased about one-half in the decade ending 1920. A proposed twentieth amendment, in 1924, forbidding interstate commerce in goods produced contrary to Federal child-labor laws, was defeated by a rather surprising revival of the states rights sentiment which had apparently not been operative when the eighteenth and nineteenth amendments were under consideration.

Turning to the matter of the rate of growth of the church as a whole, and of the several churches, some comments may be made upon the statistics for 1930 and 1931, and some comparisons with earlier tables.

There were fifty million communicant church members in this country over thirteen years old, constituting approximately 40 per cent. of the total population. Omitting from the figures for total population the children under that age, it would appear that the churches commanded the nominal allegiance of about one-half of those who were eligible to membership. This included Protestants, Catholics, Oriental Orthodox, Mormons—all organizations that call themselves churches and some that do not. These fifty millions, shepherded by 226,000 ministers and priests, succeeded during 1930 in increasing their numbers by 59,000 net. That is to say, aside from the filling of the places left vacant by death and defection, it required the combined efforts and influence of a thousand lay members and four preachers for a year to win one convert. The net increase was a trifle over one-tenth of 1 per cent. That was the smallest percentage of increase for any one year since the annual tables were first published.

Even more startling than the small net increase is the fact that some of the churches reputed to be among the most vigorous reported actual losses. That the Oriental Orthodox churches suffered a loss of 37,000 members may be accounted for by the cutting off of immigration. But the Methodist Episcopal Church lost 51,000, the Presbyterian (U. S. A.) 22,000, and the Disciples 18,000. The Reformed churches were in the red by 4,000 and the Unitarians by 5,000—almost 10 per cent. of their whole number. Here were losses aggregating 137,000—or, if we leave the Orientals out of the reckoning, an even 100,000 in five important denominations none of which was dependent on immigration to keep up its numbers and at least four of which were certainly up to the average in evangelistic fervor.

Over against these losses stood certain gains which, in some instances, were noticeably greater in the South than in the North. The southern Baptists added 40,000, the northern Baptists only 5,000. The southern Methodists gained 14,000, and the Presbyterian Church in the United States (sometimes erroneously called the southern Presbyterian) 2,000. An Episcopalian gain of 16,000 compared with a Roman Catholic gain of 18,000 showed that the former's rate of increase was about thirteen times that of the latter. What happened to the much advertised "drift to Rome"? Had the tide turned? Of course the cutting down of immigration was a factor. The most striking gain in the entire list was that of the Lutherans, who reported a net increase of 56,000, or not much less than their normal rate of increase for the last forty years. In other words, if the gains and losses of all the others, both Catholic and Protestant, had balanced (as they almost exactly did), the Lutherans may be considered as furnishing the entire increment in church membership for 1930. Or if the Lutherans were grouped with the rest to balance losses and the Baptists set by themselves, their gains would represent almost the entire gain of all the churches.

Though this mass of figures may already be a burden too great for patient endurance, still more must be added to reveal the full significance of these. The average annual rate of increase since 1890 has been 3.55 per cent. of the membership in that year. The 1930 gains amounted to about one-fourth of 1 per cent. of the 1890 membership, or only one-fourteenth of an average year's increase. The crop of converts dropped to about 7 per cent. of a normal crop.

The year 1931 may have been worse than 1930 in the stock market, but it was a better year for the churches. The net gain in membership was 433,000, or seven times that of 1930, or about one-half of the average annual percentage increase over the forty-year period. The same five denominations which contributed a hundred thousand loss to the totals for 1930 broke almost even in 1931. Most of the denominations that gained at all in 1930 gained more in 1931: the southern Methodists 38,000; the northern Baptists 23,000; the southern Baptists 87,000. No important denomination showed a greater loss, and very few had any. Only three showed diminished gains: the Lutherans gained a little less, 49,000 instead of 56,000; the Protestant Episcopal Church a good deal less, 7,000 instead of 16,000; the Roman Catholic Church, 15,000 as compared with 18,000 the year before—according to the figures furnished by G. L. Kieffer, president of the American Religious Statisticians, which I do not guarantee and which I doubt whether Catholic authorities would approve, though they furnish none more convincing.

Scanning the tables for the past forty years, one observes that, counting percentages and not absolute figures, the Mormons have grown one and a half times as fast as the Roman Catholics; the Roman Catholics (4.44 per cent. annually) a shade faster than the Jewish congregations; these and the Adventists about one-fourth faster than the Baptists (3.67 per cent.); the Baptists one and a half times as fast as the Methodists (2.46 per cent.).

One fact that emerges clearly enough from this clutter of statistics is that whatever peril confronts religion in this country, it is not the danger that some one organization will swamp all the others. The Roman Catholics, augmented by a steady influx from Europe, have increased only a little faster than the Baptists. The Lutherans have prospered chiefly by holding their own. There has been no great disparity in the rate of growth of the larger bodies. There is not the slightest statistical grounds either to fear or to hope that any one of them is going to take the field. Rather is there reason to query whether all of them together will be able to hold it.

Going still farther back into the statistical history of American Christianity, one finds data which, up to a certain point, support an optimistic conclusion. They have, in fact, often been adduced to prove that Christianity is rapidly conquering the country. Nominally Christian from the beginning, the nation was nevertheless born in an age when the proportion of church members was much less than now. The anti-religious tendencies of both English and French thought in the eighteenth century and the relaxing influences of frontier life upon the religious traditions of those who lived on the cultural and geographical margins of America, had produced a disaffection toward the church that was farther reaching than even the direst consequences of science and criticism in a later epoch. As nearly as can be ascertained in the absence of official records, only 7 per cent. of the people of the United States were church members in 1800. The proportion rose to 23 per cent. by 1860. It sank and rose again to the same level by 1890. Twenty years more brought it up to 43 per cent. Since then it has fallen to 40 per cent. That is where the church stands now—on one of the drooping sections of a curve which has shown a marked upward tendency for a hundred years. Since 1910, total population has increased a little more rapidly than church membership.

The figures are not exhilarating. They are not made any more so by adding that the number of ministers and the number of local churches increased during 1930 more rapidly than the number of members. One might hope, rather, for the gradual elimination of the more obviously unfit from the ministry and of the more glaringly superfluous and competitive from the list of churches. A great system of chain groceries, for example, on discovering that its volume of sales was diminishing, could scarcely comfort its stockholders by the assurance that anyway it had more stores and store-managers than before and a larger overhead.

But the contrasts between the church and a system of chain groceries are more important than the similarities. All of these statistical exhibits, interesting as they are, and important within limits, are irrelevant to the essential facts about the mission and vitality of the church. There was a time, though not in this country, when the church membership was practically coextensive with the total population, but it was not a time for the return of which most American Christians sigh. There have been times when the church was a purified and saving remnant. There have been situations in which the church exercised little beneficent effect even upon those who were in it, and there have been other situations in which it has wielded a great force for the betterment of those who were outside of it. Numerical increase is desirable, but it is no criterion of spiritual power. Some denominations which have made the most important contributions to the spiritual and cultural life of the country have never been notable for rapid growth or large size; for example, the Congregationalists and the Quakers. If one considers all the religious bodies together as constituting "the church," then it is obvious that the effective and working part of that church is so much smaller than the gross aggregate of its nominal membership that the enlargement or shrinkage of the statistics of total membership is no reliable index of the energy that is resident within it.

It may be that the immediate destiny of the church is not gradually to draw into its membership an increasing proportion of the population but to become relatively smaller, even absolutely smaller. If by doing so it can become clearer in its own mind as to the requirements of a Christian way of life, more resolute in its devotion to the things that make for the betterment of humanity, and more courageous in sounding the note which is prompted by its own inner conviction, it will be on the way to the only kind of success that is worthy of it. If losing one's life is a way of saving it, losing numbers may be a stage in the process of saving the world.

Chapter XVIII

FROM FUNDAMENTALISM TO HUMANISM

The prepositions "from" and "to" in this title are not intended to suggest progress from fundamentalism to humanism but rather the range of opinion between these two extremes. It is as when one says "from Dan to Beersheeba"—meaning exactly the same as "from Beersheeba to Dan." Fundamentalism and humanism are the Dan and Beersheeba of religious thought in the United States.

For more than fifty years, there has been a widening gap between the more conservative and the more liberal phases of evangelical religious thought. Throughout the greater part of the nineteenth century, the term "evangelical" was used as a convenient barrier to protect orthodoxy in all its varieties from the contamination of unitarianism. Within the last two or three decades, the word has become somewhat vague in its meaning. Its significance, like that of the word "orthodoxy" itself, depends on who uses it. It has therefore ceased to have much value for the purpose of classifying Christian thinkers into two groups.

The liberalizing of theology within the present generation has been marked by two features. The first of these is a daring modernization of theological thought beyond that which had taken place in the nineteenth century through the influence of evolution and Biblical criticism. The new changes have to do with the idea of God, the relation of Christianity to other religions, and the basis as well as the content of Christian morality. It has been influenced not only by the developments of physical science but even more by psychology and sociology; not only by the recent types of philosophy, of which pragmatism and its variations have been the most influential in America, but also and perhaps still more by a rather loose and unthinking drift toward secular interests.

I must say somewhere—and perhaps this is as good a place as any—that there is a current type of theological modernism which is not based upon rigorous thinking or upon an intellectual apprehension of the implications of proved scientific facts or deliberately accepted philosophical doctrines, but results from a shift of interest from all these things as well as from the authorities and the conclusions of the older orthodoxy. Temperamental liberals find in the contemporary social situation both an opportunity and an incentive for a type of liberalism which represents a great deal of human sympathy but very little careful thinking.

And in the second place, there has been a much wider acceptance of liberal views within the area which was formerly considered orthodox. It is no longer a question of an occasional heretic standing in peril of discipline at the hands of his church, but of a large percentage of the leading pulpits and most of the important theological seminaries advocating liberal attitudes varying all the way from a mild hospitality toward new ideas to the open advocacy of what would have seemed destructive radicalism if not sheer infidelity half a century earlier.

Union Theological Seminary in 1905 abolished the requirement that its professors and directors give assent to the Westminster Confession. The trustees of the University of Chicago voted that "it is necessary that the Divinity School be conducted in accordance with the methods and ideals of the University, in which is included freedom of teaching on the part of instructors." Many seminaries that were founded as distinctively denominational institutions have either explicitly ceased to be such or have become less so and have included in their faculties men of various religious affiliations. (The Divinity School of the University of Chicago began as a Baptist theological seminary, and technically may be one still, for all I know. But its four professors of church history, to mention only one department, are members of four denominations, and the one Baptist was a Free Will Baptist before the union of that denomination with the Northern Baptist Convention in 1909.) This interdenominationalization of theological education has not only been an expression of the tendency toward unity among the churches and an influence for the promotion of that spirit, but it has also had a definite relation to the wider acceptance of a more liberal theology.

The popularization of science which proceeded at tremendous speed after the war, not only on account of the increased attendance at high schools and colleges but also on account of the publication of a great number of popular outlines and summaries and the constant laudation of science in periodicals of every class, tended to build up the prestige of science in the popular mind. Whatever may have happened to the authority of the minister, the theologian and the ecclesiastic, there was an immense increase in the authority of the scientist—any scientist. "Science says" came to be considered by many equivalent to a demonstration. Everything relating to religion, whether an idea of God or a method of religious education, had to justify itself as scientific. The tendency of science was away from the cruder materialism and agnosticism of an earlier day, as the tendency of theology was away from a crude anthropomorphism. But many, even among the professional exponents of religion, assumed a deferential attitude toward science and seemed to consider that it was "the highest compliment to God that Eddington believed in Him."

It would be impossible, as well as superfluous, to attempt to give here any comprehensive statement of the substance of modernistic religious thought, and much more impossible to give an account of the diversity of forms in which it has appeared in different thinkers and groups. (For a summary of the more important results, see *Religious Thought in the Last Quarter-Century*, edited by Gerald Birney Smith, Chicago, 1925.) But I may state very summarily one or two characteristics of modernism—though I dislike the term, because it has ambiguous connotations either of superiority to old-fashioned error or of rebuke for apostasy from ancient truth, and I do not mean to imply either, much less to make choice between them. But what better term is there to substitute for it?

The application of critical methods to the study of the Bible has led to the conclusion that it is a book of uneven value, representing various stages of religious culture. This has led to a complete recasting of the concept of religious authority. Texts of Scripture are not quoted as final authorities. Even those who retain the idea of revelation and speak of it in the traditional terms put into those terms a different meaning—not what God has told man (using "told" in the fair and accepted sense of the word) but what man has been able to learn through his experience, including especially his experience with that ultimate Reality which is God. Not generally denying the existence of those factors which have been called supernatural, the modernist attempts to bring them into such relation to normal human life that supernatural and natural do not form separate and distinct categories. Whatever he may admit or deny, in actual practice he does not use the idea of supernatural events and a supernatural revelation of divine truths or divine commands. Every evangelical modernist will deny at once, and truly, that he has surrendered his faith in the supernatural. What he has done is to abandon that pattern of the universe which pictures two worlds of reality existing side by side—a natural world of men and events and natural causation, and a supernatural world of God and heaven and the angels from which truths and commands were once delivered to man by special revelation and which occasionally made contact with the visible world in miracles. Whether or not he believes in the possibility of miracles, the concept of the miraculous occupies little or no place in his thinking.

A very vivid picture of the direction and extent of these tendencies is presented in a study of the beliefs of 500 ministers of twenty churches in Chicago and vicinity and 200 theological students in five large seminaries widely separated. (See G. H. Betts: *The Beliefs of 700 Ministers,* New York, 1929.) Of the fifty-six points in regard to which inquiry was made, the only one upon which the entire 700 were unanimous was "that God exists." Aside from this one point, the students in every case expressed opinions more liberal, or less in accordance with the doctrines of traditional orthodoxy, than did the ministers. For example, that the New Testament is an absolute and infallible standard of religious belief was affirmed by 77 per cent. of the ministers, but by only 33 per cent. of the theological students. A little less than half of the ministers still believed that the creation of the world took place as described in Genesis, but only one in twenty among the students thought so. Two-thirds of the ministers believed that the inspiration of the Bible is different in kind from the inspiration of other great religious literature; but consider how great a change has occurred that the other third should think that the Bible has no unique inspiration—and three-fourths of the students agreed with them. It is perhaps not surprising to find that 60 per cent. of the ministers and 94 per cent. of the students find in evolution no obstacle to belief in God as creator. But it is rather surprising that the occurrence of miracles is disbelieved by 32 per cent. of the mature ministers and 76 per cent. of the students. That participation in any sacraments, or belief in the virgin birth of Jesus, or membership in any church is essential in order that one may be a Christian and a candidate for salvation, was affirmed by less than half of the ministers and by about one-tenth of the students. These tabulated replies indicate some of the changes in religious thought among the clergy.

Humanism thinks of itself as an absolutely new form of religion, characterized by the complete abolition of the supernatural and the denial of the existence of any Being which can fairly be called God. (See Charles Francis Potter: *Humanism*.) It seems to me more accurate to consider it as a variant of modernism which reverts to the earlier patterns of thought by retaining the traditional categories of natural and supernatural and declares that the latter is empty. (See the chapter on "Humanism Reactionary Rather than Radical," by W. E. Garrison, in *Humanism, Another Battle Line,* edited by W. P. King, Nashville, 1931.) In either case, humanism represents in practice the extreme left wing in current religious thought in America.

The critical view of the Bible had prepared the way for a type of Christian ethics based on other than textual foundations, and the changing social order with its new problems of conduct furnished an ample field for the newer teachers. George Herbert Palmer, as a philosopher in the field of ethics, had shown how ethical control differs radically from legal control whether the latter is based upon human statutes or on divine revelation. The discovery of new duties and responsibilities within the modern social, industrial and international situation was based not at all upon textual or exegetical considerations. G. B. Smith's *Principles of Christian Living*, a typical text-book of modern Christian ethics, supported a reasonably conservative code of behavior on grounds wholly independent of explicit divine commands and the prospect of rewards in heaven or punishment in hell. Durant Drake's *The New Morality*—which was to ethics what

Potter's *Humanism* was to theology and Haydon's *The Quest of the Ages* to comparative religion—argued for a frankly pragmatic and scientific type of ethics as a scientific study of the observable consequences of behavior.

The vast body of moderately liberal religious opinion rejects the humanistic position, and while not accepting all the conclusions of the most thorough-going modernism—and especially not accepting an antitheistic position—is hospitable toward its general principles and utilizes its concepts. But before rashly deciding that this liberal attitude is characteristic of the church as a whole, one should consider that the largest and the most rapidly growing denominations have very conservative theologies. To begin with, "Roman Catholicism is an out-and-out, thoroughgoing system of the supernatural and the miraculous. It conceives of Christianity as a body of truth supernaturally revealed, miraculously attested, and protected from corruption by supernatural means, and a body of practice supernaturally commanded and administered yesterday, today, and forever by men supernaturally endowed with authority for that purpose" (W. E. Garrison: *Catholicism and the American Mind*, p. 20). Roman Catholicism goes farther in that direction than fundamentalism, for it teaches that miracles are frequently occurring now. The Lutheran Church, in all its branches, justly prides itself on its theological conservatism. Baptists, Methodists, Presbyterians, Disciples, and Episcopalians have great areas of their membership which are untouched by any tinge of modernism. The largest Protestant denomination, and the one which is at present making the most rapid gain in numbers—*i.e.*, the southern Baptists—is also the one in which fundamentalism has the strongest hold.

The fundamentalist reaction, which received an immense impetus in the years immediately following the World War, was a militant phase of the attitudes which had long before been developed in opposition to Biblical criticism, the modification of world views through the influence of modern science, and the growing emphasis upon the social aspects of Christianity as contrasted with exclusive attention to individual conversion. It included a stress upon prophecy and upon premillennialism. The latter aspects involved a wide spread of Adventist doctrine outside of the denomination to which that doctrine had given its name. A series of "prophetic conferences" was held, beginning in 1877. Under the inspiration of these conferences there came an outpouring of literature of a quasi-apocalyptic nature. The purpose was to consolidate the forces of conservative Protestantism.

Parallel with this were the sessions of the Niagara Bible conference, beginning in 1876 and continuing to the end of the century. Its leaders included such well-known men as A. J. Gordon, Arthur T. Pierson, C. I. Scofield, and James M. Gray. The famous "five points of fundamentalism," formulated by the Niagara conference in 1895, are: the inerrancy of Scripture, the deity of Jesus, the substitutionary atonement, the physical resurrection, and the bodily return of Jesus to the earth. Similar Bible conferences were organized at Winona, Indiana, where J. W. Chapman was the leading spirit and where Billy Sunday later made his headquarters, and at Denver.

Both of these movements stressed the absolute cleavage between the Christian program and the secular world order. They represented a "crisis theology" of the most pronounced type. In their more extreme statements they manifested what, to the outsider, seemed an unholy glee in the prospect of the coming violent destruction of the unfaithful and the belief that the returning Messiah would ride bridle-deep through the blood of his enemies. Vividness was added to the picture by a sense of the imminence of the catastrophic end of the age. "Millions now living will never die."

In the Moody period of revivalism, the prophetic and premillennial movement viewed Moody as an apostate and a compromiser because he consorted with believers in evolution and Biblical criticism, though he could scarcely be accused of sharing their views. Evangelism of the tabernacle type, the dissemination of "prophetic" literature, and foreign missions of the sort represented by the China Inland Mission were its chief forms of activity.

While the established institutions of the conservative denominations for the most part did not show much sympathy with the more extreme forms of fundamentalism as promoted by the prophetic and Bible conferences, they were on their guard against what they deemed the dangerous tendencies of modern science and loose views of Biblical authority. In 1875, Alexander Winchell, an eminent professor of geology, was dismissed from Vanderbilt University (Methodist) for the "scientific atheism of the belief that the human race was older than Adam."

Liberalizing tendencies in Andover Seminary in 1885 led to the resignation of two members of the faculty who refused to subscribe to the creed submitted as a test of orthodoxy. The Andover case, which dragged on for several years and became the focus of controversy in the Presbyterian church, issued in the triumph of the more liberal group (W. J. Tucker: *My Generation*. On the other side, John A. Faulkner: "The Tragic Fate of a Famous Seminary," in *Bibliotheca Sacra*, 1923). While most of the seminaries were becoming liberalized, the fundamentalist forces were creating institutions of their own, notably Moody Bible Institute in Chicago, 1886 (at first merely conservative and evangelistic, afterward typically fundamentalist), and later the Los Angeles Bible Institute.

Two groups must be distinguished in the literature and thought of the conservative element. The first was primarily scholarly, the second evangelistic and premillennial. In the first were James Orr, Augustus H. Strong and the Princeton group of theologians, with the *Princeton Theological Review* and *Bibliotheca Sacra* as its chief organs. The second contained such men as R. A. Torrey, James M. Gray, and Griffith-Thomas, and allied with it was the Bible League of North America with its periodical, the *Bible Champion*.

Fundamentalism began business under its own name in 1909 with the publication of twelve small volumes entitled *The Fundamentals*, in which the evangelistic and prophetic wing of the ultra-conservatives gave to the world their statement of the foundations of the faith. This and other promotional enterprises were backed by the ample funds of Lyman and Milton Stewart, California oil millionaires. The literature of the movement included *Jesus Is Coming*, by "W. E. B." (Blackstone) which gained enormous circulation.

These influences had already had a wide effect throughout the church when the coming of the war and the consequent war psychology prepared their advocates for a more militant campaign within the several denominations. It was no longer deemed sufficient to carry on a general propaganda through conservative interdenominational agencies, but the denominational machinery must now be captured for the same end.

It must be sufficient here to say that vigorous fundamentalist movements were carried on among the Baptists and Presbyterians, where they were perhaps most at home; among the Disciples through the "Restoration" movement and the development of the "independent missionary agencies" apart from the United Christian Missionary Society; in the Methodist Episcopal Church with its "Essentialists"; and in the Protestant Episcopal Church. In not all of these was the premillennial feature present.

The really high-pressure fundamentalist movement began with the organization of the World Christian Fundamentals Association, in 1919, under the leadership of W. B. Riley and A. C. Dixon. Tremendous conventions were held; a flood of literature was poured forth; the services of scores of evangelists were enlisted; the Bible institutes and the "sound" colleges rallied to the task of training young workers. The Interchurch World Movement, the Religious Education Association, most of the colleges and nearly all of the theological seminaries were listed as the institutions of that "counterfeit Christianity" against which open war was declared. Soon the main strength of the Association was focused upon the task of outlawing the teaching of evolution. William Jennings Bryan became the protagonist in that fight which came to a head in the trial at Dayton, Tennessee, after the passage of laws prohibiting the teaching of evolution in tax-supported schools had been passed in some states and nearly passed in others. (The whole story of the Fundamentalist movement is told in detail and with scholarly accuracy by S. G. Cole: *History of Fundamentalism*, New York, 1931.)

The acute phase of the Fundamentalist controversy seems to have passed, for the moment; not by the settling of the questions at issue, but by a diminution of the intensity of interest in them. The suggestion, at one time seriously considered, that the fundamentalists withdraw from their denominations, since they could not dominate their machinery, and organize a new denomination, seems to have been definitely abandoned. This decision, and the failure of the anti-evolution movement, and the withdrawal of W. B. Riley, founder of the Association, from its presidency in 1930, appear to mark the end of the Association's active operations.

Chapter XIX

UNASSIMILABLE VARIETIES OF RELIGIOUS EXPRESSION

Perhaps the meaning would be clearer if I spoke of the "unassimilable varieties" as cults and isms; or as organizations upon the lunatic fringe of religion; or as fantastic and fanatical aberrations from the normal types of religious belief and behavior. But to use any of these terms would imply a supercilious and condemnatory attitude which I do not care to assume. I have no wish to sit in the seat of the scorner, even to view what must seem to me—from whatever seat I view them—bizarre and grotesque procedures in the name of religion. Besides, some of these movements, while thoroughly justifying the claim of their adherents that they are "a peculiar people," are in no sense weird or fantastic. But they have this in common: that they stand apart from the main stream of the Christian tradition. With few exceptions they set up strong claims to being "scientific." Indeed, the assertion of each that it and it alone is absolutely in harmony with modern science, especially mental science, is one thing that distinguishes them from the more traditional and regular forms of religion. The page of church announcements in any Saturday newspaper, especially in New York, Chicago, or Los Angeles, will yield a rich collection of notices of meetings representing some of the organizations that I have in mind.

In dealing with a multiplicity of movements every one of which claims to be absolutely unique, it is evidently impossible to make any classification that will command general acceptance. However, I have classified them roughly into four groups, as follows:

Occult, metaphysical, and oriental cults: Spiritualism, Theosophy, New Thought, Unity, Hinduism, Baha'ism, Rosicrucianism, Swedenborgianism, Christian Science. These represent widely varied types of reaction against the materialistic interpretation of the world, against the dominance of physical science, against the "common sense" view that things are as real as they appear to be. They have a transcendental quality and emphasize the tapping of universal reservoirs of spiritual energy for the attainment of personal ends. Some of them make healing and health the principal objective; some are very keen about getting the material rewards whose real existence they deny; some are chiefly concerned about transcending national and racial divisions; some seek to break down the barriers between the living and the dead.

Religious communities: Mennonites, Dukhobors, Shakers, House of David, Zion City, Mormons. When the religious or social ideas of any group imply practices widely at variance with the current mores of society, there are advantages in withdrawing from the world and setting up a separate community. This was an ancient and obvious discovery. Monasticism was based upon it, as were also the socialistic experiments which were popular in the first half of the nineteenth century. Such communities may be conceived either as models to show how the world could be and ought to be reconstructed, or as places of escape from its invincible ignorance and irremediable iniquity; and they may be organized for either communistic or autocratic control.

Evangelistic movements: perfectionism, Russellism, Buchmanism, the Four-Square Gospel (Aimee Semple McPherson). These are generally characterized by extreme orthodoxy, as against any form of modernism. Their primary objective is personal salvation and the winning of souls, but they also hold out promises of bodily healing and business success.

Non-religious groups: Ethical Society, Freethinkers, militant infidelity, American Association for the Advancement of Atheism. In spite of radical differences in quality, moral dignity and cultural status, these are grouped together because they are efforts to uplift humanity either without recourse to any means which they are willing to call religious or by uprooting religion.

Space will permit only a brief statement of the main facts about some of these movements. While some of them are small and growing less, others are powerful and growing stronger, and in the aggregate they constitute an important part of the picture of contemporary religion in America.

Spiritualism

It has been held that the fact of physical death is the original stimulus of all philosophy. When the voice of the church grew doubtful and unauthoritative on the subject of immortality, spiritualism arose with a claim to demonstrate the indestructibility of personality. Modern spiritualism began with the rappings of the Fox sisters at Hydesville, New York, in 1848. Later they repudiated their own performances as fraudulent, but this made little impression on the progress of the cult. It was estimated that there were 30,000 professional mediums in 1854, at which time the movement reached its zenith. Inside estimates said that there were four million followers in 1868, twenty million in 1875, and sixty million in 1884. These figures are fantastic, and could have been meant only as guesses at the number of people who believed that the soul survives death. Even at that, they were wild guesses. There were not sixty million people in the United States in 1884. The United States census reported 45,000 Spiritualists in 1900. No reports were furnished for the latest religious statistics. This is a fact of no special significance, for it is evident that there is no way of enumerating accurately those who believe in spiritualistic manifestations. Many who believe are not members of Spiritualist churches, the organization is loose, and the whole movement lends itself readily to the uses of free-lance practitioners. Undoubtedly, after the initial popularity of spiritualism there was a slump in the 'seventies, some progress toward the close of the century, then another decline until the World War doubled or perhaps trebled both its influence and the number of its adherents. The Spiritualist churches in the United States are organized in thirteen associations, eight of which call themselves national but only one of which actually is so. The religious census of 1926 listed 611 affiliated churches, but besides these there are many independent ones, each consisting of a medium and his immediate clientele. The churches, for the most part, have no property and no endowments, and the movement as a whole has no general institutions other than a headquarters at Lily Dale, New York. It has no particularly revered founder or prophet and no special body of sacred literature other than the Bible.

The Society for Psychical Research has treated spirit communications and materializations as a matter for scientific investigation. The acceptance of the genuineness of such phenomena by Sir Oliver Lodge and Conan Doyle has given strength to the cause, and the exposure of many fraudulent mediums has not greatly checked it. Spiritualism claims to be "a science, a philosophy and a religion". The gist of it as a religion is that "after death we become spirits living an eternal life very much like this earthly one in a spirit world which is a perfected replica of our own"—which may be true even if all the alleged manifestations and communications are fraudulent, or false even if they are all genuine.

Theosophy

Theosophy is the most occult of all the occult cults. What hope to condense its principles into a paragraph when its modern founder says that it is "the fruit of the work of thousands of generations of Adept Seers" who have written so many books of the higher wisdom that even the British Museum could not contain a tithe of them? For practical purposes we may say that theosophy means belief in the transmigration of souls from one embodiment to another, higher or lower according to the deeds done in the flesh, a body of practice based on this belief, and the hope of a vastly improved society through the accumulation of wisdom and the purification of souls which such reincarnations make possible.

Modern theosophy owes its origin and drive to a Russian woman, Madame Blavatsky, who came from Paris to New York in 1873 and there founded, with her pupils, H. S. Olcott and W. Q. Judge, a "miracle club" which became the Theosophical Society. She had certainly traveled widely, though the details of her odyssey are vague, and she claimed to have derived her doctrines from the "Trans-Himalayan Masters of Wisdom" whom she found in Tibet. The real existence of these teachers is a matter of some uncertainty even among theosophists. In 1887, she founded the Esoteric School of Theosophy. After her death there were published, in 1896, *The Posthumous Memoirs of Helena Petrovna Blavatsky, Dictated from the Spirit World upon the Type-*

writer Independent of All Human Contact, under the Supervision of G. W. N. Yost. Some, but not all, theosophists regard this work as authentic.

Mrs. Annie Besant became president of the Society after the death of Colonel Olcott in 1906, and the most coherent statement of the doctrines is to be found in her writings. She had been an atheist and an associate of Bradlaugh in London; then a student of spiritualism, the phenomena of which she believed genuine but the spiritualistic explanation of which she could not accept; and was converted by theosophy by Madame Blavatsky's two volumes, *The Secret Doctrine,* which W. T. Stead sent to her to review for *The Pall Mall Gazette.* Mrs. Besant established headquarters in California, but later made her home in India. The American branch of that section of theosophy which rallies around her has its central office at Wheaton, Illinois. It claims 234 lodges and 6,917 members.

Another wing makes its headquarters on Point Loma, at San Diego, California, where Katherine Tingley established a temple, a school, a university, and a colony. The present leader of this Theosophical Society is Dr. Gottfried de Purucker, who is described as the "lineal successor of the founder, Madame Blavatsky."

New Thought

New Thought began with Warren Felt Evans, who had studied and taught the doctrines of Dr. Phineas P. Quimby, from whom Mrs. Eddy either did or did not derive the initial suggestion for Christian Science according as one credits her earlier or her later statements. It was first capitalized by Doctor Holcomb, a Swedenborgian minister, and the phrase gained currency among the members of the Metaphysical Club in Boston in 1894. Like Christian Science, it includes a system of healing. Unlike it, it does not deny the reality of sickness and suffering, but teaches that these, though real enough while they last, can be overcome by right thinking and right living. Avoiding statements which would seem fanatical or extreme to the hard-headed, it clothes a spirit of Rotarian optimism in the language of an idealistic philosophy. Man has no limitations except such as he imposes upon himself. His nature is identical with the divine Nature, and it is only necessary that he concentrate sufficiently on the desired end to attain personal charm, financial success or the cure of physical ailments. The fact that it has not organized as a church has rendered its teachings the more accessible to the members and ministers of orthodox churches. There is a New Thought Alliance, but it cannot exercise any effective control over the peddlers of psychological gold-bricks who offer to teach, by mail, how to acquire a magnetic personality, develop will power, make money in real estate, know God within, and "perform miracles of healing, success, achievement, love, and happiness." O. S. Marden's *Success Magazine* was one expression of New Thought. Ralph Waldo Trine's *In Tune with the Infinite* was another. The leader of New Thought in recent years has been Mrs. Elizabeth Towne, editor of the *Nautilus*. New Thought is "the correspondence school of the soul," offering by return mail in five easy lessons not merely the spiritual growth and harmony which people ought to want but also the things that they actually do want—health, happiness, money, and friends.

Unity

The power of mind over matter has another institutionalized advocate in that oracle of truth known as the Unity School of Christianity, with headquarters at Kansas City, forty well-organized departments and a capital estimated at $3,000,000. Its heads are Myrtle and Charles Fillmore. Unity teaches that all unhappiness comes from failure to think beautiful thoughts. By the mastery of Truth, as taught by Unity, all may become Christs and have his power of resurrection. "Jesus raised his body to the fourth dimension. Every cell of his organism became a purified monad. . . . When we follow him in regeneration, our bodies will not know death; we shall become so spiritual that we shall live in the spiritual ether with Jesus; this is the great and final resurrection." But meanwhile also, even on the present plane, we may have financial prosperity and the healing of all our diseases.

The institution of Unity had its beginning about thirty years ago. It puts out booklets and tracts at the rate of 12,000,000 a year, is consulted annually by two million people, has a sales department, a correspondence course, a broadcasting station, a vegetarian cafeteria, and a phonograph record department. Each month it broadcasts a Healing Thought and a Prosperity Thought, and a booklet called *Unity Daily*

Word gives a choice selection for each day. Every day at noon and at nine o'clock in the evening the members of the School of Silent Unity meditate on these Thoughts and Words. A large plant called Unity City is under construction, fifteen miles from Kansas City, where a colony of the faithful are to live in a Unity utopia.

Hinduism

The number of Americans who have become avowed members of any Hindu cult is negligible, but the influence of the orientals who have given lectures and demonstrations of their philosophy has been a factor in rendering the minds of many Americans hospitable to the approaches of the cults that have already been mentioned. America first became India-conscious with the coming of Swami Vivekananda to the Parliament of Religions in Chicago in 1893. His liberal words about the universal elements in religion came at the psychological moment and were well received. Impressionable reporters said that he was the greatest figure at the Parliament. Certainly he was the most picturesque. From that day to this there has been a succession of greater or less luminaries from the East who have found many, especially among the affluent and bored and among the more self-conscious seekers after Culture, who were responsive to their presentation of such features of Indian philosophy as it seemed best to present to the American mind.

Baha'ism

Baha'ism is an oriental cult with some strangely modern and liberal qualities and with a claim to being a universal religion. It bears something of the same relation to Mohammedanism as the soil from which it sprang, that Christianity has to Judaism.

The Baha'is, as we know them through their propagandists in this country, stand for precisely the kind of things that liberal and socially minded Christians stand for. The latest authoritative summary of principles includes such admirable items as: the independent investigation of truth; the oneness of the human race; international peace; the conformity of religion to science and reason; the equality of men and women; universal education—and no claim whatever of special authority residing in the head of the Baha'i religion. But in another connection and to a different audience, the same spokesman—none other than Abdu'l-Baha—is quoted as saying (referring to himself as the infallible expounder of the truth): "All must obey Him; whatever He says is true. . . . Beware lest anyone declare his own ideas." It is a beautiful but borrowed system of lofty ideas of universal brotherhood and justice, with a special claim to unique authority kept somewhat in the background.

Among the Shi'ite Moslems of Persia the belief was current that there would some day appear a reincarnation of the twelfth Imam (successor of the Prophet), and that upon his appearance it would be the duty of the shah to resign to this messenger of God the control of the state. About 1850 there came one who claimed to fulfill this expectation. He was called "the Bab." The shah was not enthusiastic about a change in the government. Neither, in truth, was the Bab. He seems to have been a gentle person of a retiring nature, and the shah promptly retired him to prison. But this quiet man had very turbulent followers who took arms and went on the war path. They were suppressed, hundreds of them were killed, and the Bab was put to death for no crime of his own but to discourage his rebellious adherents. His successor was Subh-i-Azal, who moved to Bagdad by request and kept his place for ten years. Then his half-brother, Baha'-u'llah, seized the reins and declared himself the latest and greatest manifestation of God. He held his court for many years at Akka (the old Acre) where he died in 1892. He was succeeded by his son, Abdu'l-Baha, who did not claim to be a new Manifestation but only to be sole authoritative interpreter of his father's words.

Propaganda for this new faith, in a form adapted to appeal to the western mind, was started in Chicago in 1893. Abdu'l-Baha came in 1912 to dedicate the ground for a temple (still unfinished) at Wilmette, a suburb of Chicago. I personally heard the architect of the temple say that he had received the plan by direct revelation from God. Since the death of Abdu'l-Baha, in 1921, the tendency has been, even more than before, to stress the liberal and humanitarian elements more than the supernaturalistic and to hold forth Baha'ism as a way of peace for the warring followers of all religions. The present head, Sboghi Effendi, a young graduate of the American university at Beirut, is chiefly interested in the ethical and organizational aspects.

Nevertheless, it is evident that Baha'ism has a theology as well as a definite system for the control of the minds of its adherents, and any attempt to represent it as a broad and inclusive humanitarianism, or as a synthesis of the essentials of all religions, is misleading. The declaration adopted by the American Baha'i assembly in May, 1926, stated as among the requirements for voting membership: "full recognition of the station of the Forerunner (the Bab), the Author (Baha'u'llah), and Abdu'l-Baha the true Exemplar; unreserved acceptance of and submission to whatever has been revealed by their pen; loyal and steadfast adherence to every clause of Abdu'l-Baha's sacred will."

The Baha'is are not numerous. They used to talk grandiosely about millions. In Persia, it is said, they seek to give the impression that about half of Europe and America have been converted. There were 1200 in the United States (census of 1926), and there are about 10,000 in Persia, counting men, women, and children. So small a group would not be worth so much space except that it is an extraordinarily interesting movement in view of its lurid beginning and the transformation which it has undergone, and that the liberal and humanitarian aspect of its teaching has won a few very fine people in this country.

Rosicrucians

Rosicrucianism originated in Europe about 1610 as a mixture of philosophic speculation, alchemy, projects for the total reorganization of society, and the teaching of spiritual truth in the form of symbols. Its organization came later, and the present organizations in England and the United States are not continuous with those of even the eighteenth century. Its adherents always aimed to preserve the sense of being heirs of a mystery, a secret teaching, a hermetic tradition. A certain influence on freemasonry in its formative period is asserted —and denied. Like the Kabala, it wraps itself in an aura of mystery which, upon being probed, seems to have nothing much behind it.

There are two Rosicrucian organizations in the United States. The spokesman for the Rosicrucian Order, which has its "Supreme Egyptian Temple" at Rosicrucian Park, San Jose, California, dates the foundation of the movement back to Amenhotep IV (1315 B.C.), includes the Essenes, brings it to America in 1694, and lists among its officers Thomas Jefferson and Benjamin Franklin, "who carried out the plans for the work in America as outlined by Sir Francis Bacon, one of the chief officers of the organization in Europe in a preceding period" (H. Spencer Lewis, "Imperator," in J. A. Weber: *Religions and Philosophies in the United States*). The Rosicrucian Brotherhood, with headquarters at Oceanside, California, is headed by Mrs. Max Heindel, the widow of a mystic who obtained his initiation in Germany. Her account carries the foundation of the order no farther back than 1313 A.D., and she seems unaware that it existed in America until her husband introduced it in 1909, or that the San Jose group is in existence.

But in an organization where everything is *ex hypothesi* occult, it is perhaps natural that the right wing should not know what the left wing is doing, and vice versa.

Swedenborgianism

The New Church, properly called "The Church of the New Jerusalem," does not like to be called Swedenborgian, and apologies are due for using the term. It is employed only that readers may know what group I am talking about. Apologies would also be due for the company in which the New Church is placed, if I had not said in advance that there would be great contrasts within each section. Unlike the cults of the occult which have been mentioned, the New Church stresses the idea that the things which were hidden have now been revealed. The hidden sense of Scripture is made clear by Swedenborg's interpretations. By the revelations made by the Lord direct to Immanuel Swedenborg beginning in 1757, the new age was inaugurated and the plans of God were made manifest. It is not a cult of cheerfulness, material success and bodily healing, and it contains no element of orientalism or transcendentalism. God opened to Swedenborg the spiritual sense of the Word, which opening constitutes the second coming of Christ, and, as he said, "it has been granted me to be together with angels and spirits in their world as one of them." If the unbeliever counts that fantastic, so be it. Certainly there is nothing fantastic in the general body of belief and practice which issued from that revelation. Its followers are a sober, gentle, and God-fearing people, not set apart from other Christians by any sharp contrast in faith or practice, but "unassimilable" only because they date the beginning of a new dispensation from the coming of a prophet whom the others do not accept. Unlike all other modern prophets, however, Swedenborg's personality and intellectual powers command the admiration even of those who do not accept his credentials as a prophet. The membership of the church is small—about 6,000—and has not varied much in the last forty years. The great financial expert, Barron, who was a member, made a statistical study to discover whether they are holding their children and how they are gaining their converts. He found that they lose most of their children, and win most of their converts through the printed message. So he endowed a press. Their most recent historian, Marguerite Block, says that it was reported at the convention of 1931 that a missionary in Kansas had employed a large and talented family who all play musical instruments and give concerts in schoolhouses and courthouses to attract crowds, and concludes: "Perhaps the New Church in America will ultimately be transformed from theologians into troubadours of God."

Christian Science

Just because Christian Science is the most important of all these "unassimilable varieties," it is least possible to give it any fair discussion in the brief space that can be allotted to it. About all that can be done is to list it and leave it. But no apology is needed for the company in which it is listed. The appeal which it makes is similar to those made by theosophy, new thought, unity and Baha'ism; similar but not identical. Theosophy and Baha'ism drape their doctrines in the garment of a romantic and mysterious orientalism, one Indian, the other Persian. Christian Science, like New Thought and Unity, utilizes no exotic paraphernalia. Unlike New Thought and Spiritualism, it has maintained a rigid centralization of authority, an absolute discipline over its practitioners, and a perfect standardization of doctrine and practice; and in this way it not only enriched its founder and built up a powerful financial organization, but it has protected itself against such a swarm of irresponsible free-lance practitioners as trade under the names of the others. Like Spiritualism, it meets the cry of those who fear death, though it does so by merely asserting that death does not exist while Spiritualism attempts to demonstrate the continuity of life after death and to restore communication between those who are separated by a grave. Like New Thought and Unity, it catches the ear of those who are not conspicuously spiritual in their desires by promising things that the natural man wants. To be sure, it does not feature success in business or in love as among the inevitable fruits of faith, as the others do; but in promising bodily health—or perhaps one should say the absence of bodily infirmity, since body is unreal—it promises what all men desire. And like all the other cults that have been mentioned, it offers a vivid assurance of the reality of God and of the possibility of an intimate and sustaining relationship with Him. After the cavilers have finished their caviling, and the historians have shown how persistently the leaders of the movement have tried to conceal damaging facts about its early history and embarrassing ones about its founder, the significant fact remains that here is an organization including some hundreds of thousands of people of at least average intelligence who would rather believe that God has spoken through Mrs. Eddy, however improbable that may seem, than that there is no God, and who find the unreality of matter a more credible doctrine than the mechanistic view of the world.

Some hundreds of thousands, I said. The number may not be quite so large; or it may be several hundreds of thousands. No official figures are given out. In 1931, there were 2,400 churches and 4,800 persons listed as "ministers"—which in this case doubtless means readers. Most of the churches appear to be large, but what the total number of adherents is is a matter on which one person can guess as well as another. There have been some rifts—Mrs. Woodbury, and Mrs. Stetson, and the Liberal Christian Science Church with its special appeal to Jews—but the revolts against the autocracy of the centralized control have been fewer and less serious than the divisions in most other denominations. In view of the prestige which it has attained, it has more to offer (even on the basis of purely worldly advantage) to the prospective follower of any leader of revolt than the revolting leader can offer.

The metaphysics of Christian Science may be a perversion of the idealistic philosophy just as shallow and amateurish and garbled as its critics think, and as I personally think; but its adherents cannot be rated as morons when they publish and support so excellent a paper as the *Christian Science Monitor*, the only avowedly Christian daily in the United States. Its therapeutic system may in fact be only a form of mind cure, or the healing of bodily ills by personality adjustment—which it would vigorously deny—but it has perfected a technique for that purpose which has been used with satisfactory results in a great many cases. Its very rapid growth has aroused some apprehension that it may take the country. There is no probability that it will. Every religious movement with any vitality at all finds a constituency ready for it. After a period of rapid growth among this constituency, it reaches the point of diminishing returns. Christian Science has, I think, reached it. Its appeal is to bewildered intellectuals who are tired of negation and find it easier to believe the incredible than the credible; and to Jews who want to escape the synagogue but cannot bring themselves to become Christians; and to genteel sufferers from either diseases or doctors or both. There is a limit to all these classes. The requirement of gentility itself imposes a limit, and Christian Science does not go out of its way to appeal to any except the genteel.

Mennonites

With no set intention of withdrawing from the world to form separate communities, the Mennonites developed a habit of seclusiveness in Europe because of persecution and continued it in America because of the peculiar social customs which they considered essential to godliness. More adaptable than the Shakers, who have almost disappeared, they have laid aside some of their peculiarities and in doing so have lost much of their separateness. Absolute pacifism and nonresistance are among the tenets to which they have always most strictly adhered. They have now adopted the usual methods of denominational promotion and have a publishing house and a board of education, and send out evangelists at home and missionaries to India.

Plainness of dress has been traditional among the Mennonites. When the main body began to fall from grace by too great conformity to this world in the matter of clothing, Jacob Amman led a reformation which resulted in the formation of the Amish group, who abjured the use of buttons, suspenders, telephones, top-buggies, bicycles, furnaces, musical instruments, and hymn-books with notes. The neighbors of a Mennonite settlement, in central Ohio, which had divided into liberal and conservative parties on such issues, described them, respectively, as the "button Dutch" and the "hook-and-eye Dutch." The Mennonites perpetuate the teachings of the radical reformer, Menno Simons, who lived and labored in Germany in the early sixteenth century.

Dukhobors

The chief similarity of the Dukhobors to the Quakers is their refusal to bear arms. Originating in Russia, under circumstances that have never been clearly known owing to their aversion to keeping written records, many of them migrated to Canada where they have had trouble with the government intermittently on account of their refusal to record marriages and births and to record land transfers. Their doctrines, which are vague and with difficulty ascertained, are not strictly Christian. They practice a form of communism which, they say, is spiritual rather than economic. They refuse to use meat, alcohol, tobacco, medicine, or razors, and have neither lawyers nor clergymen. A more strict group eats no cooked food, and no salt, pepper, or vinegar, do not bury their dead, do not permit any form of education, and have no holidays or holy days. The Dukhobors never seek to make converts. All they ask is to be let alone.

The House of David

Benjamin Purnell, broom-maker and street-preacher, revealed himself in 1902 as the Seventh Angelic Messenger, in relation to a series of cults which had been in existence in England for about a century. With his wife and one other family he started a colony at Benton Harbor, Michigan, where he was soon joined by others. The cult has affinities with the Shakers. Sexual relations are deemed sinful and the source of all sins, but it is possible to achieve such perfection that children may be conceived without sin. Death itself is a sin, so no ceremonies are held for the dead. "King Benjamin" showed administrative ability in handling the colony, which was peaceful and prosperous, and governed his people with a firm hand, requiring detailed confession of all their actions. Exercising absolute power, he established a code of conduct for himself, as a superman, or an Angelic Messenger, and allowed to himself a degree of freedom in sexual matters which was the complete opposite of the restraints which he imposed upon his people. Charges were lodged against him in 1922; he went into hiding and avoided arrest for five years; and died a month after his trial in 1927. His followers had believed that he would never die; and when he did they expected him to rise in three days. The colony continues, with about 500 members—industrious, virtuous, devout, and friendly people—but it is now receiving no new members. Its property is the show place of Berrien County, with well-tilled farms, shops, hotels, an excellent orchestra, and a bewhiskered baseball team.

Zion City

The Christian Catholic Apostolic Church in Zion, with its colony at Zion City, Illinois, on the shore of Lake Michigan midway between Chicago and Milwaukee, is the promotion of John Alexander Dowie. A graduate in theology from the University of Edinburgh, then a Congregational minister in Australia, Dowie received a divine healing revelation in 1876 which led him to establish an independent church six years later. He came to Chicago in 1893 and began operations in a tent adjacent to the World's Fair. He rapidly won a following. The cardinal points in his teaching were divine healing, repentance of sin, no tobacco, no pork, strict obedience to himself as the Third Isaiah (John the Baptist having been the second), and payment of tithes to Isaiah. The tradition which he carried over was one of evangelical orthodoxy, and his discourse, like that of his successor, while vituperative toward all opponents and critics, was filled with terminology that was perfectly familiar to any one who ever sat under the preaching of a popular evangelist. The site for Zion City was purchased, industries were started, and hundreds of convert-colonists came and invested in the industries, or handed their money over to Dowie—which amounted to the same thing. A tremendous evangelistic demonstration was staged in Madison Square Garden in an effort to take New York by storm. New York was immensely amused, for Dowie put on a good show, but there were few converts. The cosmologic part of his doctrine —that the earth is flat and that the sun revolves around it—added to the entertainment, as always, but not to the effectiveness of the campaign. The Zion enterprises collapsed financially in 1905 and went into the hands of a receiver. Dowie was forced to resign control to

Wilbur Glenn Voliva, who became head of the church as well as of the business and got the latter on its feet by 1911. Voliva was a graduate of Hiram College and, for a short time, a Disciple preacher. He had no Isaiah complex or other claim to supernatural endowment, but he proved himself an able administrator and has held the colony together with reasonable success until the present time. Zion's chief difficulty arises from the fact that so many Gentiles have come in that it is not easy to maintain the purity of manners. Still, it is a misdemeanor to smoke even while driving through on the main highway, and during the summer of 1932 the state railroad commission sustained the objection of the city authorities, who are also the church authorities, against the stopping of through buses in Zion City on Sunday.

Mormons

When Brigham Young died in 1877, leaving an estate of $2,000,000 to be divided equally among his seventeen widows, sixteen sons and twenty-eight daughters, the *Independent* remarked that it was unedifying to see such a "coarse, brutal tyrant dying peacefully in bed . . . the incense of praise fragrant with the odor of his sanctity burned about his tomb," and expressed a preference for seeing him shot. "But," it added, "we fear that Mormonism will not suddenly collapse, as some have hoped, immediately upon his death." It has, in fact, done anything but collapse. It has not only greatly increased in numbers, wealth, and prestige, but it has to a very considerable extent become assimilated to the society which environs it. While the peculiar faith has not been surrendered, and Joseph Smith is still revered as a true prophet and martyr and the Book of Mormon is considered a genuine revelation, manners and customs have changed with the changing times, Mormons have become patriotic citizens, and modern critical scholarship is slowly having its effect upon the way in which the faith is held. The change began with the abandonment of polygamy. The fight on this practice began when President Arthur signed the first effective law against it in 1881, and when, by the strengthening of that law in 1887, men with two or more wives were practically disfranchised. In 1890, the Supreme Court sustained the decision of a lower court declaring the Mormon Church to be organized rebellion and confiscating all its property. A timely revelation forbade future polygamy, the church agreed to obey the Federal law, and the property was restored. How well the law was actually obeyed at first, and with what degree of good faith the church supported it, may be questioned. Brigham H. Roberts, congressman-elect from Utah, was excluded from his seat by vote of the House of Representatives in 1900. A little later a Senate committee reported against the seating of Senator Smoot on the ground that he favored polygamy, or was an Apostle in a church that favored it. Monogamous Gentiles perhaps did not quite recognize the difficulty of suddenly putting into effect such a radical change in the social structure. The "celestial marriage" idea is still a part of the law of the church, but the Mormons have become, to all intents and purposes, good Americans and there are few who any longer think of a "Mormon peril." They are, however, still active propagandists of their faith. While Gentiles have invaded Utah in large numbers, the Mormons have extended themselves far outside of it.

It is worth noting that the time of the rise of the "A. P. A." anti-Catholic movement was also the time when the Mormon church was in its most defiant mood toward the government. In the effort to keep Gentiles out of Utah, its officials had perpetrated the Mountain Meadow massacre in 1876. A Mormon had carried to the Supreme Court, in 1879, a test case in which he asserted—and his church backed him in asserting—his constitutional right to have more than one wife because it was a tenet of his religion. The Supreme Court decided otherwise, but polygamy continued. In 1883, a Mormon convention in Salt Lake City took a firm stand in favor of polygamy and denounced those Mormons who had put away their plural wives in deference to the Edmunds Act. In 1885, Mormon mass-meetings were held throughout Utah and also in Idaho and Arizona to protest against the "persecution" of the saints for polygamy. The claim was made that the right to trial by a jury of one's peers meant that a man charged with polygamy had a right to be tried by a jury of polygamists. Again the Supreme Court decided otherwise. Mormonism was viewed by most Christians as a menace. Even its polygamy was only an incidental evil. "It is a boil that shows bad blood; but it is the blood, not the boil, which needs to be cured." The real evil is that it is "a gigantic moneyed, political, and ecclesiastical corporation" (*Christian Union*, February 21, 1884). The members were poor, but the corporation was rich and autocratic. Opposition to it was an early part of the protest against the tyranny of corporate wealth—early because easy and safe and emotionalized by an evangelical moral indignation against polygamy. But through this whole episode, many millions of Americans were coming to believe that it is perfectly possible for a church organized under rigidly centralized control to be a dangerous element in American life. Whether or not any particular church was that, was a question of fact to be determined by the evidence, and that question was not to be hushed up by the cry of "bigotry." Anti-Mormonism thus prepared the ground for a new anti-Catholicism. The fault with the A. P. A. was not that it raised the question, but that in the main it dealt with it so unintelligently.

Perfectionism

"The twenty-three perfectionist sects on which we have two sets of census figures have practically doubled in membership from 1916 to 1926" (M. E. Gaddis: *Christian Perfectionism in America*, Ph.D. thesis, University of Chicago, 1929). The whole Methodist movement had been strongly colored by perfectionism in its early days. "Complete sanctification" and "second blessing" were familiar camp-meeting phrases. Finney, as revivalist (not a Methodist), was the perfect perfectionist. Noyes and Oneida gave perfectionism a bad name. There was always a danger of antinomianism in it. "I am so perfect that I cannot sin" easily became "I am so perfect that no matter what I do it will not be sin." As Methodism sloughed off this element, small sects sprang up to embody the idea. Some are urban and slum-missionary, perhaps under the influence of the Salvation Army. Others, though in the city, appear to be unaware of city problems. Still others, and more, are rural. All are churches of the poor and unlearned. They may be classed as either Pentecostal or moderate. All are primarily evangelistic. They are most numerous in Indiana. After that follow Delaware, Florida, Oklahoma, Kansas, Colorado, Idaho, and the Pacific coast states.

Russellism

Pastor Russell organized his Watch Tower Bible and Tract Society in 1884. Tormented in youth by the fear of hell, he had become an infidel, then a student of oriental faiths, then decided that the Bible did not teach hell. His preaching had tremendous success with the poorer class who were ready to believe in the cataclysmic end of the present order and in the setting up of a new order in which those now at the bottom might be on top. After Christ's invisible return in 1914 the Battle of Armageddon was to follow and the Lord's anointed (Russell's followers) were to become masters of the world during the millennial reign of Christ. Besides preaching constantly he poured forth immense quantities of printed material, furnished Bible lessons which were syndicated to newspapers, and put out a "Photo Drama of Creation," with a victrola attachment anticipating the talkies, which was seen by ten million people. The total circulation of his books up to the time of his death in 1916 was estimated at 12,000,000 copies. His mantle fell on Judge Rutherford, who gave a radio address in 1927 to the largest hook-up of that year, and the slogan, "Millions now living will never die," is still heard occasionally. The propaganda continues, but its place in the public eye has diminished, perhaps because of the unaccountable postponement of Armageddon.

The Four-Square Gospel

The only unique feature of Aimee Semple McPherson's special gospel is herself. Her message is a perfectly sound and conservative orthodoxy, combined with divine healing. But in addition to complete self-confidence, which plenty of evangelists have, and an equally unbounded faith in the Lord as a partner in her plans, she has a magnetic personality and a gift for stage management. Within five years after her arrival in Los Angeles, she had built her Angelus Temple and was packing it with crowds. The broadcasts from her powerful station practically crowd everything else off the air in that region when she is speaking. There is nothing crude, sensational, or vituperative in her method. She does not berate the other churches, but bespeaks their sympathy and coöperation. Smiles, spotlights, and roses enter into the picture. She preaches every night, and gives those who have been divinely healed of their infirmities an opportunity to present their testimonies once or twice a week. Her church practices immersion, without being controversial about it, and it was reported a year or two ago that she was baptizing more converts than all the Baptist and other immersionist churches in Los Angeles put together. Her personal misadventures have somewhat dimmed her luster in the public eye, but have drawn her followers more loyally to her support. Branches of her church in other cities have made fair but not striking success. The most that is to be hoped or feared from the growth of her movement is an extension of a conservative and evangelistic orthodoxy, coupled with divine healing.

Buchmanism

Twenty-five years ago Frank Buchman was the young minister of a small Lutheran church in Pennsylvania. Then he received a second conversion when, on entering a chapel in Cumberland, England, he experienced "a vibrant feeling up and down the spine." He began his soul-saving work among the students at Cambridge, who dubbed him "Old Moral Uplift" and gave him the confessions which he desired. At Princeton he was practically ordered off the campus, and this opposition gave profitable publicity to his movement. The main objective has been to reach the educated, especially college students, and the well-to-do. House-parties for personal conference have been the principal means of approach, and the securing of public confession of sin, especially sexual sin, has been the favored technique. Sexual irregularities constitute "90 per cent. of ultimate sin," according to Buchman's early teaching. Lately, perhaps as the result of criticism, less emphasis has been placed on this feature. Prosperity as well as salvation is held to be the result of putting away sin and getting into adjustment to God. Disciples receive "leadings" from God which help them in many ways. A woman testified that she was led to a sale where she "bought a $1,000 fur coat for $300," and another convert boasted that "Buchmanism enabled him not only to find God but to meet the Queen of Rumania and make a better impression on customers."

The movement has had surprising success in the Episcopal Church, and its head in New York is Rev. Samuel M. Shoemaker, Jr., rector of Calvary Church—which has become known as "the rescue mission for the Four Hundred." There has been much criticism of Buchmanism for its overemphasis on sex, for its encouragement of untrained converts to undertake the treatment of personality adjustments in cases which require the services of a skilled psychiatrist, and for its excessive emotionalism. But just how much emotion is "excessive" is a question upon which judgments will always differ. The movement has recently become more moderate in its methods and it has some striking and indubitable successes to its credit.

The Ethical Society

The first Society for Ethical Culture was organized in New York in 1876 by Felix Adler, a young professor at Cornell, whose education at German universities had unfitted him to succeed his father as rabbi at the Fifth Avenue synagogue, to which he had been called. The ideal of religion without theology soon took the form of ethics without religion. While the first appeal was to Jews, it soon passed beyond that stage. It was not intended to meet the special needs of the intelligentsia, but to give to average people the guidance which the loss of faith in their old religions left them lacking. The movement has not spread widely, but the high quality of its leadership has given it influence beyond its numbers. Its aim, as stated by the Chicago society, is "to interpret morality in the light of science, to give it reverence and devotion, and to make it a ruling influence in the lives of men." The Ethical Confession of Faith, by David S. Muzzey, includes four points: "Ethical growth is the supreme end of life; human personality is the only holy thing we can know; uncompromising intellectual honesty; man's religious duty is wholly definable in ethical terms." The American Ethical Union is a federation of the six Ethical Societies of New York, Chicago, Philadelphia, St. Louis, Brooklyn, and Boston. Its official organ is the *Standard* (New York).

Atheism, Militant and Evangelistic

Infidelity passed through many forms in the nineteenth century. An early aggressive champion of secularism was Robert Owen, the Scottish social philosopher and philanthropist, who maintained, in a debate with Alexander Campbell in 1829 that religion is an obstacle to human happiness and progress. His son, Robert Dale Owen, lectured in Chicago in 1868 (and elsewhere before and after) in favor of socialism and against religion. The early advocates of evolution, especially Huxley, gave comfort to those who ruled God out of the universe. Colonel Robert G. Ingersoll became the most famous foe of Christianity of his time. His reputation as an infidel, though still vague, cost him the Republican nomination for governor of Illinois in 1868, and from the publication of his lecture on *The Gods*, in 1872, until his *Why I am an Agnostic*, in 1896, and his death in 1899, he was the most militant champion of unbelief. In 1880, Beecher introduced him to a New York audience as "one who has worked for the right in the broad field of humanity" and as "the most brilliant speaker of the English tongue of all men on this planet." The occasion was a campaign speech for Garfield, himself a preacher. The high point in his controversial career was a theological tournament in the *North American Review*, 1887–1888, which was a succession of duels between Ingersoll and Rev. Henry M. Field, Hon. William E. Gladstone and Cardinal Manning.

Many forms of scientific and philosophic agnosticism and secularism followed, but infidelity did not become organized as well as militant until the American Association for the Advancement of Atheism was chartered in 1925. The fundamentalist movement, which was in full career at that time, and the anti-evolution campaign gave it obvious targets for attack. It took on the character of an evangelistic movement for the propagation of unfaith. Slogans were adopted. "Fight with the 4A, Kill the Beast." In a few colleges, groups of assertive deniers of religion took the title "Damned Souls." With Charles Smith as president and Hopgood as secretary, the Association put on a vigorous campaign, which met enough violent opposition to give it the feeling that it had its martyrs as well as its faith, and even sent foreign missionaries to British Columbia, Sweden and Mexico. It lacks nothing of being a full-fledged evangelistic movement except the organization of churches and Sunday schools.

Chapter XX

NEW FRONTIERS OF POLITICS AND RELIGION

For more than a hundred years it has been the proud American boast that here has been achieved the solution of a problem that has been the puzzle and the torment of political society since men first began to have both priests and rulers. We have put down the mighty from their seats of power and in their place have enthroned the collective will of the people; and we have completely separated church and state. With a government expressive of the mind of the masses and presumably devoted to the promotion of their interests, and with churches dependent for their support upon the voluntary contributions of the people who belong to them, with the institutions of religion freed from domination by the state as well as deprived of its patronage, and the state from all ecclesiastical alliances and priestly interference, we have—in so far, at least—attained an ideal social order. We have both civil and religious freedom because we have set the state on this side and the churches on that and have bidden them both to walk in their appointed paths.

And now we have discovered that we have done nothing of the sort, and that it cannot be done. The problem is back upon us in new forms, and we have to solve it all over again.

The churches are, to be sure, disestablished as we thought they were. Public education is free from ecclesiastical control, and public money is not devoted to the maintenance of church schools. We can worship as we please, or not at all if we please, and no man is required by law to contribute a dollar to the support of any religion other than his own, or even of that. Any office in the land is open to any citizen regardless of his religious beliefs or his lack of any—

provided he can get elected, and farther than that the government cannot go in guarding the religious liberty of the candidate without encroaching upon the liberty of the voter. Neither law nor social pressure nor a vague and generalized exaltation of the idea of "tolerance" can require every citizen to ignore every other citizen's religion as a possible indication of his type of mind or a possible influence upon his political behavior. We do indeed have all the religious equality that can be established by law. Still we have not solved the problem of completely separating church and state by fencing them within their respective areas of jurisdiction and guaranteeing that these areas shall not overlap. That problem cannot be solved, because, as a matter of fact, their areas do overlap. But the insolubility of that problem produces, or reveals, certain others which, in my judgment, can be solved, and must be solved on penalty of falling into deep confusion.

There are two reasons why the problem of a complete separation of the areas of church and state cannot be solved. One is that the state cannot set limits to its own jurisdiction. It may be reasonably expected to abstain from asserting its absolute authority over every field of conduct and opinion, or from acting upon the assumption of such omnipotence, but it can scarcely be expected to set up precise criteria by which its own competence shall be limited. It is therefore likely that there will always be a somewhat hazy boundary to the field of the state's actual or possible control. The other reason is that the churches are unwilling, and of necessity must always be unwilling, to limit the scope of their interest to matters about which the state can have no possible concern.

The reawakening of the church within the last fifty years to its responsibilities in the domain of social ethics has revived this problem in new and acute forms, but it is not a new problem. Except at periods of extreme and temporary subservience on the part of one or the other, there have always been complaints of mutual encroachment by both church and state. The frequent charge against the church has been that it meddled with the affairs of the state, as sometimes it obviously did. In the medieval period, the church frankly took the whole area of life as its own. More recently, the customary defense has been that church and state cannot conflict because they occupy two different fields and move upon different planes. But their areas of interest obviously do overlap. This is as true of Protestantism as of Catholicism. Calvin's Genevan state enacted into law and enforced by the police power the church's whole code of individual morality. The Puritan governments in colonial New England, as well as other governments elsewhere, made disregard of Sunday observance a misdemeanor. The churches took sides upon the slavery question on the ground that it was a moral issue, while the government legislated upon it as a political issue, and neither denied the other's right to participate in the controversy. With the multiplication of questions in our own time upon which the churches are convinced that they must make their voices heard, and with the quickening of the social conscience, still more general has become the belief that religion has something to say about the behavior of men in society and about the structure and processes of the social order, though these are the very things with which government is most vitally concerned. Let the dangers of interference or of intolerance be what they may, there is no escape from them by retreat into the ivory towers of dogma and mystical devotion.

Whether one looks at our civilization's most urgent problems from the standpoint of the professed religionist or from that of the avowed secularist, it is impossible not to realize that religion has a legitimate part in their solution if it has a right to exist at all. The chorus of testimony from ministers, theologians, and other professional exponents of Christianity, to the effect that religion must make its contribution to social and moral betterment in concrete ways, is so familiar and so unanimous that it would be superfluous to cite examples. But on the other hand also, we find such a thinker as Mr. H. G. Wells—who is certainly anything but a partisan of the churches —assigning to religion a great and objective task. "Religion, modern and disillusioned, has for its outward task to set itself to the control and direction of political, social, and economic life. If it does not do that, then it is no more than a drug for easing discomfort, an 'opium of the people' " (*What Are We to Do with Our Lives?*, p. 33, New York, 1931).

"Control" and "direction" are brave words. Used by churchmen in such a context, they would seem arrogant words. Their meaning need not be pressed farther than that religion must play a part in the determination of these matters.

Let us take a sweeping view of the main outlines of that total process of American thought and culture in which it has been the business of the churches to take an influential part, even though perhaps not a controlling or directing part, and to which it must now make its contribution. The general curve of that development has exhibited a transition through three stages:

1. An uncritical optimism prevailed from the early part of the nineteenth century until well after the middle of it, persisting longer in some circles and some areas than in others. The Civil War brought it to an end in the South but gave it a new lease of life in the North. Its ground was partly religious in the evangelical way; partly the luminous but unsubstantial clouds of Emersonian transcendentalism; partly economic, springing from the rapid growth of wealth, population and the statistics of almost everything by which the temporal welfare of nations is measured; and partly patriotic. It seemed little less than treason not to believe that God's in his heaven, all's right with the U. S. A., the most favored corner of his footstool. The beginning of the industrial age had already brought prosperity—to all except the least fortunate of the workers, and the comfortable and pious could write off the miseries of these as the manifest results of addiction to string drink or other vices—and it had not yet brought the acute problems which were implicit in it. Evolution gave the orthodox some tremors of uneasiness, but the reconcilers of science and religion soon appeared to show that the theory of evolution, with its recognition of the resistless upward and onward movement of everything, reinforced faith in the goodness and the power of God by showing that a benevolent Deity and the cosmic evolutionary force were operating in the same direction. The triumph of righteousness in the freeing of the slave, and the abounding prosperity which followed this virtuous exploit and which accompanied the exploitation of the resources of the West and the development of new industries (especially steel and oil) in the East, confirmed this optimistic view.

2. A period of disillusion and doubt ensued. The delayed problems of the industrial revolution became too manifest to be ignored.

The swollen clouds could no longer be held in suspension by the winds of westward expansion. Labor troubles multiplied. In the effort to solve them on terms acceptable to labor, effective unions came into existence. Capital, already conscious of its power and increasingly devoted to its increasing profits, would not yield. The struggle was marked by bitterness and violence. Politics was corrupted by wealth and by the struggle to obtain it. Science grew less complacent toward orthodoxy. It even abandoned its own early optimism and was no longer willing to testify that evolution would, in the long run, take care of everything. Perhaps, after all, we have a meaningless cosmos that goes around in circles, or one that is gradually running down like a clock, or coming to a stop like a spent bullet. The momentum of the pre-critical optimism with its flavor of mystical transcendentalism could no longer prevail against the drag of a civilization primarily interested in profits. Those who undertook to interpret the world as they saw it could no longer give an encouraging account of either the present or the future, and faith in supernaturalism had so far faded that those whose voices were most influential left it out of account entirely. A literature of disillusion took the place of the literature of romantic optimism. The Great War furnished an interlude and a somewhat hectic revival of faith in the worth of humanity, the validity of non-materialistic ideals and the triumph of justice and righteousness. But this turned out to be largely inspired propaganda, or war hysteria, and when this fever was over and the dupes learned how sordid had been the purposes which all their suffering had served, the disillusion was more desperate than ever.

3. A critical realism is rising out of this disillusion and is finding sufficient certainties to form the basis for a new idealism more durable and satisfying than the romantic optimism of our age of innocence. It began far back with the voices of isolated thinkers even when disillusion was at its darkest. It nourished itself upon the practical sympathies and indomitable hopes of those who promoted enterprises of good will and social betterment. The pioneers of the "social gospel" were sowing the seeds of it. The religious and sometimes fanatical zeal of those who preached crusades of economic, moral and political reform contributed to it. The fervor of the populists, the single tax of Henry George, the trust-busting of Roosevelt, the idealism of Wilson,

regardless of the wisdom or folly of any of the specific programs involved, exhibited the spirit that takes things at their worst and still believes that the best is possible because man, whatever may have been his terrestrial ancestry, and whatever may now be his economic disabilities, has in him a value that must not be lost.

The conservation of all the human values is the avowed objective of all these enterprises, not one of which can be carried through by government except as government takes into account those moral and spiritual considerations which are admittedly the legitimate concern of religion; and not one of them can be carried through by religion without governmental action. Not a statesman who is a candidate for high office can urge his own candidacy without phrasing his appeal in terms which declare his devotion to the principle that men are more than money, that justice and good will and fair dealing among individuals and classes are the foundation of public policy, and that morality in the highest sense in the conduct of the government's affairs is of the essence of his platform. (At the very instant when this paragraph is being written, there comes over the radio the voice of a presidential candidate declaring that his expectation of success in the approaching election is predicated upon the belief that the country is ready for a "spiritual awakening" to a new concern for the underprivileged and the overburdened among our people.) And not a religious leader dares to express the object of his hopes without including aspects of betterment in the conditions under which men live and in the adjustments among men and nations which can be attained only by appropriate legislation.

Let us survey some of these new frontiers upon which politics and religion meet and mingle. First, consider the economic system. During the past twenty years church assemblies and the Federal Council of Churches have constantly been reiterating their demand for "social justice" toward labor—a type of justice which does not flow from unrestricted bargaining between unorganized labor and concentrated capital, or from the use of injunctions to prevent peaceful picketing during strikes, or from permitting men on the verge of starvation to be compelled to sign away their right to organize on the excuse of protecting their "freedom of contract." The Federal Council's "social creed of the churches," the Roman Catholic "Bishops' program of social reconstruction" issued by the administrative committee of the National Catholic War Council, and the Pope's labor encyclicals, all agree in this—that there are certain forms of action which the government must adopt and certain others from which it must refrain in order to meet the reasonable demands of a religion which is sensitive to the rights of labor. Church and state are here dealing with the same materials.

Consider race relations. Religious opinion is still confused and discordant, no less than secular opinion, for it is largely determined by the same traditional prejudices and behavior patterns as well as by the same desire to preserve institutions of tested value. But it is also partly determined by some considerations which are leading it toward more generous attitudes than those which are common in the community as a whole. Race relations are partly governed by laws which are crystallizations of the dominant sentiment of the community. The state thus voices public sentiment and makes it effective in specific situations. But it often occurs that a considerable body of religious opinion, influenced by what it believes to be the teaching of Jesus about the equal value of all men or moved by experience or reflection, gets in advance of secular opinion and the laws. Then a condition of conflict may arise between church and state.

Or consider the case of prohibition. It needs no argument to prove that the free and unlimited circulation of liquor produces moral consequences to which neither the churches nor any other organizations professing any interest in moral conditions can be indifferent. There was a liquor problem long before there was a prohibition problem. For nearly a hundred years the churches have furnished a great part of the initiative and energy that have supported the various methods of attempting to curb or prevent the evils of this business by law. There have been limitations of the hours of sale, Sunday closing, elimination of bar-maids and other women from the premises, high license, local option, state prohibition, and finally national prohibition. All these are legal methods of dealing with the question. So, also, were the laws in every state before 1903 requiring that the physiological effects of alcohol be taught in the public schools, and the Federal law to the same effect for the territories. The church also gave support to various voluntary plans of temperance education and pledge-signing campaigns. But it has been a long while since any one seriously proposed that all legal restrictions be removed and that the whole matter be left to individual decision subject only to such verbal persuasions as may be used for the encouragement of temperance. Some of the arguments for "personal liberty" sound as if they meant that, but they do not. Nobody wants *all* restrictions removed. It is a moral question which is also a legal question. The church must do something about it because it is a moral question. The state must do something about it because it is unescapably a question of laws. But what shall the laws be? It is impossible to expect that element in the community which is most definitely interested in the moral results to be unconcerned about the laws by which, at least in part, those results must be obtained.

I am not arguing for any particular form of control, but am trying to show only that the representatives of religion are doing no unreasonable thing when they take an active and organized part in trying to secure the passage and enforcement of such laws as seem to them likely to be most effective for the purpose.

The churches are not in entire agreement about this matter. Most of the evangelical Protestant churches have arrived at a sufficiently unanimous sentiment in favor of prohibition so that the resolutions of their general conferences or assemblies and the activities of their boards which have to do with that matter fairly represent a consensus of opinion. For these churches to bring their influence to bear with Congress or with state legislatures or in the election of dry candidates is not "clericalism," for this opinion has not been imposed upon the churches by their clergy but has been as democratically formed as any opinion in any group. If and when the opinion of the members of these churches changes, there is nothing to prevent them from passing other resolutions, directing their boards into other activities, and supporting other policies. But there are other churches which have a different view. This is especially true of the Roman Catholic Church, and to a large extent of the Lutheran and Protestant Episcopal churches. These also are within their rights in throwing the weight of their influence on the other side. The Roman Catholic Church has not, so far as I know, made any official pronouncement against prohibition. Its members are free to take whichever side they please. But the weight of the influence of the press and the clergy is against; and in a church in which the voice of the clergy is law in so many matters, it naturally carries more weight with the laity in this than the voice of any body of Protestant clergy would with its constituency. Both the Catholic Church and the Protestant churches are in the prohibition fight, though on different sides, and they are probably there to stay so long as there is a fight. They both have a perfect right to be there, because the question of public and private morals is inseparable from it. It is a field in which church and state are alike interested.

Consider the family. It is the usual religious belief that the family is a divinely ordained institution and that, whether or not particular marriages are made in heaven, the institution of marriage was. The Roman Catholic Church holds that the church by right has sole jurisdiction over marriage. The Second Plenary Council of Baltimore, in 1866, declared: "No state law can authorize divorce so as to permit the parties divorced to contract new engagement." And the Third Council, 1888, decreed: "Nor has 'legal divorce' the slightest power, before God, to loose the bond of marriage and to make a subsequent marriage valid." A church which considers marriage a sacrament can scarcely admit that the control of it is in other hands than its own. The Protestant Episcopal Church opposes divorce to the extent of refusing to admit to communion persons who have remarried after divorce. Most Protestant churches content themselves with general declarations against the "divorce evil" and do not attempt to declare that legal divorces are invalid. Even as early as the period immediately after the the Civil War the frequency of divorce became the occasion for alarm, and most of the church assemblies have from time to time passed resolutions of disapproval. The increase in the divorce rate has been fairly constant. In 1914, it was about one to each ten marriages; in 1928, one to six.

Among the causes for this increase may be mentioned: (1) The growth of a sense of independence on the part of women. The unattached woman is no longer an oddity. (2) Increasing economic independence through the opening of new occupations to women. (3) The passing of the habit of deriving moral codes from detached verses of scripture. People unhappily married are not silenced or satisfied by texts. (4) The decreasing authority of ecclesiastical pronouncements; and with this the rise of new codes and mores, pragmatic rather than authoritarian. (5) The rise of the social sciences has given ground for the common belief that the whole question of family stability and of social and individual welfare as involved in domestic relations is a matter to be studied as a part of the total social situation and not one to be decided arbitrarily on the basis of an inherited code. Pending such study—which is still in its infancy—there has been a good deal of rather reckless experimentation. That "marriage is sacred" is a statement still not likely to be challenged in the best circles, but the word "sacred" has come to have a meaning not unrelated to human welfare.

But whether the churches take the absolutist position of the Roman Catholics or yield in some measure to the pressure of what seems to be a demand for the approval of at least some divorces, it would be absurd to think that they can be indifferent to the question.

On birth-control the Roman Catholic Church is equally uncompromising. Among the Protestant churches there is a strong tendency to take a favorable attitude, with warnings and limitations. Here again the end sought by both is a moral end. The means employed by those who hold what may be considered conservative views on the subject is legal prohibition of giving information. In this case, strangely enough, it is the Catholics who favor Federal prohibition most strongly and the Protestants who are beginning to doubt its value and efficacy.

Most important, perhaps, of all the subjects upon which the churches are making their voices heard in a field where only governmental action can be determinative, is that of international relations with all its ramifications—the ethics of war, the building of the institutions of peace, militarism, "preparedness," disarmament, and the legal status of the pacifist. When the end of the war came, the churches were as enthusiastic for peace as they had been for war while the war was on. The Federal Council, many denominational conventions and a great part of the religious press urged the ratification of the Treaty of Versailles, the joining of the League of Nations, and entrance to the World Court. The Kellogg-Briand Pact for the outlawry of war had the practically unanimous support of the churches. A vast body of absolute pacifist sentiment has grown up among both ministry and laity, based on the conviction that war is always and under all circum-

stances wrong. In general, the Protestant churches in the years since
the war have approximated the position that has been held by the
Quakers since their beginning and that their general conference of
1924 reaffirmed in these words: "We believe the whole system of
determining right by violence and destruction rather than by friendly
conference and negotiation is fundamentally wrong, inefficient, and
irreligious."

The interdenominational conference held in Columbus, Ohio, in
March, 1929, declared in its published report entitled *The Church and
World Peace*, that "war means everything that Jesus did not mean
and means nothing that he did mean. We therefore hold that the
churches should condemn resort to the war system as sin, and should
henceforth refuse as institutions to sanction it or to be used as agencies
in its support. . . . We further hold that the churches should now
regard war as a crime. . . . We hold that the churches should support
and sustain with moral approval individuals who, in the exercise of
their right of conscience, refuse to back up any war or military training." The volume and variety of such pronouncements from leading
churchmen, from the religious press and from denominational conferences and assemblies leave no doubt but that the church's patriotism has entered upon a new phase. It is no longer in the mood to
back the government in whatever war may be declared. Perhaps it
would be if a war should come, but it is not now. And its repudiation
of war shows every sign of being made of sterner stuff than the vague
generalities in praise of peace that did duty during the intervals between wars before 1917.

The central issue was brought to a sharp focus in the case of
Professor D. C. Macintosh, of Yale Divinity School, to whom naturali-
zation was refused because he would not expand the oath of allegiance
into a categorical declaration that he would yield unconditional obedience not only to all present laws but to any law that might hereafter
be enacted, such as a law demanding service in war which he might
deem unjust. In that case, the sentiment of the churches with almost
entire unanimity supported Professor Macintosh in the claim that,
while the state has a right to punish any citizen for disobedience to
any law whether he considers it a just law or not, it has no right to

demand of any citizen in advance a promise to disregard his conscience
if a conflict should arise between conscience and the law.

The institutions and spokesmen of religion in America are, at the
present time, cultivating millions of consciences to be sensitive to
certain aspects of social morality which are also subjects of legislation.
Because of a diversity of private interests and of inherited attitudes, as
well as the natural variability of human judgments, the well-meaning
are not in agreement on all of these topics, but they are in earnest
about them. What part shall religion play in these matters, and how
shall it be played? Can it be done without again lighting the fires of
intolerance? Religion played a sorry part in the 'sixties. Will we be
meeting the present problems any more wisely—prohibition, for example, and disarmament, and social and economic reforms, and divorce
—if we get God so definitely aligned on both sides, or even on one,
that we turn the whole enterprise into a crusade? When the spirit
of the crusade comes in, the spirit of tolerance goes out. "Hades," said
the philosopher who recently imaginatively visited Socrates in that
region, "is a great place if it can teach the good to be tolerant."
And America will be even a greater place than hades if it can teach
the good to be both tolerant and in earnest about those concrete enterprises of social reconstruction which they believe to be essential elements in a sound religion.

Sources and Bibliography

The principal sources from which material has been derived for this book, and which may profitably be used by students for further research, are the following:

SOURCE MATERIALS

Files of the *Independent*, New York, 1865–1890.

Files of the *Christian Union*, New York, 1873–1893.

Files of the *Christian Advocate*, the *Congregationalist*, the *Advance*, the *Christian-Evangelist*, and the *Literary Digest* for various extended periods, and of other religious papers for briefer periods.

Files of the New York, Boston and Chicago daily papers for various periods.

Files of *The Christian Century*, 1900–1932.

Minutes of the Methodist General Conferences, the Presbyterian General Assemblies, the National Councils of Congregational Churches, the General Conventions of the Protestant Episcopal Churches, Yearbook of the Churches, Federal Council, 1931.

BOOKS ON THE GENERAL FIELD

P. G. Mode: *Source-Book and Bibliographical Guide for American Church History*, Menasha, Wisconsin, 1921.

E. P. Oberholtzer: *A History of the United States Since the Civil War*, three volumes, New York, 1922.

V. L. Parrington: *The Beginnings of Critical Realism in America, 1860–1920*, New York, 1930.

C. A. and Mary R. Beard: *The Rise of American Civilization*, New York, 1927.

H. U. Faulkner: *American Economic History*, New York, 1924.

E. C. Kirkland: *A History of American Economic Life*, New York, 1932.

W. W. Sweet: *The Story of Religions in America*, New York, 1930.

Daniel Dorchester: *Christianity in the United States*, New York, 1888.

L. W. Bacon: *A History of American Christianity*, New York, 1897.

H. K. Rowe: *The History of Religion in the United States*, New York, 1924.

L. M. Hacker and B. B. Kendrick: *The United States Since 1865*, New York, 1932.

BOOKS ON CHAPTERS

CHAPTER I

Allan Nevins: *The Emergence of Modern America, 1865–1878*, New York, 1927.

Lewis Mumford: *The Brown Decades*, New York, 1931.

Washington Gladden: *Applied Christianity*, New York, 1886, pp. 255ff.

G. R. Crooks: *The Life of Bishop Matthew Simpson*, New York, 1891.

Files of papers for July, 1865.

CHAPTER II

Claude Bower: *The Tragic Era*, New York, 1928.

H. K. Beale: *The Critical Year*, New York, 1930.

Avary: *Dixie After the War*.

S. L. Davis: *Authentic History of the Ku Klux Klan, 1865–1877*, New York, 1924.

J. M. Mecklin: *The Ku Klux Klan*, New York, 1924, Chap. III.

L. P. Stryker: *Andrew Johnson*, New York, 1929.

H. E. Luccock and P. Hutchinson: *The Story of Methodism*, New York, 1926.

Files of the *Independent*, New York, 1865–1870.

C. H. Phillips: *History of the Colored M. E. Church*, Jackson, Tennessee, 1925.

CHAPTER III

P. G. Mode: *The Frontier Spirit in American Christianity*.

P. G. Mode: *Source-Book*.

W. E. Garrison: *Religion Follows the Frontier*, New York, 1931.

Denominational Histories in American Church History Series, New York, 1898.

F. M. Briston: *The Life of Chaplain McCabe*, New York, 1908.

CHAPTER IV

E. P. Cupperly: *Public Education in the U. S.*, New York, 1919.

L. Abbott: *Life of Henry Ward Beecher*, New York, 1903.

P. Hibben: *Henry Ward Beecher*, New York, 1926.

H. W. Morrow: *Tiger! Tiger! The Life Story of John B. Gough*, New York, 1930.

E. Sachs: *The Terrible Siren*, New York, 1928.

Herbert Schneider: *The Puritan Mind*, New York, 1930.

Arthur Train: *Puritan's Progress*, New York, 1931, Chaps. XIII and XIV.

Lewis Mumford: *The Brown Decades*, New York, 1931.

H. U. Faulkner: *American Economic History*.

CHAPTER V

Gorham: *Camp Meeting Manual*, 1854.
A. B. Bass: *Protestantism in the United States*, New York, 1929.
G. Seldes: *The Stammering Century*, New York, 1928.
G. C. Loud: *Evangelized America*, New York, 1923.
Dorchester: *Christianity in the U. S.*
W. R. Moody: *D. L. Moody*, New York, 1930.
T. D. Bacon: *Leonard Bacon*, Chap. XVI on Beecher, New Haven, 1931.
D. L. Moody: *Gospel Awakening*, sixteenth edition, Chicago, 1883.
L. Denison: "The Rev. Billy Sunday and His War on the Devil," in *American Magazine*, LXIV, 1907, pp. 451-468.

CHAPTER VI

Lyman Abbott: *Life of Beecher*, New York, 1903.
W. Lawrence: *Life of Phillips Brooks*, New York, 1930.
G. A. Gordon: *My Education and Religion*, Boston, 1925.
Washington Gladden: *Applied Christianity*, New York, 1886.
S. G. Cole: *The History of Fundamentalism*, New York, 1931.
W. E. Garrison: *Catholicism and the American Mind*, Chicago, 1928.
Minutes of Congregational National Council, February, 1876. (On Beecher.)
W. N. Rice: *Christian Faith in an Age of Science*, New York, 1903.
F. J. McConnell: *Borden Parker Bowne*, New York, 1929.
The *Outlook*, LXXV, 1903, p. 927. (On trial of Bowne.)
H. G. Mitchell: *For the Benefit of My Creditors*.

CHAPTER VII

G. J. Slosser: *Christian Unity, Its History and Challenge*, New York, 1929.
Wm. Adams Brown: *The Church in America*, New York, 1922.
J. T. McNeill (ed.): *Community Religion and the Denominational Heritage*, New York, 1930.
A. B. Bass: *Protestantism in the U. S.*, New York, 1929.
H. K. Rowe: *History of Religion in the U. S.*
J. W. Suter: *The Life and Letters of William Reed Huntington, a Champion of Unity*, New York, 1925.
William Lawrence: *Memories of a Happy Life*, New York, 1924.
William Lawrence: *Fifty Years*, London, 1926.

CHAPTER VIII

A. M. Schlessinger: *The Rise of the City, 1878–1898*, New York, 1930.
E. P. Oberholtzer: *A History of the U. S. Since the Civil War*.
R. Maury: *The Wars of the Godly*, New York, 1928.
C. A. and Mary R. Beard: *The Rise of American Civilization*.
Mark Sullivan: *Our Times*, three volumes, New York, 1927.
L. B. Paton: *Recent Christian Progress*, New York, 1909.
G. C. Loud: *Evangelized America*.
W. E. B. DuBois: *The Negro Church*, Atlanta, 1903.

C. G. Woodson: *The History of the Negro Church*, Washington, 1921.
Files of the *Christian Union*, New York, 1873–1893.
William Lawrence: *Life of Phillips Brooks*, New York, 1930.
C. G. Woodson: *The History of the Negro Churches*, Washington, 1921.

CHAPTER IX

E. P. Cubberly: *Public Education in the U. S.*
A. M. Schlessinger: *The Rise of the City.*
C. A. and Mary R. Beard: *The Rise of American Civilization.*
Mark Sullivan: *Our Times.*
V. L. Parrington: *The Beginnings of Critical Realism in America.*
L. B. Paton: *Recent Christian Progress*, New York, 1909.
T. W. Goodspeed: *William Rainey Harper*, Chicago, 1928.
E. E. Leisy: *American Literature, an Interpretative Survey*, New York, 1929.
J. T. Howard: *Our American Music*, New York, 1931.
R. L. Kelly: *Theological Education in America.*
V. Vogt: *Art and Religion*, New Haven, 1929.
Leon H. Vincent: *John Heyl Vincent*, New York, 1925.
L. J. Sherrill: *Presbyterian Parochial Schools, 1846–1870*, New Haven, 1932.
M. W. Brabham: *Planning Modern Church Buildings*, Nashville, 1928.
E. M. Conover: *Building the House of God*, New York, 1928.

CHAPTER X

Washington Gladden: *Applied Christianity*, New York, 1886.
W. A. Brown: *The Church in America.*
H. U. Faulkner: *American Economic History.*
Shailer Mathews: *The Church and the Changing Order*, New York, 1909.
G. B. Smith: *Religious Thought in the Last Quarter Century*, Chicago, 1925. Chapter by Shailer Mathews on "The Development of Social Christianity."
S. Miller, Jr., and J. F. Fletcher: *The Church and Industry*, New York, 1930.
Brand Whitlock: *Forty Years of It*, New York, 1914.
Graham Taylor: *Pioneering on Social Frontiers*, Chicago, 1930.
C. W. Gardner: *The Doctor and the Devil, or the Midnight Adventures of Dr. Parkhurst*, New York, 1894, 1931.
P. H. Odegard: *Pressure Politics*, New York, 1928.
Justin Stewart: *Wayne Wheeler, Dry Boss*, New York, 1928.
H. U. Faulkner: *The Quest for Social Justice*, New York, 1928.
Charles Stelzle: *A Son of the Bowery*, New York, 1926.
Charles Stelzle: *The Workingman and Social Problems*, New York, 1903.
C. B. Thompson: *The Churches and the Wage-earners*, New York, 1909.
Kerr: *Catechism of Catholic Social Principles*, 1927.
American Magazine, LXVIII, 1909. Ray Stannard Baker: "The Spiritual Unrest," "The Gap Between Labor and the Church."

Everybody's Magazine, XIX, 1908, p. 54. (On the tenements of Trinity Church.)

CHAPTER XI

Walter Millis: *The Martial Spirit*, New York, 1931.
C. A. and Mary R. Beard: *The Rise of American Civilization*.
Mark Sullivan: *Our Times, III.*
L. B. Paton: *Recent Christian Progress*, New York, 1909.
H. F. Pringle: *Theodore Roosevelt*, New York, 1931.

CHAPTER XII

H. K. Carroll: *Religious Forces of the U. S.*, revised edition, New York, 1912.
Federal Council: *Year Book of the Churches*, New York, 1931.
J. T. McNeill (ed.): *Community Religion and the Denominational Heritage*, New York, 1930.
D. Dorchester: *Christianity in the U. S.*
S. D. McConnell: *History of the American Episcopal Church*, Milwaukee, 1916.
H. E. Luccock and P. Hutchinson: *The Story of Methodism*, New York, 1926.
W. W. Sweet: *History of American Methodism*, New York, 1932.
H. C. Vedder: *The Baptists*, New York, 1902.
W. Walker: *History of Congregational Churches in the U. S.*, New York, 1894.
E. H. Gillett: *History of the Presbyterian Church in the U. S. A.*
W. E. Garrison: *Religion Follows the Frontier, a History of the Disciples*, New York, 1931.
A. R. Wentz: *The Lutheran Church in American History*, Philadelphia, 1923.
C. G. Woodson: *The History of the Negro Churches*, Washington, 1921.
John Lanahan: *The Era of Frauds in the Methodist Book Concern*, Baltimore, 1896.
V. Ferm: *The Crisis in American Lutheran Theology*, New York, 1930.

CHAPTER XIII

W. E. Garrison: *Catholicism and the American Mind*, Chicago, 1928.
T. O'Gorman: *History of the Roman Catholic Church in the U. S.*
J. G. O'Shea: *History of the Catholic Church in the U. S.*
J. S. Moore: *Will America Become Catholic?*, New York, 1931.
James Cardinal Gibbons: *A Retrospect of Fifty Years*, Baltimore, 1916.
R. Maury: *The Wars of the Godly*, New York, 1928.
Michael Williams: *The Shadow of the Pope*, New York, 1932.
J. M. Mecklin: *The Ku Klux Klan*, New York, 1924.
C. W. Ferguson: *Confusion of Tongues*, Chaps. 12 and 13, New York, 1928.
National Catholic War Council: *Social Reconstruction*, Washington, 1919.

Peter Guilday: *A History of the Councils of Baltimore, 1791–1884*, New York, 1932.
Elliott: *Life of Father Hecker*, New York, 1888.
A. S. Will: *Life of Cardinal Gibbons.*
C. H. Moehlman: *The Catholic-Protestant Mind*, New York, 1929.

CHAPTER XIV

G. J. Slosser: *Christian Unity, Its History and Challenge*, New York, 1929.
Federal Council: *Year Book of the Churches*, 1931.
W. A. Brown: *The Church in America*, New York, 1922.
E. R. Hooker: *United Churches*, New York, 1926.
J. T. McNeill (ed.): *Community Religion and the Denominational Heritage*, New York, 1930.
E. B. Sanford: *Origin and History of the Federal Council of Churches*, Hartford, 1916.
C. S. Macfarland: *The Churches of the Federal Council*, New York, 1916.
C. S. Macfarland: *The Progress of Church Federation to 1922*, New York, 1922.
A. B. Bass: *Protestantism in the U. S.*
D. R. Piper: *Community Churches*, Chicago, 1928.

CHAPTER XV

W. A. Brown: *The Church in America.*
W. P. King (ed.): *Social Forces and Christian Ideals*, Nashville, 1931.
W. M. Tippy: *The Church as a Community Force*, New York, 1914.
R. L. Johnson: *Western Baptists in the Age of Big Business*, Ms., Ph.D. thesis, Chicago, 1929.
The World Service of the Methodist Episcopal Church.
Messages of the Men and Religion Movement, seven volumes, New York, 1912.
H. U. Faulkner: *The Quest for Social Justice*, New York, 1931.
W. E. Garrison: *Religion Follows the Frontier*, Chap. XV.
Mark Sullivan: *Our Times.* 4 vols. New York, 1928–1933.
Ernest Gordon: *When the Brewer Had the Strangle-hold*, New York, 1930.
C. H. Moehlman: *When All Drank and Thereafter*, New York, 1930.
C. C. Regier: *The Era of the Muckrakers.* Chapel Hill, N. C., 1933.
Anti-Saloon League Yearbooks.
U. S. Brewers' Association Yearbooks.

CHAPTER XVI

A. R. H. Miller: *The Church and War*, St. Louis, 1931.
W. H. P. Faunce: *Religion and War*, New York, 1918.
P. W. Slosson: *The Great Crusade and After*, New York, 1930.
Kirby Page: *Jesus or Christianity*, New York, 1930.
H. E. Fosdick: *The Challenge of the Present Crisis.*
A. C. F. Beales: *History of Peace.*

S. W. Gulick: *The Christian Crusade for a Warless World*, New York, 1923.
N. M. Thomas: *The Conscientious Objector in America*, New York, 1923.

CHAPTER XVII

P. W. Slosson: *The Great Crusade and After*.
F. L. Allen: *Only Yesterday*, New York, 1931.
C. A. and Mary R. Beard: *The Rise of American Civilization*.
R. S. and H. M. Lynd: *Middletown, a Study in Contemporary American Culture*, New York, 1929.
A. Blumenthal: *Small-Town Stuff*, Chicago, 1932.
A. B. Bass: *Protestantism in the U. S.*
S. Mathews: *The Church and the Changing Order*.
Federal Council: *Year Book of the Churches*, 1931.
World Survey by Interchurch World Movement, New York, 1920.
National Catholic War Council: *Social Reconstruction*, Washington, 1919.
Methodist Review, 1921, p. 405, W. W. Sweet: "Negro Churches in the South."

CHAPTER XVIII

S. G. Cole: *The History of Fundamentalism*, New York, 1931.
Shailer Mathews: *The Faith of Modernism*, New York, 1925.
G. H. Betts: *The Beliefs of 700 Ministers*, New York, 1929.
G. A. Gordon: *My Education and Religion*, Boston, 1925.
W. P. King (ed.): *Humanism*, Nashville, 1931.
W. P. King (ed.): *Behaviorism*, Nashville, 1930.
G. B. Smith: *Social Idealism and the Changing Theology*, New York, 1913.
Paxton Hibben: *The Peerless Leader, W. J. Bryan*, New York, 1929.
R. G. Ingersoll: *Works*, twelve volumes, New York, 1900.
Clarence Darrow: *The Story of My Life*, New York, 1932.
C. Y. Harrison: *Clarence Darrow*, New York, 1931.
G. B. Smith: *Religious Thought in the Last Quarter-Century*, Chicago, 1925.
Cosmopolitan, XLVI, 1909, pp. 665–676, H. Bolse: "Blasting at the Rock of Ages."

CHAPTER XIX

C. W. Ferguson: *The Confusion of Tongues*, New York, 1928.
G. Seldes: *The Stammering Century*, New York, 1928.
A. B. Kuhn: *Theosophy*, New York, 1930.
George Lawton: *The Drama of Life after Death, a Study of the Spiritualist Religion*, New York, 1932.
E. Sachs: *The Terrible Siren* (on Spiritualism).
Georgine Milmine: "The Life of Mary Baker Eddy," New York, 1909, *McClure's Magazine*, 1907–1908.
Sibyl Wilbur: *Life of Mary Baker Eddy*, Revised edition, Boston, 1913.
E. F. Dakin: *Mrs. Eddy, The Biography of a Virginal Mind*, New York, 1929.

E. S. Bates and J. V. Dittemore: *Mary Baker Eddy, the Truth and the Tradition*, New York, 1932.

L. P. Powell: *Mary Baker Eddy, a Life Size Portrait*, New York, 1930.

A. K. Swihart: *Since Mrs. Eddy*, New York, 1931.

W. A. Linn: *The Story of the Mormons.*

Cosmopolitan, LX, 1910, p. 439; *McClure's*, XXXVI, 1911, pp. 245, 449. (Attacks on Mormonism.)

R. Harlan: *J. A. Dowie and the Christian Catholic Apostolic Church in Zion*, Evansville, Wisconsin, 1906.

Literary Digest, XXVII, 1903, pp. 532, 572, 820. (Dowie.)

E. Worcester and S. McComb: *The Christian Religion as a Healing Power*, New York, 1909.

J. A. Weber: *Religions and Philosophies in the U. S.*, Los Angeles, 1931.

W. M. Miller: *Baha'ism, Its Origin, History and Teachings*, New York, 1931.

Shoghi Effendi: *The Dawn-Breakers, Nabil's Narrative of the Early Days of the Baha'i Revelation, translated from the original Persian*, New York, 1932.

M. Block: *The New Church in the New World*, New York, 1932.

Maurice Magre: *Magicians, Seers and Mystics*, New York, 1932.

Elwood Worcester, *et al.*: *Religion and Medicine*, New York, 1908.

Success Magazine, 1897–1911, and *New Success*, 1918, edited by O. S. Marden. (New Thought.)

The *Forum*, November, 1931, E. W. Mandeville, on Buchmanism.

CHAPTER XX

H. W. Schneider: *The Puritan Mind*, New York, 1930.

W. E. Garrison: *Catholicism and the American Mind*, Chaps. V and VI.

Files of *The Christian Century*, 1917–1932.

Kirby Page (ed.): *Recent Gains in American Civilization*, New York, 1928.

P. H. Odegard: *Pressure Politics.*

C. C. Morrison: *The Outlawry of War*, Chicago, 1927.

Devere Allen: *The Fight for Peace*, New York, 1930.

F. L. Allen: *Only Yesterday*, New York, 1931.

C. S. Macfarland: *International Christian Movements*, New York, 1924.

Index

.

CPSIA information can be obtained at www.ICGtesting.com
Printed in the USA
LVOW02s2319271013

358850LV00004B/78/P

9 781179 102139